Monarchs of the Sea

Monarchs of the Sea

THE GREAT OCEAN LINERS

Kurt Ulrich

TAURIS PARKE

'OH, THESE JOURNEYS! THE HUSTLE AND BUSTLE OF A SUDDEN DEPARTURE,
ALMOST NOT KNOWING WHERE YOU'RE GOING – I KNOW ALL THAT ...
HOW MANY TIMES HAS MY WHOLE LIFE BEEN BROUGHT TOGETHER IN THIS
ONE SINGLE FEELING OF UPHEAVAL; TRAVELLING, FAR, FAR – AND THAT FIRST
AWAKENING UNDER A NEW SKY!'

RAINER MARIA RILKE IN
'RAINER MARIA RILKE/ANDRÉ GIDE, LETTERS 1906 – 1926'

Contents

High-tech nostalgia: the 1,996 square metres of sail on the Wind Song *are computer-controlled. Sensors control the position of the sail, trim it when the wind comes up and start the engine when the vessel is becalmed.*

Tradition and Change

Luxury liners have sailed all the world's oceans, but it is the Atlantic which has been their favourite place for pageantry and racing. This is where the battle to be biggest and fastest was fought, where companies vied to outdo one another with ever bigger, faster and more luxurious passenger ships. They became media stars when they won the legendary Blue Riband for breaking a speed record or else were celebrated as the most powerful means of transport ever created by man. This brought with it prestige for the nation and profits for the shipping lines. Even today, the 'floating palaces' and the 'grand hotels' are still symbols of elegance and glamour, stylish travel and refined luxury, even though they have long been supplanted by the jet aircraft.

In his film *Amarcord*, Federico Fellini created what is probably the most beautiful portrayal of a luxury liner ever: the *Rex*, colossal in size and bedecked with lights, looms out of the darkness, its black hull topped by a white superstructure and two mighty funnels. The people of Rimini, who have been waiting around in small boats for hours to greet the ship on its maiden voyage, break into cries of delight. Fellini's *Rex*, an unmistakably stylised model, expresses in a visual metaphor the absolute fascination of the passenger steamers of yesterday better than any words could do.

In the rush of nostalgia we often forget that right into the 20th century, liners had two faces: whilst a minority of privileged people travelled in luxury, the majority, many of them European emigrants on their way to America, had to sleep in cramped steerage accommodation.

The era of Atlantic shipping is irrevocably over, yet names like the *Normandie*, the *Bremen* or the *Queen Mary* live on in our memories; these maritime giants were not anonymous means of transport but personalities with a life story. They were 'baptised', suffered misfortune, aged and usually landed up in a ships' graveyard.

Liners were followed by cruise ships. These travel from destination to destination carrying holiday-makers eager for pleasure and relaxation and they try to inject some of the glamour of yesterday into these closing years of the 20th century. They are no longer the famous and highly-subsidised national flagships trying to outpace all competitors, but rather floating holiday resorts for the leisure society of our high-tech age. In addition to being mere items in the history of transport, liners and cruise-ships also document technical developments, social changes, changes in fashions and the transition between travel for the elite only and modern mass tourism.

We explore in this book the ships that made history and journey back to the age of luxury liners and into the present and future worlds of the floating resorts.

Royal Caribbean's Sun Viking *which has been running as* SuperStar Sagittarius *for Star Cruises since January 1998, is ready for departure. The passengers are looking forward to the exciting cruise to far-eastern destinations.*

Masterful film director Federico Fellini re-created the maiden voyage of the Rex *on 28 October 1932 in his film 'Amarcord'.*

The cruiser Sea Godess II, *which only holds 116 passengers yet stands comparison with luxury yachts across the world, docked in Monaco.*

Posters for sea voyages are part of contemporary and cultural history. Some matter-of-factly describe the shipping routes, whilst others appeal to our yearning for faraway places.

The shipping lines' posters of yesteryear tempted us with inexpensive sea voyages to exotic destinations and also showed stylised illustrations of their liners.

13

Introduction: under sail

'The unfurled top sails fluttered in the wind, making softly rounded shapes like white clouds caught up in the tangle of ropes. Then the sheets were braced up and the yards hoisted until the ship rose up to form a great, lonely pyramid, gliding along brilliant white in the hazy sunshine.'

The appeal of a sailing ship on the high seas has never been more beautifully described than in this passage from Joseph Conrad's novel *The Nigger of the 'Narcissus'*; no one has ever described sailing ships and sea travel, storms and calm with quite the same mastery as Polish-born Joseph Conrad (1857-1924). To the poet and sea captain, the sailing ship was a 'sensitive creature' demanding to be handled 'with understanding and experience' and which 'we have to a certain extent brought into the world with the aim of proving ourselves through it'. However these were a far cry from the clippers

James Cook (1728-1779), the English seafarer and explorer, travelled tens of thousands of nautical miles between the Arctic and the Antarctic on his three Pacific voyages.

and windjammers, the most stylish and technically perfect of all the sailing ships, which traversed the oceans during the second half of the 19th century.

People were taking to the sea as early as the third millennium before Christ – first rowing, then sailing. Journeys gradually became longer, the ships more refined, nautical knowledge more extensive. Yet there was always deadly danger lurking on these voyages, which often lasted for several months: the ships foundered on reefs, sank in storms, caught fire, were attacked by pirates, illnesses and epidemics decimated crew and passengers. Very few people took on the rigours and uncertainty of a sea voyage voluntarily. The first passengers were usually soldiers, merchants and adventurers, and later pilgrims, explorers, scientists, whalers, missionaries, colonial officials, emigrants and deportees. Fearless seamen sailed across unknown oceans in nutshell-sized ships whose names were to become no less famous than they themselves; they discovered, described and charted unknown oceans and islands. Among the most famous of these were the 24-metre-long three-master *Santa Maria*, in which Genoese explorer Christopher Columbus set sail westwards in 1492 in search of East Asia; Ferdinand Magellan's *Trinidad*, the flagship of a fleet of five sailing vessels, which set out in 1519 and were the first to circumnavigate the world by sea; the *Endeavour* and the *Resolution*, two converted coal transporters, in which the Englishman James Cook undertook three voyages to the South Seas, Alaska and the Antarctic between 1768 and 1779.

The ships' logbooks recorded the voyages in the brief style of the seaman, reports described regions that no European had ever seen before, sometimes in more and sometimes in less detail. But contemporary accounts of everyday life and the accommodation on board are rare. Marco Polo, who reached Asia by land at the end of the 13th century, noted:

'Of all the remarkable things we found in India, we want to start by describing the merchant ships. These are made of spruce and have only one deck; under this, the space is divided into sixty small cabins – sometimes more, sometimes less depending on the size

In 1774, when Ludolf Backhuyzen (1631-1708) painted the 'Port of Amsterdam', sea voyages were dangerous journeys with an uncertain outcome. Hardly anyone went on-board voluntarily.

Designed by H. A. Moth

The Santa Maria, Christopher Columbus' flagship in 1492, was a three-master just 24 metres in length. It ran aground in the Caribbean on Christmas Day, just four months after leaving home, and had to be abandoned.

of the ship – which are intended for the accommodation of the merchants.'

Descriptions of pilgrimages to the Holy Land in the late 15th century have been handed down to us. The well-to-do slept in the cabins in the stern whilst *hoi polloi* slept in cramped conditions below deck – their heads along the sides of the ship, their feet pointing inwards towards the middle. There were two meals a day, announced with a trumpet call, and three religious services. Everyone was given a swig of malmsey (a sweet wine) every morning to combat sea-sickness.

In 1553, merchants from London financed a journey of three ships to forge trading relations with Russia and to open up a northern trading route to the Far East. The sailors and eleven merchants had to undertake in writing to obey the captain, to hold morning and evening prayers, and not to indulge in 'blasphemy or heinous swearing' or 'the games of the devil' such as 'dice, cards and *doppelkopf*. Paragraph

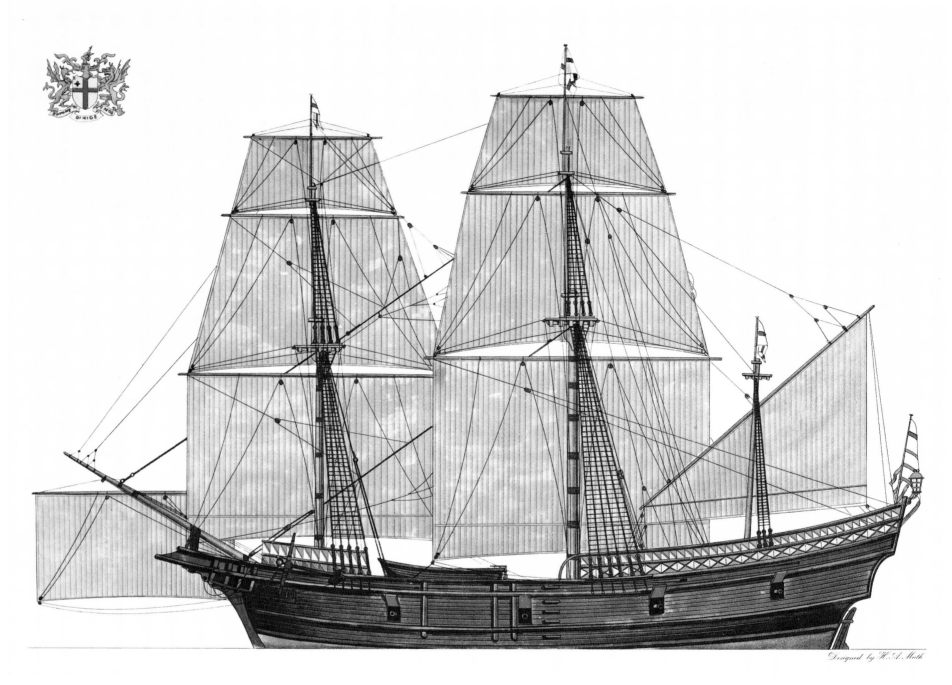

Designed by H.A. Muth

19 of the contract stated that 'if it is any person's destiny that he should die or be otherwise lost during the course of the voyage, 'the deceased's clothes and other possessions shall be registered and preserved for the later use of his wife and children.'
Sixty-six of the 116 participants died and only one ship made the return journey to London. In 1609 the *Sea Venture* was stranded in a hurricane on a coral reef off the coast of Bermuda. The 150 English emigrants made it to the shore, built two new ships, the *Deliverance* and *Patience*, from the wreckage, and continued on their way to the New World. It would have been one shipwreck amongst thousands, had it not been for the fact that William Shakespeare had read about it and used it as

Conditions must have been painfully cramped aboard the Mayflower, *which was probably only 28 metres in length, in which the Pilgrim Fathers reached Plymouth in what is now the State of Massachusetts in the USA, after a turbulent three-month crossing.*

The world of maritime travel at the beginning of the 16th century: the 'Carta Marina Navigationa' by Martin Waldseemüller (1470–1518); overleaf.

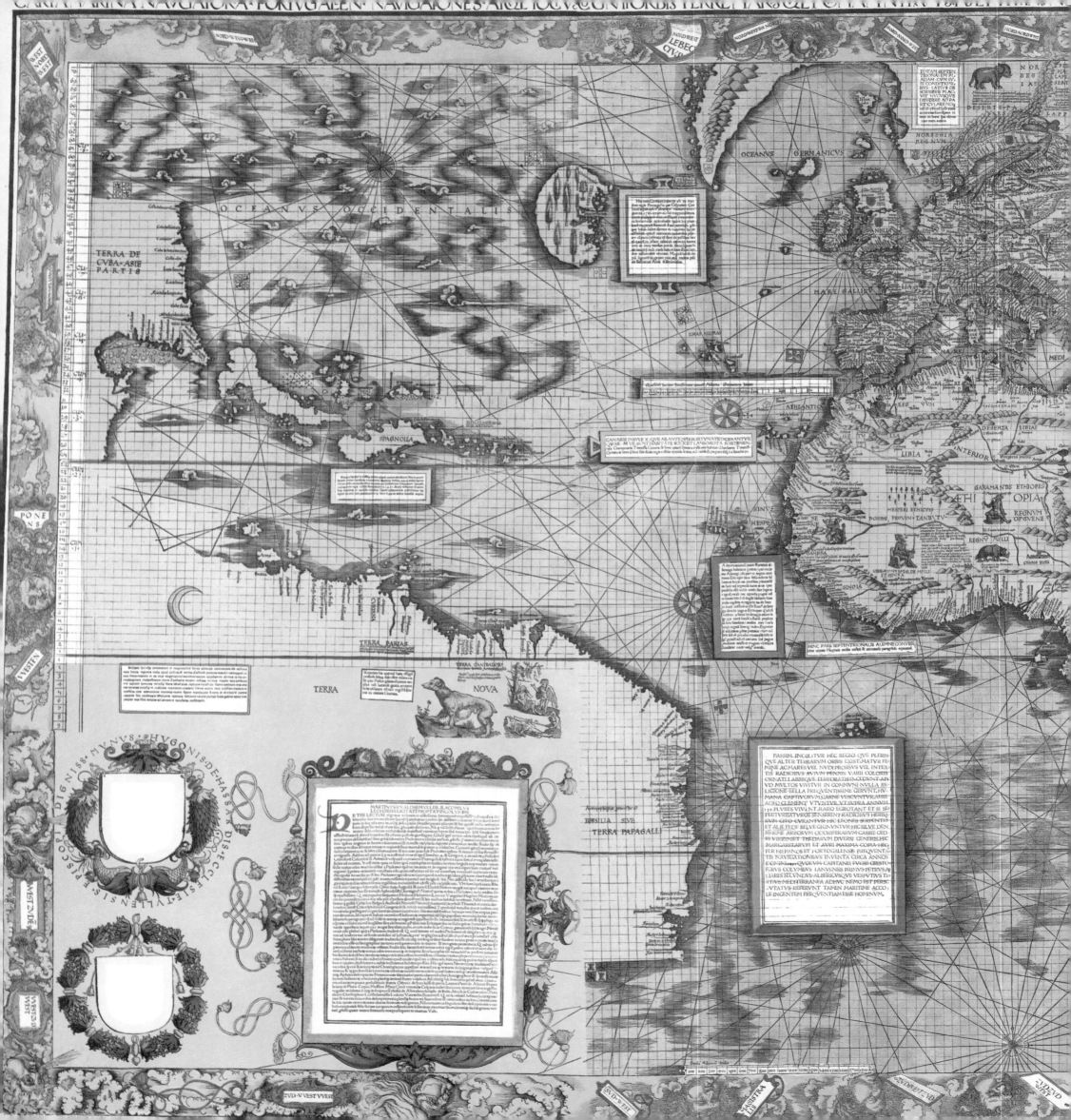

the inspiration for his play *The Tempest*, which was premiered in 1611. A life-sized replica of the *Deliverance* today stands in St. George's Harbour in Bermuda.In the autumn of 1620, the *Mayflower* left England carrying the Pilgrim Fathers – 50 men, 20 women and 32 children. They had a stormy crossing, were at sea for 3 months and finally anchored off the coast of what is now Plymouth in the American state of Massachusetts in mid-December. Conditions on board the ship, which historians estimated to have been no more than 27.5 metres in length, must have been desperately cramped with the 102 passengers and a crew of at least 20. Four families slept in cabins, whilst the rest tried to create a little privacy by hanging up sails. Any remaining space was used to keep goats and chickens and food supplies, as well as furniture and household goods.

Conditions in the infamous slave transporters were far more precarious. During the 18th century, millions of people were shipped from Africa to the Caribbean and north America; they were chained up in four rows below deck from stem to stern, and not infrequently only half of them survived the crossing. A law was passed in England in 1799 which was intended to ameliorate the very worst abuses, and set out a formula to establish the maximum number of people permitted in this human cargo: length x width of a deck ÷ 8. Thus up to 375 slaves could be housed in a space 100 feet long and 30 feet wide. The slave trade was only outlawed at the beginning of the 19th century.

Anyone wanting to embark upon a sea voyage at the beginning of the 19th century first had to enquire at quayside pubs, sailors' homes or the offices of shipping companies about sailing vessels which were bound for the desired destination, and then had to negotiate

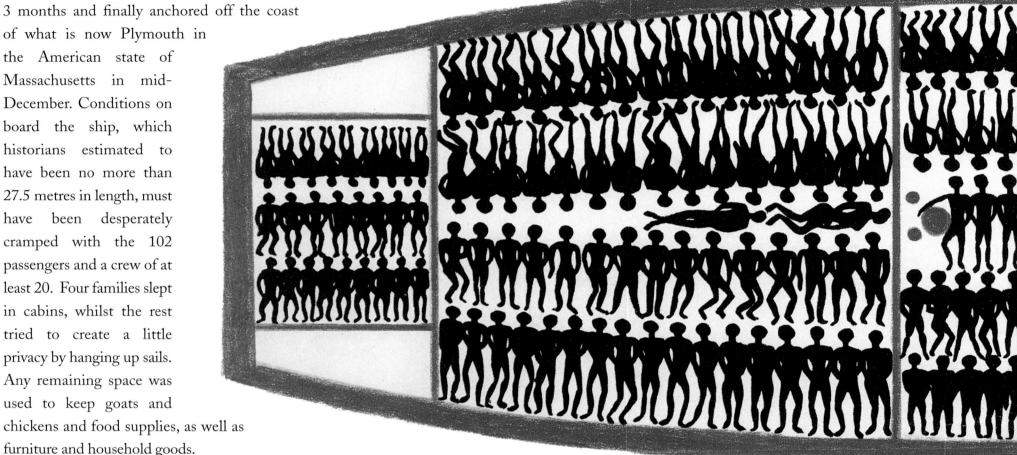

the price with the captain and wait patiently until favourable winds allowed the ship to set sail. Passengers slept in narrow bunks or hammocks and candles provided light at night. Once the goats, cows, sheep and hens which they had taken with them had all been slaughtered, it was pickled salted meat on the menu every day. Experienced travellers not only brought their own furniture but also their own live animals on board. To protect themselves from pirates, merchant and passenger ships carried as many as 30 cannons; male passengers were expected to help defend the ship by manning the cannons or hand-weapons in the event of an attack.

Slave ships like the Brook, *built in Liverpool in 1881, carried up to 600 Africans to North America and the Caribbean. The plan of the bottom deck shows how desperately tightly the human cargo was crushed in.*

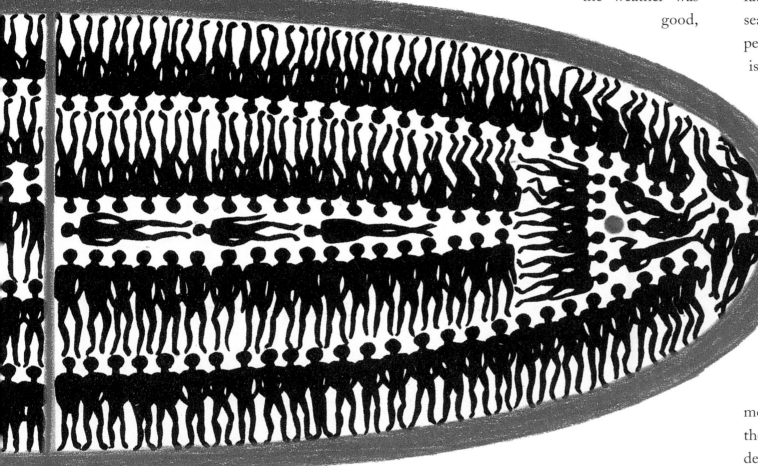

The French author François-René Chateaubriand, who sailed to North America in April 1791, later described his sea voyage, which lasted several weeks, in *Voyage en Amérique* (*Voyage to America*):

'The passengers ate in the cabin. When the weather was good, a sail was raised on the poop and we ate under it with a view of the blue sea which here and there threw up "white horses" whipped up by the breeze. The passengers on board a ship differ from the crew in that they are rooted in a different element; their fate is rooted in the earth. The one is searching for good fortune, the other for peace. The one is returning home, the other is leaving it in order to become acquainted with the customs of different people and to study science and the arts. People can get to know one another at their leisure in this floating hotel, experience an adventure or two, develop dislikes and forge friend-ships.'

Chateaubriand returned in December of the same year; the ship sailed into a storm in the English Channel:

'A shipwreck seemed unavoidable. The passengers had gathered up their most valuable possessions in order to save them. Passengers, sailors, everyone was on deck, some had climbed onto the rigging, others onto the side walls, some onto the capstan and others onto the ground tackle, in order not to be washed away by the waves or thrown into the sea by the rolling of the ship. The captain cried "An axe! an axe!", to chop down the masts. […] The following day we arrived at Le Havre.'

On 27 October 1817, an advertisement in the New York newspaper the *Evening Post* announced that the undersigned had 'set up a shipping line between New York and Liverpool which would set out from one of these ports on specific days of the month throughout the year in order to provide a fast and regular goods and passenger service.' The 'undersigned' were two

A slave auction in the USA, a contemporary painting. There were four million black slaves in the American South in 1860.

On 22 September 1862, US President Abraham Lincoln (seated left) signed his Emancipation Proclamation in which he declared the slaves in the rebellious southern states to be 'forever free'.

"Yo- Ho-Ho, and a Bottle of Rum!"

We call them pirates, marauders, corsairs, buccaneers, freebooters or filibusters, but these all mean the same thing: bandits of the seas who captured ships, ransacked towns, extorted ransoms and sold prisoners as slaves.

Ever since ships have been sailing the seas, they have been victims of this scourge. The Vikings, the Arabs, the Germans, the English or the French – everyone was at it, because profits were high and risks were low. As governments were too weak to guarantee the safety of the sea routes, they were quite happy to act as accomplices. Angered, the Venetian envoy to the court of the English king wrote to the Doge of Venice in 1603: 'England's reputation and strength is based on a large number of small corsairs.'

Pirates pursued their criminal activities on all the world's oceans, but none were more famous or more feared than the pirates of the Caribbean. In Walt Disney's fun parks they pursue their criminal activities as quaint little plastic figures drinking and shooting; and in front of the Treasure Island Casino Hotel in Las Vegas, the pirate ship *Hispaniola* and the frigate *Britannia* engage each other in loud explosive skirmishes every 90 minutes. Robert Louis Stevenson made pirates into literary salon material in his classic adventure novel, *Treasure Island* Whenever the 'Jolly Roger', the black flag with the white skull and cross bones, was flying on the top of the mast, the bottle of rum would be round on deck and the singing would get underway with alcoholic fervour:

'Fifteen men on the dead man's chest,
Yo-ho-ho, and a bottle of rum!
Drink and the devil had done for the rest,
Yo-ho-ho, and a bottle of rum!'

Right up into the 18th century, pirates had permanent bases in the Bahamas, Haiti and Jamaica, where they turned Port Royal into the 'Sin

Bartholomew Roberts, born in Wales in 1682, is said to have captured 400 ships off the African coast and in the Red Sea.

Charles Vane, who had his headquarters in the Bahamas, was notorious for his cruelty. He died on 'the gallows in Port Royal, Jamaica, in 1719.

Edward England, an Englishman, pursued his crimes in the Caribbean and off the coast of Africa during the first half of the 18th century.

Capital of the West': these included Francis Drake, who later became Sir Francis, Henry Morgan, who was later promoted to become Governor of Jamaica, and William Kidd, who was financed by New York bankers. There were also female pirates like Mary Read and Ann Bonny. Both were captured in November 1720; only the fact that they were pregnant saved these 'wild ladies' from the gallows. This 'fallen crowd' may have lived outside the constraints of normal society, but they did follow their own code of honour: anyone who refused to obey was rejected, mutilated or even sentenced to death. Women and gambling were forbidden on board. Booty was distributed amongst the crew according to a specific pattern, the loss of a limb in a fight was compensated for

Pirates Ann Bonny and Mary Reed were sentenced to death by hanging in Jamaica in 1720.

according to specific rates. Captain Drake ordered those guilty of uttering 'dirty phrases at mealtimes' to be whipped; Captain Roberts allowed his crew one day off a week.

Piracy was still flourishing at the beginning of the 19th century, as a result of which the 1815 Congress of Vienna put forward the 'successful combating of African piracy' as a matter of urgency. It was not until the introduction of steam-powered warships, the abolition of slavery and better communications that this criminal activity was eradicated.

But not forever. The International Maritime Bureau registered 224 pirate attacks on commercial ships in Asian, South American and West African waters in 1996.

Henry 'Long Ben' Every came from Plymouth and terrorised the Caribbean and the Indian Ocean in his ship the Fancy.

Howell Davis was one of the most cunning of all the pirates. He pretended to be a merchant or a pirate hunter so that he could sell his booty without risk.

Stede Bonnet, the 'Gentleman Pirate', was born in Barbados in 1688 and ended his life on the gallows in 1718.

Americans and three Englishmen, owners of the newly-established Black Ball Line which had four sailing ships – the *James Munro*, the *Courier*, the *Amity* and the *Pacific*.

The three-master *James Munro* had cabins for 28 passengers and space for 400 tonnes of cargo. When it set sail from New York on its first transatlantic crossing on 5 January 1818, the cargo holds were half empty and there were only eight passengers on board. The Black Ball Line was the first line to offer large-scale regular shipping links between the old and new worlds, for which they asked higher prices than other shipping lines, which initially frightened off many customers. However, the regular timetable and the speed of the ships – from east to west in 40 days and from west to east in an average of 24 days depending on the wind – easily made the higher price worthwhile.

The company augmented the fleet with larger ships, doubled the number of monthly departures and made the ships more comfortable. Steerage passengers still had to make do with sparsely furnished but cheap mass accommodation, whilst cabin class passengers were served four meals a day and three different table wines. The cabins were tiny, measuring just six square metres, but they had two beds, a commode and a washstand with jugs of hot and cold water. If the sea was not too choppy, shuffleboard was played on deck, there was pistol shooting with bottles as targets and even rat hunts. After dinner, the men withdrew to the smoking room and the ladies to the Lady Salon.

The Dutch sailing ship Kolumbus *sank in a storm in 1822. A French ship rescued the passengers.*

24

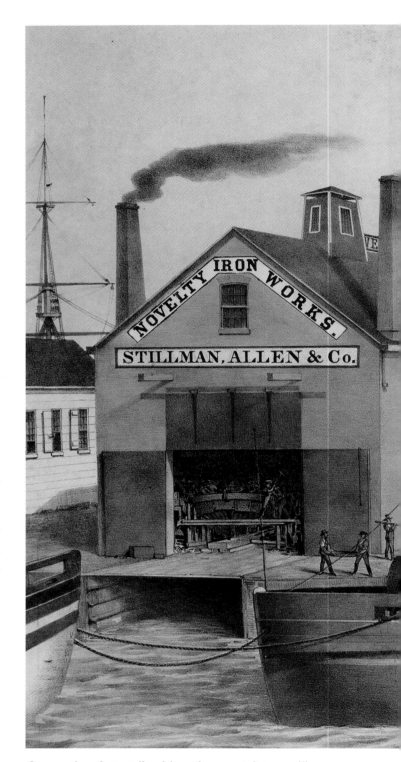

On 17 June 1819, a burning ship was reported off the southern coast of Ireland. A rescue cutter was immediately sent out from Queenstown, but it was not able to catch up with the smoking three-master. The *Savannah*, sailing under the American flag, was however by no means in distress – it was in fact the first steamer to cross the Atlantic. The wooden ship had originally been built as a sailing ship in a New York shipyard and had later been converted to steam. A 90 hp engine drove the two propellers which could be folded together and stowed away on deck in order to lessen resistance when travelling under sail. The top part of the funnel was located between the first and second masts and could be rotated to keep the smoke and sparks away from the sails.

On 2 May, the 34-metre-long *Savannah* left the port of Savannah carrying 75 tonnes of coal and 25 bundles of wood, but no passengers or cargo – no one had the courage to board this new-fangled ship, which was derided as being a 'steam coffin'.

The steamship stopped off in New York, started its historic crossing on 24 May and reached Liverpool in 29 days and 11 hours. However, it

Cross-section of a propeller-driven three-masted steam sailing vessel from the 1880s (left). Installing a boiler in the fitting-out quay of a New York steel works in 1848 (above)

had used sail for most of the voyage and only travelled under steam for 85 hours. The Savannah Steam Ship Company tried unsuccessfully to sell the ship in Europe, and it returned to America. The *Savannah* was offered for sale for $300 with the advice that if the new owner were to remove the machinery, it would 'sail as well as any other ship'.

Despite its commercial failure, America celebrated the first transatlantic crossing by a steamer as a symbol of progress. A contemporary poem read, 'The greatest wonder ever seen/The *Savannah* was the Ocean Queen'.

In 1933, US president Franklin D. Roosevelt declared 2 May, the day on which the *Savannah* had set sail, as National Maritime Day. On 2 May 1958, the keel of the first atomic-powered cargo ship was laid in New Jersey and

THE LANGUAGE OF THE SEA

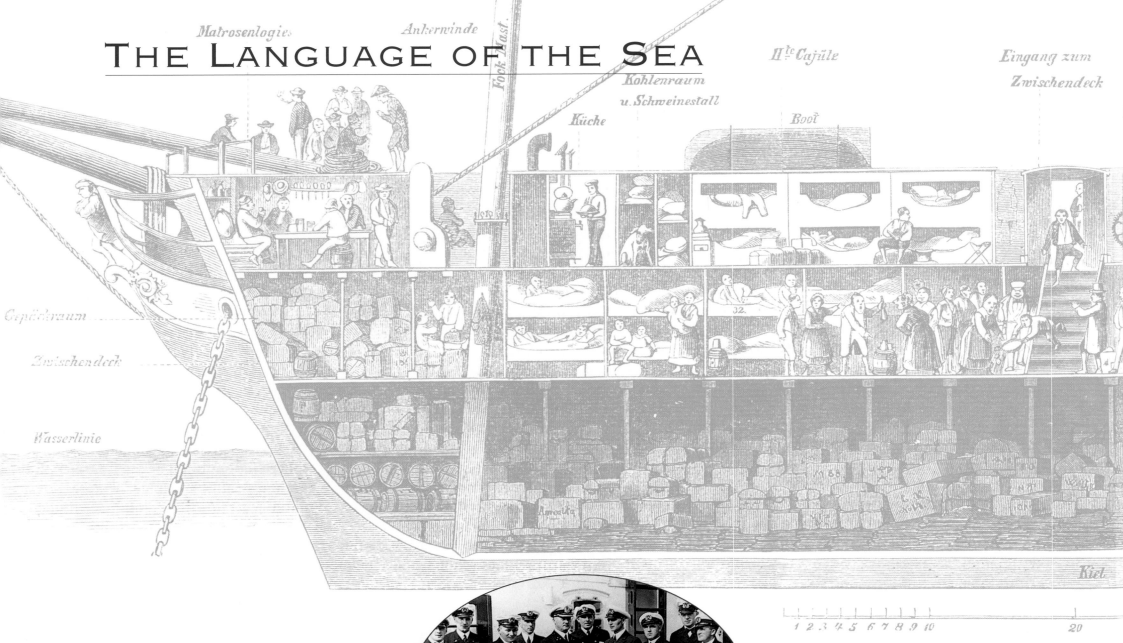

Matrosenlogis   *Ankerwinde*   *Fock Mast.*   *II.te Cajüle*   *Eingang zum Zwischendeck*

Kohlenraum u. Schweinestall

Küche   *Boot*

Gepäckraum

Zwischendeck

Wasserlinie

Kiel

1 2 3 4 5 6 7 8 9 10   20

Leopold Ziegenbein (1874 – 1950; centre) was captain of the Bremen *when Norddeutscher Lloyd's high-speed steamer won the 'Blue Riband' on its maiden voyage.*

Every professional has his own jargon and the sailor is no exception. For the sailor, it's *bulkhead*, *deck* and *overhead* and not *wall*, *floor* or *ceiling*. The sailor is a traditionalist – he still measures distances in nautical miles, speed in knots and depth in fathoms.

Some nautical terminology has found its way into everyday use. Today the expression 'devil to pay' is used primarily to describe having an unpleasant result from some action that has been taken – someone has done something they shouldn't have and, as a result, 'there will be the devil to pay.' Originally, this expression described one of the unpleasant tasks aboard a wooden ship. In wooden ships, the devil was the longest seam in the hull. It ran from the bow to the stern. *Caulking* was done with *pay* or pitch (a kind of tar).

The task of 'paying the devil' (caulking the longest seam) by squatting in the *bilges* was despised by every seaman. When the devil had to be caulked, the sailor sat in a bosun's chair to do so. He was suspended between the devil and the sea – the 'deep' – a very precarious position, especially when the ship was underway.

Often we use 'took the wind out of his sails' to describe getting the best of an opponent in an argument. Originally it described a battle manoeuvre of sailing ships. One ship would pass close to its adversary on its windward side. The ship and sails would block the wind from the second vessel,

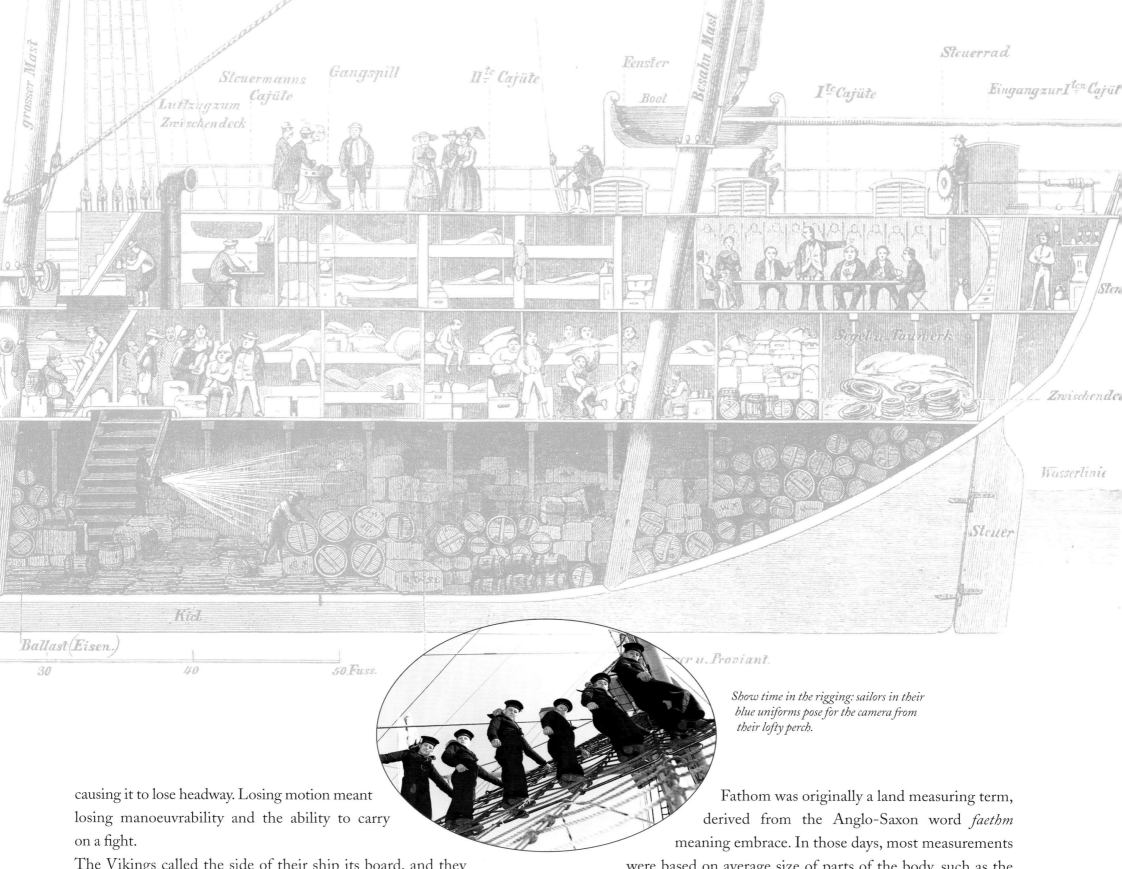

Grosser Mast　*Steuermanns Cajüte*　*Gangspill*　*II^{te} Cajüte*　*Fenster*　*Besahn Mast*　*Boot*　*Steuerrad*　*I^{te} Cajüte*　*Eingangzur I^{ten} Cajü...*

Luftzug zum Zwischendeck

Segeln Tauwerk

Ste...

Zwischende...

Wasserlinie

Steuer

Kiel

Ballast (Eisen.)

...r u. Proviant.

30　　40　　50 Fuss.

Show time in the rigging: sailors in their blue uniforms pose for the camera from their lofty perch.

causing it to lose headway. Losing motion meant losing manoeuvrability and the ability to carry on a fight.

The Vikings called the side of their ship its board, and they placed the steering oar, the *star*, on the right side of the ship, thus that side became known as the *starboard*. It has been that way ever since. And, because the oar was in the right side, the ship was tied to the dock at the left side. This was known as the loading side or *larboard*. Later, perhaps because larboard and starboard were too similar, especially when trying to be heard over the roar of a heavy sea, the phrase became the 'side at which you tied up to in port' – the *port* side.

Fathom was originally a land measuring term, derived from the Anglo-Saxon word *faethm* meaning embrace. In those days, most measurements were based on average size of parts of the body, such as the hand or the foot. A fathom is the average distance from fingertip to fingertip of the outstretched arms of a man – about six feet. A fathom remains six feet. The word was also used to describe taking a measurement – 'to fathom' something. Today, when people are trying to work something out, they are trying to fathom it.

The Royal William, *a 54 metre three-master with propellers, was the first ship to cross the Atlantic almost exclusively under steam (above). – James Cook went on his third Pacific voyage in 1776 with the* Resolution *and the* Discovery *(right), two converted coal ships.*

On 23 April 1838, the *Sirius* anchored in New York, having arrived from Queenstown and London. The two-master was the first ship to cross the Atlantic making continual use of its engines and in the new record time of 18 days and 10 hours. Just hours later, the four-master *Great Western* also arrived from England, beating the *Sirius*'s record by 3 days. It was thus proven, as a New York newspaper stated, that 'it is possible for steamships to cross the Atlantic in safety and comfort and with punctuality, even in bad and turbulent weather. Even the most sceptical observer can doubt this no longer'.

Historians may argue whether the *Savannah*, the *Royal William* or the *Sirius* was the first steamer on the Atlantic, but the important issue is the fact that the age of steam had begun on the oceans as well as on land, on rivers and in coastal traffic. The benefits of the steamer were obvious: they were independent of the vagaries of the wind, they guaranteed passengers shorter journey times and scheduled departure and arrival dates. On the other hand, sailing vessels did not need costly engines or expensive fuel,

was given the name *Savannah* a year later. However, British marine historians complained that the *Savannah* had travelled without passengers and most of the way under sail to boot, so they claim the kudos for the first transatlantic steamer crossing for their country: in August 1833, the *Royal William*, a 54-metre-long three-master with propellers, set sail carrying 324 tonnes of coal and 7 passengers from Pictou, Nova Scotia, and arrived in London after 25 stormy days. Captain MacDougall declared that his ship 'was the first steamer to cross the Atlantic, as it had steamed the entire way'. However, MacDougall did not admit that he had stopped the engines on at least 4 days to clean the steam boiler, and presumably travelled under sail during this time. The *Royal William* never made the return journey – it was sold to Spain as a warship.

James Cook sailed on his first journey across the Pacific on the
Endeavour *in May 1768.*

"THEY HAVE THE POWERFUL SEA BENEATH THEIR
BELLIES AND THE CLOUDS AND STARS ABOVE THEM.
THEY ARE DRIVEN BY A HEAVENLY BREATH
WITH A GENTLEMAN'S VIEW INTO THE DISTANCE.

THEY SWING COQUETTISHLY INTO THE HAND OF FATE
LIKE DRUNKEN BUTTERFLIES. BUT THEY CARRY
FROM LAND TO LAND PRECIOUS THINGS WITH CARE."

JOACHIM RINGELNATZ, IN
"SEGELSCHIFFE" (SAILING SHIPS), 1920

crews were smaller and as there were no engines there was more space for cargo.

No sooner had the first steamships, which were part sailing ship, part steamer and thus maritime hybrids, caused a stir on the Atlantic, than first American shipyards and later British ones started building a new generation of sailing ships: the clippers (from the word 'clip', high speed). With their sleek wooden hulls, their very pointed prows and as many as four towering masts carrying up to 3,000 square metres of sail, they could easily outrun any steamer. They had names like *Flying Cloud*, *Flying Fish* or *Sovereign of the Sea*s, and in ideal wind conditions could reach speeds of up to 22 knots. The fastest steamers at that time could only achieve 13 knots.

Never before had there been faster, more beautiful or bigger sailing ships sailing the world's oceans. People spoke in awe of 'sky-scrapers on the water' and 'greyhounds of the seas', which could make use of their outstanding

speeds especially on the long voyages to Asia and Australia. Clippers were usually cargo ships which brought their owners massive profits, particularly in trade with China – on the outward journey they carried opium to China, and on the return journey freshly harvested China tea to England and the USA.

They carried immigrants to Australia and in a very short time became highly desirable passenger ships after the gold rush started in California in 1848. The fastest route from the Atlantic to the Pacific before the trans-

The Royal Sovereign, *the former* Sovereign of the Seas, *destroyed by fire in 1696 (left). – The* Cutty Sark *is the most famous of all the clippers. Its 3,000 square metres of sail helped it race across the oceans at a speed of 17.5 knots (above).*

The legendary American clipper Flying Cloud *left New York for San Francisco on its maiden voyage in 1851, travelling via Cape Horn (left).*

A contemporary caricature shows the imaginative vehicles used by soldiers of fortune to get to California as quickly as possible to dig for gold in 1849 (above).

continental railway was completed was not the 5,230 km trip overland but the 13,200 nautical mile (24,446 km) route around the much-feared, stormy Cape Horn. The fastest clippers completed this journey in less than 100 days.

Contemporary travellers who kept diaries described the accommodation in first-class: 'All cabins are furnished differently, and the furnishings reveal superior taste. Every room has a rectangular window in the side wall, and there is a sieve-like ventilator between the deck beams providing as much light and air as one could wish for. The dining room next to the cabins contains a large mahogany dining table running the whole length of the room with padded, sofa-like benches along the sides.'

When the sea was calm, they felt 'no more movement than when one was sitting at home in one's own lounge', although during storms things became uncomfortable – and not only in the dining room: 'a boiled leg of mutton jumps out of the dish like a flying fish and lands on a gentleman's shirt; someone else has a beef pie stuck to his breast, and the mustard potatoes are being distributed evenly across the whole table.'

After the clippers, the second half of the 19th century saw the arrival of the windjammers

33

The shipping line J.F.W Iken & Co.'s racy Bremen, *built in 1853, was regarded as extremely seaworthy and took thousands of emigrants to the New World. This painting from 1861 shows it in the Caribbean.*

(from the verb 'to jam', meaning to jam the sailing ship up against the wind). With their steel hulls, masts and yards, they were the first floating giants, less elegant perhaps than their wooden predecessors, the clippers, but much more robust and efficient.

Ironically it was at this time, when sailing ships had reached the climax of thousands of years of perfecting, that they were overtaken by technological developments. Not only were the rival steamships superior in terms of speed, punctuality and safety; sailing ships were also hugely handicapped by the opening of the Suez Canal (1869) and the Panama Canal (1914); they were not able to navigate these man-made waterways, and had to make time-consuming detours via the Cape of Good Hope and Cape Horn. They were thus no longer competitive for passenger traffic.

In *The Mirror of the Sea*, Joseph Conrad, that great champion of the sailing vessel, lamented the end of an era in 1906:

> 'Sailing is an art which, already separated from its highest form, appears to set off down the path towards the shadowy valley of oblivion. To sail a modern steamer does not require the same close relationship with nature (although the responsibility should not be under-estimated), which is an essential requirement for the coming about of

art. Modern sea travel is more impersonal and more methodical in its requirements, which are not as tough but also not as satisfying, because this service is lacking the close contact which binds the artist with the medium of his art. In short, it is no longer so much a matter of love.'

However, sailing ships have not entirely disappeared from our oceans. In World War I, the German three-master *Seeadler* caused problems for the allies as an auxiliary cruiser under the command of Lieutenant Felix Graf von Luckner. Between the two World Wars and subsequently right into the late 1950s, an ever-diminishing fleet of windjammers continued to sail the oceans carrying coal, cement and wheat. Thereafter, any of these ships which had not already sunk or run aground were broken up. Only a handful survived the mass extinction of sailing ships: the *Passat*, the *Peking* and the *Cutty Sark* are moored as museums in Tarvemünde, New York and Greenwich respectively; the *Eagle*, the *Krusenstern*, the *Statsraad Lehmkuhl* and the *Gorch Fock* are used as training ships for trainee sailors. As Joseph Conrad said, and which still rings true today in this age of high-tech, would-be sailors only really get to know the weather, wind and the sea at first-hand on a sailing ship.

Officers of the Polish merchant navy are trained on the sailing ship Dar Mlodziezy *(literally: gift of youth), built in 1982 with 2,936 square metres of sail (top). – Australian Alan Villiers set sail for the New World in a replica of the* Mayflower *in the wake of the Pilgrim Fathers in 1957. The three-master now lies in Plymouth, Massachusetts, as a museum (right).*

SHIP CARVING UPSTAIRS

Travelling by liner

THE RISE, GLORY AND FALL OF THE TRANSATLANTIC LINERS

Samuel Cunard (1787-1865) was the first to offer a regular North Atlantic connection.

Samuel Cunard – pronounced Kunaar – was described by his contemporaries as 'shy, taciturn, brilliant and having an endearing manner'. He was born in 1787 in Halifax, Nova Scotia, to a ship-owner. In 1814, he took over his father's business, whose ships delivered mail, freight and passengers along the west coast of America. But he also traded in wood and coal, financed whaling fleets and developed revolutionary ideas for Atlantic traffic: 'Correctly constructed and properly managed steam ships can depart with the same punctuality, and arrive at their destinations as reliably as railway trains on the mainland. We don't need to drill tunnels, dig away hills or build roads. All we need is to have steam-driven ships.'

This was an audacious concept in the 1830s! The North Atlantic, which was feared by sailors and passengers alike, was still dominated by sailing ships; one out of every six sailing ships never reached its port of destination. Sailing plans were illusory, because arrival times were dictated by the vagaries of the wind and of captains' navigation skills.

In 1839, when the British Admiralty was looking for a contractor to carry mail on scheduled steamship routes between the Old World and the New World, Cunard travelled to England and submitted his tender. To the amazement of his competitors, this ship-owner from abroad, who was quite unknown in London, won the contract. He undertook to set up a shipping line whose steamers would travel twice monthly in summer and once monthly in winter between Liverpool and Boston.

Now, although Samuel Cunard had a contract worth £60,000 per year, he had no ship. He joined forces with three trading partners, founded the British and North American Royal Mail Steam Packet Company, and commissioned construction of four identical ships at a Glasgow yard: *Britannia*, *Acadia*, *Caledonia* and *Columbia*.

When the *Britannia* was launched in February 1840, the *Glasgow Courier* wrote: 'We can report today on an event which will probably represent a milestone in the history of this country, inasmuch as it represents the start of a new kind of transport between the Old World and the New World, which will bring the two worlds together by halving the previous travelling time.'

On 4 July 1840, the national annual celebration day of the United States, the stage of progress was such that the *Britannia* was ready to sail from the port of Liverpool: it was a wood-construction paddle steamer with a strongly protruding bow-sprit, gold plated stern decorations, three gigantic masts, one black funnel with a red band on its top, and cabins for 115 passengers.

At 2 pm, Captain Henry Woodruff gave the order to cast off for the voyage across the Atlantic, approx 3000 nautical miles. On-board, there were 63 passengers, including Samuel Cunard with his daughter and one cow, three cats and some hens. Space was uncomfortably restricted on the ship, which was only 63 metres long, and below decks, the engine took up almost one-third of available space, the mails were carried in the bow, and the wine-cellar was astern. Passengers sat in the lounge together with the captain and the ship's doctor on benches along two long tables: breakfast was at 10 am, lunch at 4 pm, followed by the evening meal three hours later. The cow, who spent her voyage in a pen, provided fresh milk, the hens laid eggs every day, and the cats hunted down the rats. The lounge served as a sitting room

In July 1840, Samuel Cunard's paddle-steamer the Britannia *sailed from Liverpool to Halifax and Boston. This historic voyage was the start of routine transatlantic shipping under steam.*

The brilliant ship builder Isambard Kingdom Brunel designed the first of the ocean-going giants, the Great Eastern *(above), and the* Great Western, *England's first steamship constructed specifically for operation on the North Atlantic (right).*

between meal-times, the ladies did their knitting and embroidery, and the men read or played whist. When the passengers withdrew to their appointed cabins, the steward would give them two candles, and 'lights out' was around midnight.

The *Britannia* steamed at 8.5 knots across the 'Big Pond', anchored off Halifax after 12 days and 10 hours and sailed on to Boston, where she moored late in the evening of 18 July. On 1 August, she started the return voyage, and moored in Liverpool 10 days later. This was the birth of scheduled transatlantic shipping under steam, which continued to develop transportation history with ships of increasing size and speed. In 1841, Samuel Cunard's foursome of ships was complete, and they sailed with astonishing punctuality and reliability. In the

first 14 years, they transported more than 100,000 passengers, without losing one passenger, damaging one item of baggage or damaging any ship. Cunard promised his passengers 'Speed, comfort and safety', but set priorities: safety was disproportionately more important than speed and comfort. The English writer Charles Dickens, who crossed the Atlantic on the *Britannia* in the perennially stormy winter month of January, wrote in his *American Notes*, a highly graphic description of the spartan interior of the ship, that the lounge reminded him of 'a gigantic hearse with windows', in the cabin he felt like a 'giraffe in a flower pot', and the bunk appeared extremely narrow to him – 'nothing is tighter to sleep in than a coffin', in brief: 'An experience which left an impression'.

"Before we climbed down into the body of the ship, we had to pass from the deck through an extended, narrow passageway, not dissimilar to the inside of a gigantic hearse, but with windows, and at its other end there was a comfortless stove, at which 3 or 4 freezing stewards endeavoured to warm their hands."

Charles Dickens in
"American Notes" on his Atlantic Crossing on the Britannia in 1842

One decade later, the paddle steamer fleet of the British and North American Royal Mail Steam Packet Company, which in 1847 also ran to New York, for the first time, virtually held a monopoly for transport of freight, mail and passengers between England and the USA. Then, however, it encountered competition from America.

Edward Knight Collins was born in 1802 in Truro, Massachusetts, and was – like Samuel Cunard – the son of a ship-owner. Like him, he also took over his father's fleet of sailing ships and firmly believed that the future on the sea

Edward Knight Collins

belonged to steamships. The American government, to whom Cunard's position of predominance on the Atlantic had long been a thorn in the side, gave Collins a 10-year contract for postal service between New York and Liverpool, and annual subsidies; he founded the United States Mail Steam Company and commissioned four steamships – *Atlantic, Pacific, Arctic* and *Baltic*.

Whilst Samuel Cunard contented himself with small, robust but functional ships, Edward Knight Collins insisted on size, speed and a high standard of equipment. The *Atlantic*, which set

In autumn 1848, the Hamburg-Amerikanische Packetfahrt-Actien-Gesellschaft started its line service between Hamburg and New York with the three-master sailing ships the Deutschland *(left) and the* Nord-Amerika *(right)*

43

out on her maiden voyage from New York on 27 April 1850, was also the first 'floating palace': she was longer (91 metres), faster (12 knots) and bigger (250 passengers) than the *Britannia*. The cabins had running water, hot-air heating, a ventilation system and bell-pulls to ring for the steward. There were bathing cabins

In 1885, the Cunard's Line's Etruria *was the last steamship on the Atlantic still to be equipped with ancillary sails. Then, as now, the owner of the ship was indicated by the colours on the funnels and the shipping company's flags.*

and a hairdressing salon, the men had their own smoking room, and the ladies their own 'ladies' salon'.

Although the American-registered stern-paddle-steamers were quick and almost luxurious, they were completely uneconomic. Whilst the 'Cunarders', as Samuel Cunard's ships were called, consumed 37 tons of coal daily, the 'Collins Liners' gobbled up 87 tons per day and steamed ever further into the red. In 1858, Edward Knight Collins had to declare bankruptcy. The winner of the first duel between shipping lines on the Atlantic was Samuel Cunard. He became Sir Samuel, retired to Canada a rich man and enjoyed living on land until he died in 1865. Collins died in poverty

and obscurity, in 1878. The end of the United States Mail Steam Company simultaneously represented America's premature withdrawal from the North Atlantic. The USA concentrated on opening up the 'Wild West' with railways and riverboats.

In the middle of the 19th Century, in Europe, under the impetus of an upsurge in nationalism and the onset of industrialisation, three shipping lines were founded within one decade, and these were to battle for market shares on the North Atlantic: in 1847 there was the Hamburg Amerikanische Packetfahrt-Actien-Gesellschaft, in 1857 Norddeutscher Lloyd, in 1861 Compagnie Générale Transatlantique. These were shortly followed by the Ocean Steam Navigation Company (1869), which was later to be the White Star Line, and the Nederlandsch Amerikaanische Stoomboot Maatschappij (1873), which is now the Holland-Amerika Lijn or Holland America Line.

This was the cue for a battle for time-saving and tonnage, glitter and glamour on the Atlantic, which lasted right into the 1950s. The 'big pond' became the 'street of floating hotels', the racetrack for the 'Blue Riband', the symbolic distinction for the quickest crossing, which rewarded shipping lines with passengers and nations with prestige.

'The purpose of the Hamburg-Amerikanische Packetfahrt-Actien-Gesellschaft is to provide a regular connection with Hamburg and North America, using Hamburg-registered sailing ships'. This is what was set out in the foundation charter, of 1847, of the Hanseatic Shipping Line, which was later to abbreviate its long-winded name to Hapag and was also called the Hamburg-Amerika Line. 17 years after the Atlantic premiere of the paddle steamer *Britannia*, the Germans still distrusted the new-fangled propulsion system.

In October 1848, the three-master *Deutschland*,

Hamburg–Amerika Line, Hamburg

Hamburg–Bremer Afrika-Linie, Bremen

Deutsche Levante Linie, Hamburg

Deutsche Ost-Afrika-Line, Hamburg

Norddeutscher Lloyd, Bremen

Aug. Bolten, Hamburg

Leonhardt & Blumberg, Hamburg

Hamburg–Südam. Dampfschiff.-Gesellschaft

Arnold Bernstein, Hamburg

Rob. M. Sloman jr., Hamburg

Woermann–Linie A.-G., Hamburg

Tankdampfer-Ges. «Ossag» GmbH, Hamburg

Cunard Steam Ship Co., Liverpool

White Star Line, Liverpool

Atlantic Transport Co., Ltd., London

Blue Star Line, London

Aberdeen & Commonwealth Line, London

Anchor–Line Ltd., Glasgow

Canadian Pacific Steamships Ltd., London

Gen. Steam Navigation Co., Ltd., London

Royal Mail Lines, London

Union Castle Line, London

Pacific Steam Navigation Co., Liverpool

Prince Line, London

Compagnie Générale Transatlantique, Paris

Cie. Fraissinet, Marseille

Cie. Des Messageries Maritimes, Paris

Cie. de Navigation Paquet, Marseilles

Cie. Française de Nav. à Vapeur, Paris

Cie. de Navigation Mixte, Marseilles

Cie. de Nav. Sud-Atlantique, Paris

Cie. de Navigation D'Orbigny, Paris

Holland-America Line, Rotterdam

Rotterdamsche Lloyd, N.V., Rotterdam

Utd. Netherlands Navigation Co., Den Haag

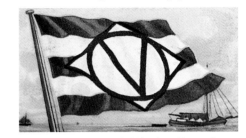

Phs. van Ommeren's Shipping, Rotterdam

Lloyd Triestino, Trieste

Lloyd Sabaudo, Genoa

Cosulich, Soc. Triestina di Nav., Trieste

Navigazione Libera Triestina, Trieste

Wilh. Wilhelmsen, Oslo

Fred-Olsen & Co., Oslo

Westfal-Larsen & Co., Bergen

Norske Amerika Linje, Oslo

United States Lines Co., New York

Morgan Line, New York

Canadian Pac. Railway Co., Montreal

Vaccaro Line, New Orleans

Dollar Steamship Lines, Inc., San Francisco

Isthmian Steamship Co., New York

C.D. Mallory & Co., Inc., New York

Grace Steamship Co. Inc., New York

Japan Mail Steamship Co., Tokyo

Mitsui & Co., Tokyo

Kokusai Kisen Kabushiki Kaisha, Tokyo

Katsuda S.S. Co., Kobe

from Hamburg, performed her maiden voyage to New York, followed in mid-November by the *Nord-Amerika*, and by the *Elbe* in March of the following year. These were ships that could carry 220 passengers but were just 100 m long. Line director Adolph Godeffroy praised the interior fittings as being 'as attractive and as comfortable as one could ever wish, whilst avoiding all superfluous luxury.' However, this trio of sailing ships was much slower than the Cunard steamers, as a passage from Hamburg to New York and back would take 88 to 98 days.

In 1853, the AGM of the shareholders of Hapag decided by 47 votes to 11 to order two 'steamers' from a British yard. Three years later, this Hanseatic line also entered the steamship age with *Hammonia* and *Borussia*. Step by step, they phased out their sailing ships so that eventually, by 1867, they were able to offer weekly transatlantic voyages, with their 8 steamers. The Hamburg-Amerikanische Packetfahrt-Actien-Gesellschaft was celebrating its ten-year anniversary when in 1857 Norddeutscher Lloyd was founded by Bremen business people in order to 'set up regular steamship connections with European and transatlantic countries'. The new line differed from the Hamburg company from the outset in that it relied on propeller steamers and had two pairs of sister ships constructed in Scotland. *Bremen* and *New York*, *Hudson* and *Weser* were intended to provide a 14-day line service across the Atlantic. When, in the following year, the *Bremen*, the first of six ships of that name, first entered the mouth of the Weser, the local *Weser Zeitung* (*Weser Times*) rejoiced: 'Anyone who is German at heart must feel his pulse race at the thought that this magnificent steamer is to carry the German flag across the ocean and become a pioneer for further products of national trade.' It did, however, go on to raise the following questions: 'Can it succeed, where its own home country has not yet shown any willingness to provide government subsidy as in other countries where such endeavours are aided?' It did succeed, and not least because Norddeutscher Lloyd was far quicker than Hapag to concern itself with a lucrative market: In the 'tween-deck', between the main deck and the holds, emigrants to America were transported, whilst on the return voyage supplies of tobacco and cotton were brought back to Europe.

French investors Emile and Isaac Péreire, who had made millions out of railway construction and the banking business, had virtually no understanding of shipping business but, like good businessmen, they recognised the opportunity to make money out of the sea: 'The time is ripe to invest capital in the major shipping companies.'

In 1855, in Paris, they founded the Compagnie Générale Maritime, constructed a representative

In 1858, the Bremen *was the first ocean-going ship of Norddeutscher Lloyd, which had been founded one year before, by Bremen businessmen. She crossed the Atlantic in 14 days and 13 hours.*

THE GREAT EASTERN – THE FIRST OF THE OCEAN GIANTS

Isambard Kingdom Brunel.

What English engineer Isambard Kingdom Brunel had designed in 1852 was six times bigger than anything that had previously sailed the world: she was 211 m long, had six masts, five funnels, two side paddles, a stern screw and cabins for 4,000 passengers.

Her name was planned to be *Leviathan* (giant) but it was soon changed to *Great Eastern*, whilst Brunel always referred to her as 'the big ship'. On the slipway in November 1857, however, the giant, weighing in at 18,915 tons, seemed remarkably averse to water: she slid forwards all of 120 cm, then refused to budge. Three months later, the ship was moved forwards by a few metres; not until the end of January 1858 did she feel water under her keel. 'The big ship' cost twice what had been originally calculated to build her.

Six months later, the 'mega ship' was finally ready. But on the trial voyage, the fo'c'sle was destroyed by an explosion, which also ravaged one funnel and catapulted a stoker overboard, who was then crushed by the paddles. Work continued for a further two years on the iron giant. Finally, in June 1860, she set off for her maiden voyage to New York, where she arrived ten days later and was celebrated as a wonder ship. You could buy *Great Eastern* lemonade, drink *Great Eastern* beer and stay at the *Great Eastern* hotel which had been built.

The brief period of euphoria was followed by a long one of misery. The superb creation was apt to roll and pitch so seriously that only a trickle of passengers would venture on board. So the shipping line sold its bird of ill fortune. Next, she was used for laying telegraph cables across the North Atlantic and in the Far East, and was then left to rust for 12 years until David Lewis, the owner of a Liverpool chain of warehouses, took pity on her. From then on, the world's largest ship, with shops, restaurants and a music hall, was used as a floating showcase for her owner's business. When that novelty had worn off and visitors stopped coming, the former glory of Great Britain was scrapped.

In her short career, the liner had proven to be the worst case of design misconception and the worst example of unshakable bad luck in the history of shipping in the Christian world. Her engines had been under-powered, her paddle drive prone to malfunction, and the strength of her construction had been open to question. *Great Eastern* had caught fire, run onto a reef, rammed ten ships, experienced one mutiny, ruined her owner and caused the premature death of her builder from worrying about the whole fiasco. Superstitious sailors believed they knew why the *Great Eastern* had had such a tragic fate in store: when the double-bottom was opened up for scrapping, the skeletons of two yard employees were discovered – they had inadvertently been welded in there during the construction of the ship.

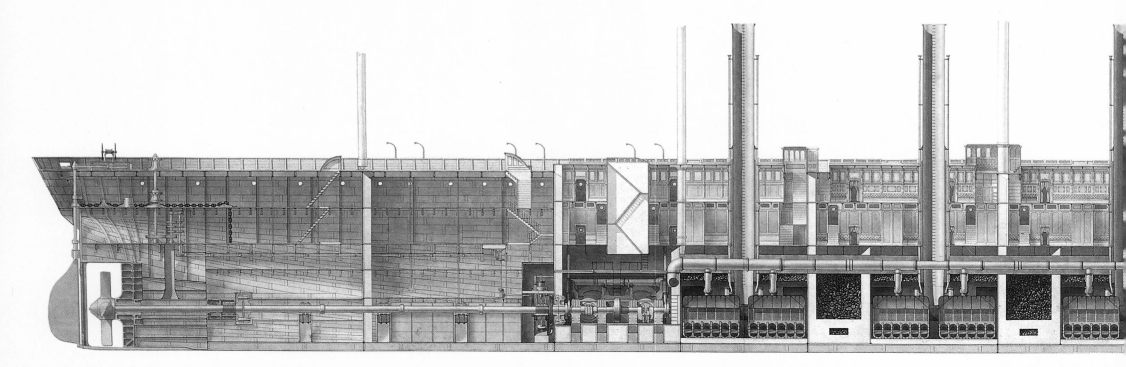

The Great Eastern, *constructed in the mid-19th century by Isambard Kingdom Brunel, was the first ocean-going giant of all time: 211 metres long, with 6 masts, 5 funnels, 2 side paddles, a stern screw and cabins for 4000 passengers.*

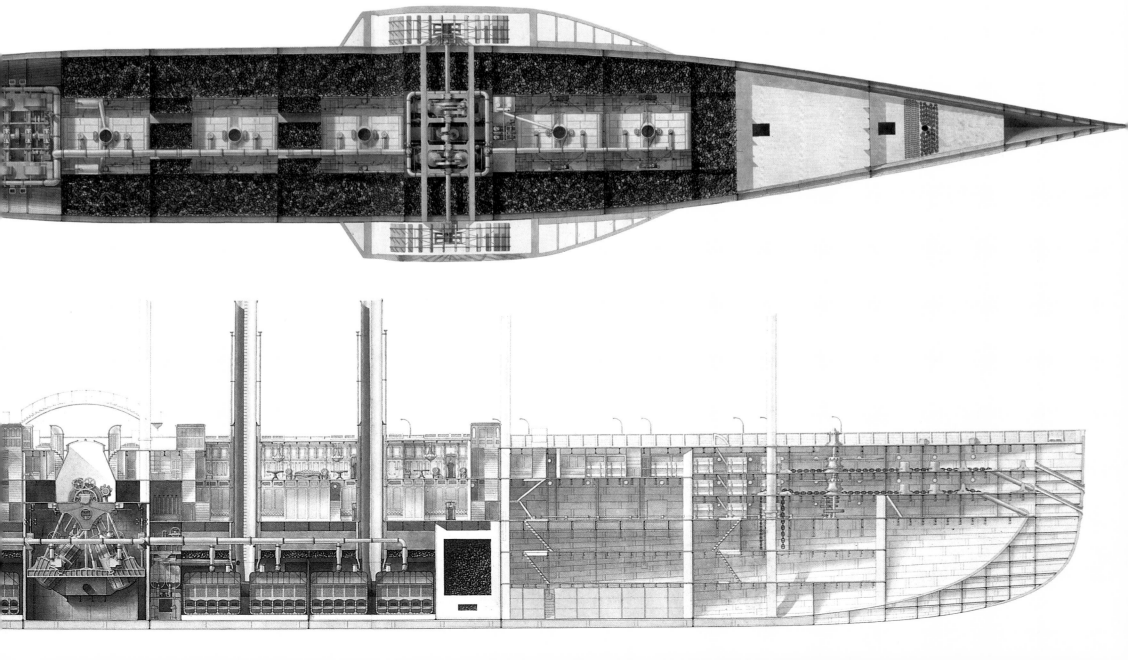

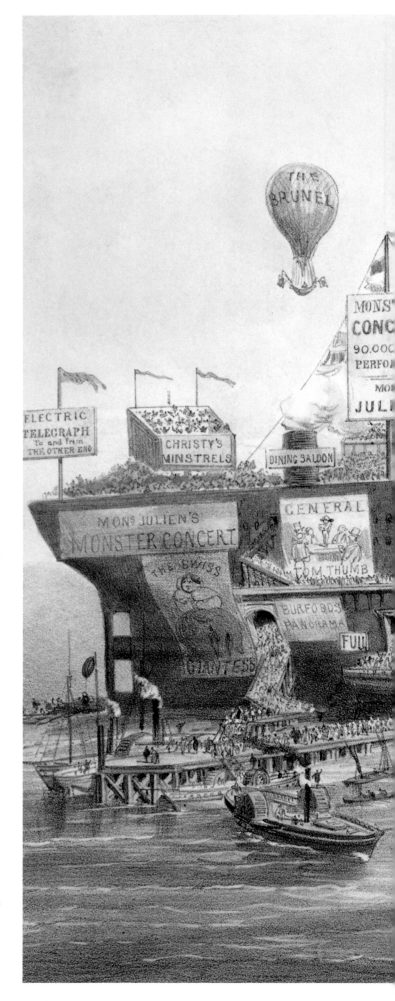

After the Great Eastern *was de-commissioned in America, she became a tourist attraction which people paid to visit (above), and later in England she was converted to a leisure centre with a variety theatre and souvenir shop (right).*

building in the best position, No. 15 Place Vendôme, the present location of the Ritz Hotel, as the head office and – within two years – purchased a fleet of 33 sailing ships and six steamships. In 1860, they received from the Emperor Napoleon III a mail contract for a steamer connection to North America and interest-free credit for construction of 14 passenger ships. The Péreire brothers constructed their business machine and gave it a new name in 1861: Compagnie Générale Transatlantique, abbreviated to Transat, and known as the French Line in the USA. In June 1864, the *Washington*, a paddle-steamer with an iron stern, and 105 m overall length, equipped with two funnels and cabins for 400 passengers, set out from Le Havre on her first voyage to New York. Later, the *Lafayette* and *Europe* were to follow across the Atlantic, flying the tricolour from their sterns.

Despite German and French competition, it was England that kept the lead on the Atlantic until the 1880s. In 1888, 30 'Royal Mail Steamers' of the Cunard Steam Ship Company, the previous British and American Royal Mail Steam Packet Company – later to be known as the Cunard

Kaiser Wilhelm II coined the phrase: 'Germany's future is on the water!'

Line – maintained scheduled voyages from Liverpool, with calls at Queenstown in Southern Ireland, now known as Cobh, to New York and Boston. The schedule laid down the transport conditions, as posted on the 'tween-deck': 'Each passenger has his own bed provided, and married couples are housed together with their children in the same compartment. Women and men travelling on their own have separate accommodation but there is no segregation during the day. Passengers have to bring their own plates, cups, knives, forks, spoons and bed linen. These are available at reasonable prices in Liverpool and Queens Town. Each passenger receives one container of water daily and as much food as he can eat, all of the best quality.' Top-drawer passengers travelled more comfortably, in the first class. A contemporary raved with enthusiasm about the Cunard ships *Umbria* and *Etruria*, whose accommodation was '…thoroughly superb. There are single and double beds, which – as in the case of a Pullman carriage – can be stowed away during the day, so that the cabin is converted into a comfortable lounge. Instead of jugs, there are taps for hot or cold water. You press a button, and the steward arrives immediately. You turn a switch and there is electric light.'

In the 1880s, transatlantic passenger travel was dominated by England, and the 1890s was the decade of the new giants of the sea. Between 1881 and 1891, New York's harbour statistics record 738,668 passengers carried by Norddeutscher Lloyd, 525,900 with the Hamburg-Amerika Line, 371,193 with White Star, with Cunard following in fourth place with 323,836 passengers.

When, in March 1897, Norddeutscher Lloyd's *Kaiser Wilhelm der Grosse* finally left the slipway at the Vulkan yard, at Stettin, in the presence of Kaiser Wilhelm II and more than 30,000 jubilant spectators, Germany was seen not only to have constructed the world's largest passenger ship (14,329 gross tonnage, abbreviated to GT), but also the first four-funnel ship. The new profile created a sensation, and over the succeeding years the image of four funnels became the symbol of quality for an ocean-going steamer, with much the

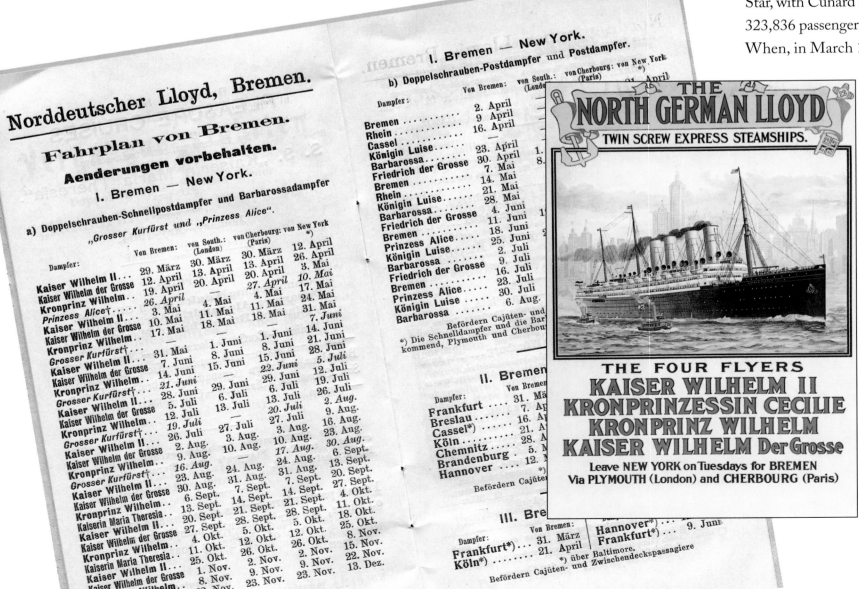

Schnelld. „Kaiser Wilhelm der Grosse" den Rothesand-Leuchtthurm passirend.

Norddeutscher Lloyd's Kaiser Wilhelm der Grosse, *in 1897, was the first 'floating palace' and the first four-funnel ship (above). - In 1900, the* Deutschland *was launched, the only 4-funnel ship constructed by Hapag (below).*

same cachet as the stars on bottles of cognac. In passengers' eyes, they symbolised luxury, speed and safety, and for that reason many preferred to book their passages on four-funnel craft.

Until then, Atlantic travel had been operated with 'floating boarding-houses', but the age of the 'floating palace' was begun by the *Kaiser Wilhelm der Grosse*, also dubbed the 'Tubby Wilhelm' and the 'Grosser kaiser' in German nicknames of the time. Norddeutscher Lloyd was the first shipping line to take on a designer

GROSS REGISTERED TONNAGE?

GROSS REGISTERED VOLUME?

GROSS TONNAGE?

In 1848, the English marine engineer Moorsom invented a survey formula for ships, which gradually came to be used worldwide: Gross Tonnage (GT), equivalent to the German BRT (Bruttoregistertonne - gross registered tonnage). However, a gross registered tonne was not a unit of weight but a volumetric unit: 1 BRT corresponded to 100 cubic feet or 2.83 cubic metres.

'Moorsom's Rule' comprised a survey of enclosed ship accommodation from the keel up to the top deck, but excluded the kitchen, toilets or superstructures for additional equipment. This survey provided the basis for fees for registration, ports, pilots, tugs, canals and locks. Since July 1994, after a 12-year transition period, a new survey system has been applied internationally and is bound to cause confusion: the registered tonne at 2.83 cubic metres remains, but the innovation is that the total volume of the hull is surveyed and corrected according to a conversion factor which varies according to the ship's size and function. Whilst Gross Tonnage is still referred to in English, in German the gross registered tonne has been replaced by the new gross volumetric figure which is abbreviated to BRZ.

Traditionally, military ships are not surveyed according to their volumetric capacity but according to their displacement of water in tonnes, in English: 'Displacement Tonnage'. Thus, for example, a 10,000 tonne cruiser displaces 10,000 tonnes of water.

The German ship the Kronprinzessin Cecilie, *a Norddeutscher Lloyd 4-funnel ship, which was constructed in 1907, made up a popular foursome of ships together with her 'near sister ships' the* Kaiser Wilhelm der Grosse, *the* Kronprinz Wilhelm *and the* Kaiser Wilhelm II.

54

for interior fitments, in this instance in the form of Johannes Georg Poppe. This interior designer, who had previously designed several representative buildings in Bremen, made his mark with plush and pomp, cherubs and tassels, gold stucco and stained glass. Poppe's exaggerated 'Bremen baroque', also pejoratively known as 'brothel baroque', complied with the taste of the age, proved to be an encouragement to first class passengers and was quick to be imitated by the competition. The *Grosser kaiser's* triumph was complete when in 1898, for the first time, the 'Blue Riband' was won by Germany for the quickest Atlantic crossing, which had been a firmly held English prize for more than three decades.

The promotional effect was tremendous. In one blow, Norddeutscher Lloyd became the leading line: in 1897 it transported 36,145 passengers to New York, and in 1898 it was as much as 76,118, just one quarter of all Atlantic passengers. However, the world's quickest and largest ship had an hourly coal consumption of 20 tonnes when travelling at 22 knots, and this unmistakably narrowed down the profit margin. At the same time, she wallowed in a troublesome way, even on a calm sea; American passengers nick-named her 'Rolling Billy' which was 'Willi' in the equally disrespectful German nickname, but they remained loyal to her. This prompted Bremer Lloyd to commission three craft that were virtually sister ships: *Kronprinz Wilhelm* (1901), *Kaiser Wilhelm II* (1903) and *Kronprinzessin Cecilie* (1907), which were

The legendary Captain Charles Polack.

"FOR MANY CAPTAINS ON THE LARGE PASSENGER SHIPS IN NORTH ATLANTIC TRAFFIC, THE SOCIAL COMPONENT OF THEIR DUTY WAS A BURDEN. NOT FOR CHARLES POLACK. HIS SHIP WAS NOT THE QUICKEST, AND NOT THE MOST LUXURIOUS; BUT THE POSITION HELD BY THE KRONPRINZESSIN CECILIE WAS UNDISPUTED AS ONE OF THE MOST POPULAR ON THE GOLDEN ROUTE. PASSENGERS LOVED THIS MOUSTACHIOED GIANT, ESPECIALLY AMERICANS. THERE WERE PASSENGERS WHO HELD TRUE TO HIM FOR 20 YEARS. TO THEM HE WAS KNOWN SIMPLY AS 'CHARLY'."

SANDRA PARETTI, IN "THE MAGIC SHIP", 1977

Cie Gle TRANSATLANTIQUE
FRENCH LINE

SS « ROCHAMBEAU » (Pont-promenade).

T. S. S. „ Zeeland "
Length 580 feet. Beam 60 feet.
Tonnage 11,904 gross.

A Ship is a 'She'

'When a ship lies in harbour, she is always surrounded by hordes of men. She has fine curves, a slim waist and a steel corset, she needs a lot of paint in order to look her best, and her upkeep costs a lot of money. And it takes the right man for the job. That's why a ship is a "she".'

This is the explanation, kept framed and under glass, in the warehouse of the cruiseship the Royal Star.

A different explanation sounds more credible: In the early days of sea travel, sailing ships usually had feminine, quite often full-breasted figureheads. The exclusively male crew, who were often at sea for months on end, experienced erotic dreams and transferred their yearning for femininity to the ship. In German and in English parlance, ships are feminine, but not in French. When, in the 1930s, Compagnie Générale Transatlantique wanted to re-name their newly constructed ship after the Western French region of Normandy, which in French is feminine, 'La Normandie', sailors protested. They wished to adhere to the French tradition of male ship names and insisted on Le Normandie. Finally, a compromise was reached: Normandie without 'Le' or 'La'.

In former days, ships were adorned with figureheads.

publicised by a shipping line poster as 'The ocean hounds of the four winds'.

Furthermore, arch-rivals Hapag, from Hamburg, flourished, expanded and recruited Albert Ballin, the man who was to make the company the world's greatest shipping line. Ballin, who was born in 1857, started work as an emigrant passenger agent, was the manager of the Hapag Passenger Department by the age of 29, rose to the rank of Director and from 1899 to 1918 was the Managing Director. He weeded out the older craft and replaced them with faster and more comfortable high-speed steamers such as the *Deutschland*, which was launched in January 1900. This was the only four-funnel steamer ever constructed by the Hamburg-Amerika Line, and won the 'Blue Riband' on her maiden voyage. For two years, she remained the fastest

ship in the world (23 knots) and for three years she was Germany's largest (16,502 GT). This giant Hamburg craft, with her transport capacity of 2,050 passengers, one half of which were accommodated on the 'tween-deck, brought the line prestige in the shortterm but no profit in the longterm. The over-developed engine system was uneconomic and prone to faults, and when the *Deutschland* was steaming under full power, the vibrations would annoy the passengers. Albert Ballin took the consequences, Hapag withdrew from the 'Blue Riband' race and from then on placed comfort over speed.

After a yard overhaul at Belfast, Ballin stopped over at London, dined in the grill room of the recently opened Carlton Hotel and was inspired by the combination of refined cuisine with immaculate service in an intimate atmosphere;

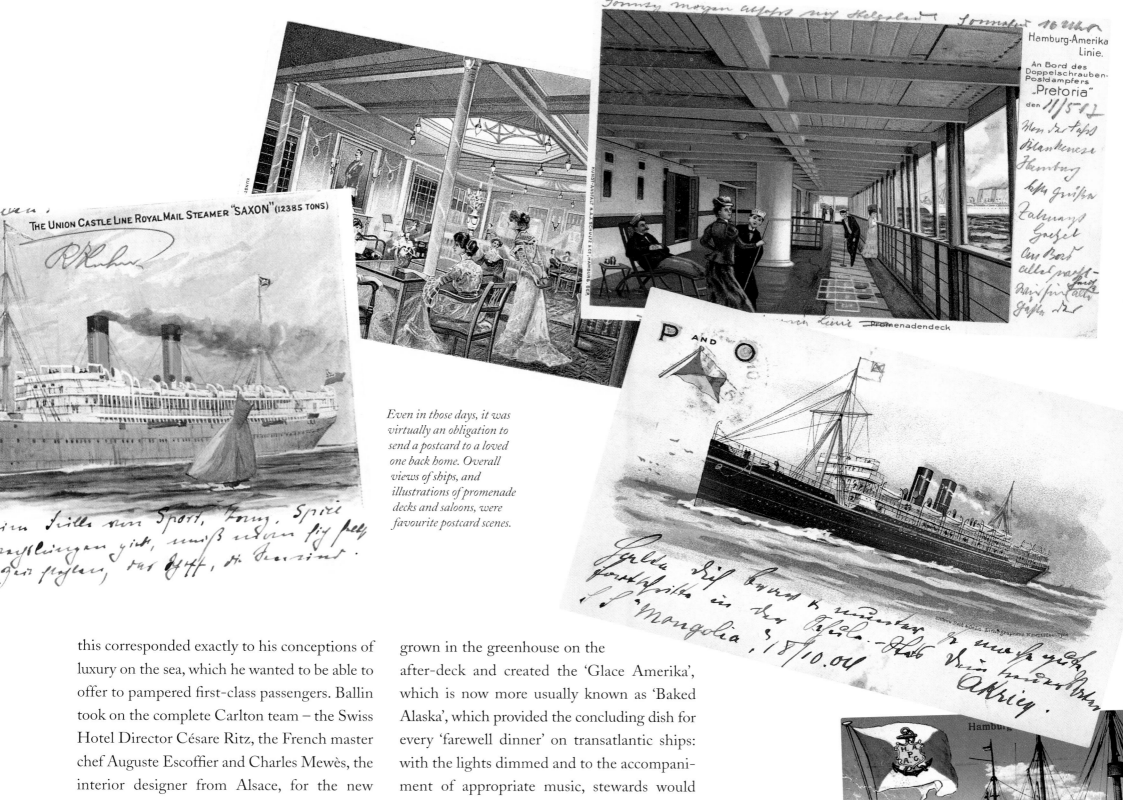

Even in those days, it was virtually an obligation to send a postcard to a loved one back home. Overall views of ships, and illustrations of promenade decks and saloons, were favourite postcard scenes.

THE UNION CASTLE LINE ROYAL MAIL STEAMER "SAXON" (12385 TONS)

Hamburg-Amerika Linie. An Bord des Doppelschrauben-Postdampfers "Pretoria"

this corresponded exactly to his conceptions of luxury on the sea, which he wanted to be able to offer to pampered first-class passengers. Ballin took on the complete Carlton team – the Swiss Hotel Director Césare Ritz, the French master chef Auguste Escoffier and Charles Mewès, the interior designer from Alsace, for the new Hapag creation, the *Amerika*.

Mewès designed lounges, cocktail bars, a palm-garden and the first floating 'Ritz-Carlton Grill': an exclusive restaurant with its own kitchen, reached via six marble steps, glazed on three sides and adorned with a soft pink shade of Louis XVI furniture. Passengers luxuriated in a small circle of four-place tables rather than sitting at long tables as in the main dining room. The stewards were trained by Ritz, Escoffier monitored the gastronomy, had vegetables

grown in the greenhouse on the after-deck and created the 'Glace Amerika', which is now more usually known as 'Baked Alaska', which provided the concluding dish for every 'farewell dinner' on transatlantic ships: with the lights dimmed and to the accompaniment of appropriate music, stewards would totter into the dining room with the illuminated delicacy made from ice cream and egg-white. Passengers were enchanted, and the 'Ritz-Carlton Grills' on the Hapag Steamers *Amerika* (1905) and *Kaiserin Auguste Victoria* (1906), despite the extortionate prices, were always booked out, although a single meal here cost as much as the complete crossing to a 'tween-decks passenger.

At around the turn of the century, Germany had the largest, finest and fastest liners on the

In the a-la-carte restaurant (above) and the palm garden (bottom right) of the Amerika. *The dining room of the* Kaiser Wilhelm II *(top right). These pictures of the accommodation of the* Cap Arcona *(bottom left and opposite) show how plush was the style of the 1920s.*

TRANSATLANTIC VOYAGES IN 1899

'The average price of a good cabin on a good steamer in the first class is between 75 and 125 dollars, in the second between 30 and 65, in the 'tweendeck between 20 and 30. It is a general rule that the slow "steamers" have more favourable prices, but are often quite rudimentary in the matter of comfort. The average voyage over the Atlantic takes from six to nine days. Passengers should pack clothes and anything else they will require on the crossing in small, shallow cases (not clothes bags), for ease of storage in the cabin. Large cases will be stored in the hold. Shipping lines provide luggage labels for this purpose, marked "Cabin" and "Not Wanted". A deck chair can be purchased or rented before the ship sets sail. It can be booked with the shipping line agent upon boarding, until the return trip. It is common practice to give the restaurant/cabin steward a tip (two and a half dollars).'

From: The United States with an excursion into Mexico, Handbook for Travellers edited by Karl Baedeker, 1899.

Cunard ships the Aquitania *(at top) and the* Mauretania *(above) are amongst the most famous liners on the North Atlantic. - On 7th May 1915, the* Lusitania *(right) made political headlines when she was torpedoed and sunk by a German submarine*

Atlantic, and Hapag at 117 and Norddeutscher Lloyd at 113 ships constituted the world's largest shipping lines. Their fleets sailed all the seas of the world, but the North Atlantic remained as the parade ground of the liners, and the place where they hit the headlines with a consistent succession of new speed and size records.

Germany's success caused sleepless nights for the managers of the Cunard Line and damaged England's pride as a seafaring nation. One of the subordinate employees in the office pool grumbled: 'We must challenge these German monsters and hit them hard.' The Admiralty and Cunard signed an agreement which was equally satisfactory to both sides. The latter promised to have the entire fleet converted into ancillary ferry craft in the event of war, whilst the former provided extensive financing for construction of the giant ships *Lusitania* and *Mauretania* and guaranteed annual subsidies. The two sister ships, England's first four-funnel craft, were the largest (31,938 GT), the longest (240 m), the fastest (26 knots) and also the most powerful (78,000 hp) of any ocean-going large ships to date. Despite their imposing bulk, the names given them by the English were almost affectionate: *Lucy* and *Maury*. *Lucy*, which was three months younger than *Maury*, was launched from the slipway in June 1906, having taken only 13 months to build, and left Liverpool in September 1907 for her maiden voyage, and put the nation into a fever of excitement. 'For all classes', enthused the specialist journal *Marine Engineering*, 'the *Lusitania* offers the last word in luxury and comfort. She is a floating hotel, whose comfort exceeds all other ships, with the exception of one

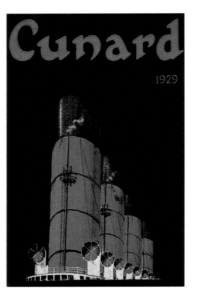

or two luxury palaces in well-to-do cities on land, and the *Lusitania* was constructed to British plans in Great Britain.'

However, the maiden voyages were disappointing: three out of the five days were covered by dense fog, which meant that for some of the time Captain Watt had to throttle back the speed and just missed winning the 'Blue Riband'. On her second voyage, the *Lusitania* made up for this loss by forging across the Atlantic at an average speed of just 24 knots and was the first ship to arrive in New York in less than 5 days, winning the 'Blue Riband' back for England.

The Cunard Line celebrated, and Norddeutscher Lloyd gave its congratulations: 'Naturally Norddeutscher Lloyd is reluctant to part with this Riband which is the symbol of speed and superiority on the sea. Although we must relinquish it, however, we have the consolation of knowing that only one ship in the world is faster than the *Kaiser Wilhelm II*.' As soon as the following year, the figure would be two, because after *Lucy*, *Maury* was also faster than the *Kaiser Wilhelm II*. The two speed queens vied with each other for the record, until September 1909, when the *Mauretania* crossed the 'big pond' at 26.06 knots, taking four days, 10 hours and 51 minutes for the crossing. It was not until 20 years later that this record was excelled by Norddeutscher Lloyd's *Bremen*, which was 22 years younger.

The *Corsair*, the yacht of American finance mogul J Pierpont Morgan, exceeded the size and opulence even of such magnificent steamers as the German Kaiser's *Hohenzollern* or the English King's *Victoria & Albert III*. But the American financier also entertained maritime

Here, the artist has made two errors simultaneously: what this picture illustrates, although the name Titanic is marked on the bow, is not the legendary liner on her maiden voyage in April 1912 – which ended in catastrophe – but her sister ship the Olympic which can be identified by the entirely open promenade on the A deck. On the Titanic, the front section of the promenade was enclosed and fitted with windows. Also, the rearmost funnel could not be smoking, because it was just a dummy.

THE TITANIC – THE END OF A DREAM

Monday, 15 April 1912 at 0045 hrs, one hour after the Titanic's collision with an iceberg: the first white distress rocket explodes in the night sky.

The 'largest ship on the seas and the most magnificent work of human hand', constructed according to the latest state of the art and operated by experienced officers, sailed across the Atlantic on a cold April night, rammed an iceberg and sank.

The *Titanic*? No, the *Titan*, whose fate was described by the barely-known author Morgan Robertson in 1898 in his short story 'Futility' (*Titan - A love story on the high seas*). But the surprising similarities are not just limited to the name and fate of the ships: the real and the fictitious liners were of the same length, the same size and the same speed, both had insufficient lifeboats and both were equipped with watertight bulkheads. It was perverse to have asserted that the new ship, the *Titanic*, which set sail on 10 April 1912 from Southampton on its maiden voyage to New York, was 'unsinkable'. But the English specialist publication *The Ship Builder* in 1911, in its special *Titanic* supplement (page 26, first column, seventh line from the bottom), unmistakably claims that thanks to 16 watertight compartments, the craft was 'practically unsinkable'. The

In the American press, the White Star Line had advertised the first West–East Atlantic crossing of the Titanic, *the new 'Queen Of The Ocean' for 20 April. The voyage never took place.*

WHITE STAR LINE
ROYAL & UNITED STATES MAIL STEAMERS

FIRST SAILING OF THE LATEST ADDITION TO THE WHITE STAR FLEET

The Queen of the Ocean

TITANIC

LENGTH 882½ FT.   OVER 45,000 TONS
TRIPLE-SCREWS   BEAM 92½ FT.

This, the Latest, Largest and Finest Steamer Afloat, will sail from
WHITE STAR LINE, PIER 59 (North River), NEW YORK

Saturday, April 20th At 12 Noon

All passengers berthed in closed rooms containing 2, 4, or 6 berths, a large number equipped with washstands, etc.

Spacious Dining Saloons
Smoking Room
Ladies' Reading Room
Covered Promenade

THIRD CLASS FOUR BERTH ROOM

THIRD CLASS DINING SALOON

Reservations of Berths may be made direct with this Office or through any of our accredited Agents

THIRD CLASS RATES ARE:

To PLYMOUTH, SOUTHAMPTON, LONDON, LIVERPOOL and GLASGOW. **$36.25**
To GOTHENBURG, MALMÖ, CHRISTIANIA, COPENHAGEN, ESBJERG, Etc. **41.50**
To STOCKHOLM, ÅBO, HANGÖ, HELSINGFORS **44.50**
To HAMBURG, BREMEN, ANTWERP, AMSTERDAM, ROTTERDAM, HAVRE, CHERBOURG **45.00**
TURIN, $48.   NAPLES, $52.50.   PIRAEUS, $55.   BEYROUTH, $61., Etc. Etc.

DO NOT DELAY: Secure your tickets through the local Agents or direct from
WHITE STAR LINE, 9 Broadway, New York

TICKETS FOR SALE HERE

The Titanic's *passengers entered the first class dining-room on D deck (above) by lifts or via a ceremonial staircase. – Captain Edward J Smith lost his life when the ship went down. It is said that he refused to climb into a lifeboat (below).*

floating 'grand hotel' had been under way for just 110 hours when, on the night of 15 April, it grazed an iceberg to the south of Newfoundland at 22.5 knots, to sink 160 minutes later.

The tragic end was recorded by London teacher Lawrence Beesley from lifeboat No. 13: 'Some leapt into the water, but most clung to the railings and deck structures. The ship tipped up further and further, until it was almost on end with the stern up in the air. It remained motionless for some time, perhaps five minutes, but it may have been less, then it slowly slid into the water and the sea closed behind it. 1500 people who had not been able to find places in lifeboats fought a hopeless battle for their lives in the icy water. Their cries are not only cries for help but also an appeal to the world to prevent the possibility of such a catastrophe in the future'. Of the 2,201 passengers and crew members, it is probable that 711 were saved (the precise figures are unknown). The sinking of the *Titanic* shocked the world as no other shipping catastrophe has done before or since. The blind confidence in technology, progress and the scope of future possibilities was permanently shaken.

In 1985, the American marine biologist Robert Ballard located the *Titanic* 4 km below the surface. One year later, he dived down to the wreck in a small submarine, took photographs and video recordings and left behind a panel requesting that 'All who follow us here should leave this ship in peace'. This

Third-class passengers (see photo) had the lowest chance of survival, and 75% of them died. Only 37% of first-class passengers lost their lives.

did not prevent French souvenir hunters from salvaging 900 items from the *Titanic* such as plates, visiting cards and shaving brushes, and making gifts of them as ghoulish conversation pieces.

ambitions: he wanted to own the world's largest fleet and use it to control shipping on the North Atlantic. Morgan bought American, Belgian and English shipping lines, including the renowned White Star Line, which he combined into one umbrella holding company in 1902: the Mercantile Marine Company ('IMM'). But his plans to include the Hamburg-Amerika Line, Norddeutscher Lloyd and the Cunard Line in his shipping empire were doomed to failure.

IMM possessed more than 100 Atlantic liners and transported one third of all passengers to America; what it now lacked was giant craft to win renown and cast a comprehensive shadow over competitors who did not wish to be taken

Naufrage du « Labourdonnais »

Before the First World War, ship sinkings were favourite topics of the gutter press. Artists gave full rein to their imagination in depicting the struggle for survival.

THE CONTINUING STORY OF THE TITANIC

1997 was a 'Titanic' year: in the Spring, the musical 'Titanic' premiered on Broadway in New York, and once again the White Star liner went down on the stage of the Lunt-Fontanne Theater, 46th Street, to the accompaniment of singing and dancing. This spectacle, costing 10 million dollars to produce, won 5 'Tony Awards' for script, music, choreography, orchestration and best musical. In the autumn, history's most expensive film, 'Titanic', reached the cinema. For more than 200 million dollars, director James Cameron (whose other works include 'Aliens', 'Terminator 1', 'Terminator 2') was able to produce a superlative disaster movie, one of 12 re-makes that have been made since 1912. For filming work at Rosarito in Mexico, the ill-fated ship was reconstructed as a mock-up 230 metres in length, and that was only 39 metres shorter than the original. Titanic exhibitions in Hamburg and in Memphis, in the American state of Tennessee, exhibited

hundreds of items salvaged from the wreck. Book titles such as Raise The Titanic!, The Message Of The Titanic *or* The Titanic Conspiracy *- the latter work making the audacious claim that it is not the* Titanic *but her sister ship the* Olympic *which lies at the bottom of the North Atlantic - make up a stack of works available about the* Titanic. *In some cases they are reprints, in others they are new editions, for example the* Last Dinner On The Titanic, *with recipes to recreate at home and tips for a macabre* Titanic *meal at home. In CD shops, there is souvenir music such as Gavin Bryar's oratorio 'The Sinking of the Titanic' and the collage of sounds from the 'Titanic Expedition'.*

A virtual tour of the luxury liner can be made with the CD-ROM 'Titanic - Adventure Out Of Time', and 150 Titanic home-pages are available to those who surf the Internet. Marketing is total, and the legend of the Titanic *is still unbroken, 85 years after her sinking.*

LA PERTE DU PLUS GRAND PAQUEBOT DU MONDE
Le "Titanic" a sombré après être entré en collision avec un iceberg.

over. The American holding company financed a trio of ships for the English White Star Line, intended to place all previous craft in the shade, the four-funnel craft *Olympic*, *Titanic* and *Britannic*. In June 1911, one month after the launch of the *Titanic*, the *Olympic* set out for its maiden voyage to New York. This 'super liner', which was 269 m long, was 29 m longer than the world's highest skyscraper, the Woolworth building in New York. And, with a tonnage of 45,324, she was conspicuously bigger than the previous record holder the *Mauretania*, which on the other hand could travel 4 knots faster. J Pierpont Morgan declared no ambition to win the 'Blue Riband', rather he was concerned with winning 'publicity' by imposing size and extravagant equipment. In the first class, there were three lifts to transport passengers to cabins, suites and common rooms, reflecting more expense than good taste. A passenger walking through here would stroll through the European history of art, with an excursion to Arabia thrown in. A luxury suite cost 4,350 dollars, which was four times more than the average annual income of an American citizen. The newspapers, greatly impressed, referred to 'the largest movable object ever manufactured by human hand'.

The maiden voyage of the *Titanic* on 10 April 1912 was initially overshadowed by the continuing euphoria about the older sister ship the *Olympic*, which, although 30 cm shorter, was otherwise virtually identical. But four and a half days later, an iceberg 600 km to the south-east of Newfoundland made the White Star Liner the most famous of all ships since Noah's Ark.

Upon the sinking of the 'practically unsinkable' ocean-going giant, on the night of 15 April, more than 1500 people lost their lives, frozen in the icy cold water, drowned in the labyrinth of corridors below decks, crushed by the collapse of the forward funnel or fatally injured by the leap from 60 m into the sea from the steeply angled stern. Sailor and novelist Joseph Conrad, who had already, beforehand, described the *Titanic* as a 'monstrous Atlantic ferry managed by a hotel syndicate', summed up world-wide reaction to the catastrophe in one sentence: 'Blind faith in scientific progress has suffered a terrible shock'.

The catastrophe, caused by human frailty, defective equipment and disastrous ill fortune, has long become the symbol of human hubris and a metaphor for disaster. For the American Walter Lord, who wrote the classic *Last night of the* Titanic after interviewing 63 survivors in

1956, it even amounts to a 'classic Greek tragedy'. The assessment made by American marine expert William Garzke, today, is no less extreme: 'Simply everything that could go wrong did go wrong'.

The 'myth of the *Titanic*' makes it easy to forget that far worse tragedies have taken place at sea. In January 1945, a Soviet submarine sank the *Wilhelm Gustloff*, which was steaming westwards

LE SAUVETAGE DES MILLIONS DE L'"OCÉANA"

APRÈS LA COLLISION DE L'"OCEANA" ET DU "PISAGUA"
Les chaloupes de sauvetage trop chargées chavirent

On 16 March 1912, the German sailing ship the Pisagua *rammed the P&O liner* Oceana *in the English Channel. The accident was reported on with copious illustrations by the French* Le Petit Journal.

out of the Bay of Danzig with 6,600 German refugees. 5,348 people, including 3,000 children, were killed. Five days before the end of the war, British fighter aircraft attacked the *Cap Arcona*, in the Bay of Lubeck, which capsized, being totally overloaded with more than 6000 POWs, and burnt out: 5,500 people were burnt to death or drowned.

Only five days after the sinking of the *Titanic*, and thus virtually unknown outside of France, the *France*, owned by Compagnie Générale Transatlantique, set out on its maiden voyage to New York. France's first and last four-funnel

The Imperator *gained the title of the 'World's longest ship' by a beak's length, by using this monstrous eagle as a figurehead*

ship was only half the size of the *Titanic* and had the charm of a Loire chateau. The 'chateau on the Atlantic' celebrated 'haute cuisine', offered 'joie de vivre' and excelled with its elegant interior furnishings. In the first-class grand salon, there was a painting of the 'Sun King' Louis XIV, and a hinged staircase led down into the dining room, which extended over three decks. After dinner, one would be served coffee in the 'Moorish saloon' by stewards, each one wearing a fez and baggy trousers.

One month after the *France* had left Le Havre

The Imperator, *illustrated here at Cuxhaven in 1913, was not only the longest ship in the world, at 280 metres, but also the biggest at 52,117 GT.*

The Imperator – Glory of the Kaiser on the Atlantic

Glorious pomp for first-class passengers. They could swim about the Pompeian style swimming pool on B deck or sit in the visitors' gallery and watch the bathers (left). The lush greenery of the palm was a pleasant setting in which to chat or pass the time (right).

On the eve of the First World War, the Hamburg-Amerika Line could congratulate itself on possessing fame as the world's largest shipping line. For Managing Director Albert Ballin, it was therefore a question of national prestige for Germany also to possess the world's largest passenger steamer. He commissioned the construction of 3 giant ships which were launched within 3 years – the *Imperator* (1912), the *Vaterland* (1913) and the *Bismarck* (1914).

When the *Imperator* was first launched in June 1913, she broke almost all records: with cabins for 4,594 passengers, she even exceeded the capacity of the *Great Eastern*; no ship of such large capacity has been built since. At 52,117 GT, she effortlessly exceeded the previous maritime record set by the White Star Line's *Titanic* (46,329 GT). And, at 280 m, the *Imperator* was also the longest ship. But she achieved this distinction only by a trick:

when Ballin heard it rumoured that Cunard's *Aquitania* would be longer, he hastily had a monstrous bronze eagle mounted on the bow. Thanks to this ferociously scowling, crowned figurehead which held in its claws·a globe representing the world and inscribed with the shipping line's motto 'My field is the world', Hapag won by a beak's length. Before long, however, an Atlantic storm tore one of the wings off the eagle, whereupon the heraldic beast was removed.

The 'floating palace' *Imperator* made its impression thanks to the glorious pomposity of the first class: the pseudo Louis-XV-style furniture, the dining room capped with a glass cupola, the Pompeian-style swimming pool with a visitors' gallery, and, behind the bridge, the Kaiser suite together with its own private veranda. But the passengers of the three lower classes had to get by with far more humble accommodation.

The 3-funnel ship Imperator was intended to give the impression of Germany's glitter & glory on the Atlantic. - There was a greenhouse on the stern deck so that first-class passengers could always enjoy fresh flowers and eat fresh vegetables.

The Kaiser-style glory made the giant ship top-heavy, so that it rolled and pitched seriously even in the calmest sea; therefore the three funnels had to be shortened by just 3 m, marble had to be removed by the ton and 2,000 tons of cement had to be poured into the bilges to provide ballast.

But the three 'mega liners' of the *Imperator* class were only to spend a short time flying the Hapag flag: after the First World War, the *Imperator* was taken over by Cunard and renamed the *Berengaria*, and together with *Aquitania* and *Mauritania* she belonged to the 'Big Three'. The *Vaterland* went to the United States Lines and was renamed *Leviathan*, and as such she became America's largest passenger ship. *Bismarck* went to the White Star to become the *Majestic*, and together with the *Olympic* and *Homeric*, which had previously been Norddeutscher Lloyd's *Columbus*, formed a popular trio on the North Atlantic.

The pomp and splendour of the Kaisers' Germany for first-class passengers on board the Imperator: *The writing and reading room (top left); a luxury apartment (top right), a luxury cabin (bottom left) and the bridge, showing the wheel and the machine telegraph system (bottom right). All photos date from 1913.*

for her maiden voyage, the German Kaiser baptised a new Hapag giant with the name of *Imperator*. Her precise tonnage was 52,117 GT, making her twice as large as the last new ship from the Hamburg-Amerika Line of 1906. For two decades, *Imperator*, together with her sister ships the *Vaterland* and *Bismarck*, known as 'The Big Three', led the league table of largest ships, but after the First World War, all three of them sailed under different flags by the names of *Berengaria*, *Leviathan* and *Majestic*. This unique imperial trio was not overtaken until 1935 – by the *Normandie* – and even today they rank at 6th, 7th and 9th. In 1914, Hapag had still been the largest line at 175 seagoing ships, together with Norddeutscher Lloyd at 116. The First World War stopped the planned construction of new ships, and transatlantic traffic collapsed.

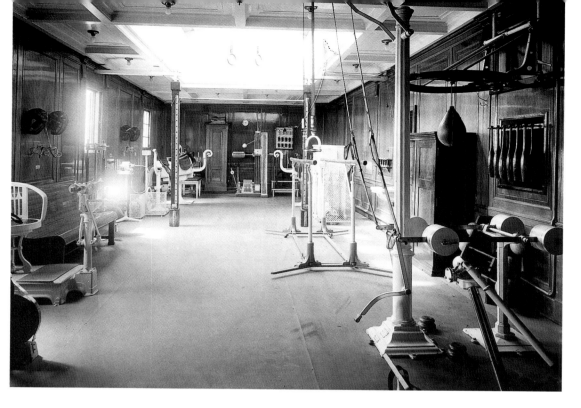

The exercise room with pre-First World War fitness equipment (top left), a glass-roofed saloon (top right), the large banqueting room with a coloured glass cupola, which could accommodate all 908 of the first-class passengers (bottom left), and the seating accommodation in a cabin (bottom right).

Liners were hastily converted to troop carriers, floating hospitals and ancillary ferries.

The troop transporter *Olympic* rammed and sank a German submarine in the English Channel, and the *Britannic*, the sister ship to the *Titanic*, was serving as a floating hospital in the Aegean when she hit a German mine and sank. The *Mauretania* was just able to avoid a torpedo when she was carrying 3,500 soldiers,

but the *Lusitania*, which was travelling from New York to Southampton carrying civilian passengers, sank with the loss of 1,195 lives, having been hit by a torpedo.

In 1919, there was no German passenger fleet remaining, as the victorious allies had confiscated all ships of more than 1,600 GT as part of the reparations. The richest spoils went to the USA and England, whilst France received

"HUNDREDS OF POLISH EMIGRANTS ALSO TRAVELLED ON THE 'TWEEN-DECK.
THEY WERE BERTHED DOWN THERE AMONGST THEIR BRIGHT BAGS & BAGGAGE
AND CHILDREN & NAPPIES, IN A PATHETIC TUMULT. [....] AROUND US ALL THERE
WERE THE SHIP'S CREW. THE RICH PASSENGERS TRAVELLED WITH THEIR
ELEGANT CLOTHES, GOURMET MEALS AND LEISURELY GAMES AND
CELEBRATIONS WITH MUSIC AND EVERY CONCEIVABLE LUXURY. TWO OPPOSITES
LIVING IN CLOSE JUXTAPOSITION."

JOACHIM RINGELNATZ IN
"MEIN LEBEN BIS ZUM KRIEGE" (MY LIFE BEFORE THE WAR), 1931.
IN 1902, RINGELNATZ TRAVELLED ON HAPAG'S COLUMBIA AS AN ORDINARY SEAMAN.

a couple of smaller craft. The First World War was not only a watershed for shipping on the Atlantic. The joyous 'belle époque' was a thing of the past, and the post-war period, with the 'Roaring Twenties' and 'Swinging Thirties', brought in fresh ideas, new concepts and new liners for a new public.

In just eight decades, ship construction had passed through a rapid phase of development, from paddle steamers which were only a little larger than the inland lake pleasure craft of today, to the 'floating palaces' of the turn of the century. The first steamers, with their clipper-

The majority of passengers crossing the Atlantic were emigrants (right : photo from 1905).

THE GREATEST MIGRATION OF PEOPLES OF ALL TIME

There are no statistics to record how many Europeans migrated to North America between 1820 and 1920, firstly on sailing ships and later on steamships. Estimates vary between 30 and 70 million. The migrants, driven by political and religious persecution, hunger, unemployment and adventure, hoped for a better future in the 'land of unlimited opportunity'.

It must have been a floating hell to cross under sail, which took two months if the winds were not favourable: migrants in their hundreds were perched like living cargo in mass quarters, they slept on mattresses on the floor or in tightly packed bunks on straw pallets. In the same room, they cooked the food they had brought with them, and ate it out of table napkins. The toilet was a couple of cubicles behind a partition. Transportation of emigrants was a gold-mine. As recorded in a centenary document of Norddeutscher Lloyd in 1957, it constituted the 'basis for continuous and ever-accelerating growth'

The English artist Ford Maddox Brown gave the title of 'Last View Of England' to this painting of 1852/1855, an illustration of an emigrating couple.

in shipping companies. For that reason, they constructed larger steamers for up to 3500 'tweendecks passengers; the crossing time became shorter, competition drove prices down and there

was a gradual improvement in the inhuman conditions.

The shipping-lines would pamper the well-to-do minority of passengers and spoil them with pomp and splendour. This brought them prestige, but the main source of profit was from the majority in the 'tweendecks. In 1913, 1,228,216 passengers sailed for New York, and 152,416 of them travelled first-class, 230,437 second-class and 955,363 in the 'tweendecks. The English writer Robert Louis Stevenson observed the following distinction during a crossing in 1879 : 'In the 'tweendecks there are men & women, but in the first and second classes there are ladies & gentlemen.' When the USA drastically reduced its immigrant quotas in 1921, the migrant passenger trade collapsed overnight. The 'tweendecks disappeared and were replaced by the tourist class. Migrants were replaced by middle-class passengers who were out to enjoy travelling.

On board S.S. „Vaterland" H.

Transatlantic voyages on Hapag's Vaterland *in 1914 : Passengers would seek out a place in shelter from the wind, to sit in an armchair and survey the sea, waiting for lunch or dinner.*

type sharp bows, their wooden hulls, their high masts replete with yard-arms and the smooth upper deck, still looked like sailing ships. Gradually, side-mounted paddles gave way to the more efficient propeller drive. Firstly iron was used as the material for construction, later giving way to steel, and coal-firing gradually gave way to oil-firing. However, sailors valued their tradition and did not want to give up sailing power for a long time yet. It was not until 1893 that Cunard constructed a liner with no auxiliary sails.

The most pioneering innovations came from the English engineer Isambard Kingdom Brunel, the Director of the Great Western Railroad Company and the builder of three steamships which made history. The *Great Western* (1838) was England's first steamer constructed specifically for the Atlantic, and the *Great Britain* (1846), which is now stored in Bristol as a museum ship, was the first ship with an iron hull and propeller drive to navigate the 'big pond', whilst the *Great Eastern* (1860) was for 41 years the world's largest ship.

In the 1870s, steam ships acquired their characteristic profile, by the addition of super-structure for cabins and public rooms. Now, ship designers at last had space for roomy cabins,

Crossing on the White Star Line's Doric *in 1914: Passengers would wrap themselves up in their rain-coats on the promenade-deck, sitting on armchairs, and read a book until a steward served them a bouillon.*

plush lounges and pomp-laden dining rooms, scope for indoor pools, fitness rooms and à la carte restaurants. They constructed sea-going museums, and there was hardly any decorative style that was forgotten, ranging from Gothic through Baroque and Classical style to Tudor and Chippendale. Everything was imitated, be it German castles, French chateaux or English cottages.

Arthur Davis, an employee of Charles Mewès, who had designed the public rooms of the Cunarder *Aquitania*, answered, when asked why a ship never looked like a ship from the inside, that: 'Passengers are neither sailors nor "yachties", nor people who enjoy the sea. Their only wish is to forget that they are on board a ship.' The main people to benefit were the first-class passengers, who, although they constituted a minority, took up as much as 75% of the accommodation. As hoped, the plush equipment did bring prestige for the shipping lines, but their profit was made from the masses in the second, third and 'tween-deck classes. The division between the wealthy few in the first-class, the less rich second-class and the impoverished third-class and 'tween-decks was strict. 'Ocean steamers,' as the *New York Times* wrote in 1923, 'function in the same way as the

Bremen, 16 August 1928: final preparations for the launch of Norddeutscher Lloyd's rapid steamer Bremen *at the Weser yard, Bremen. Far below in the bowels of the ship, firemen and stokers would have the dirtiest job on board the ship to do (right).*

caste system. Even in India, class distinctions have never been more sharply outlined. The captain, officers and crew have formed the bureaucracy, the first-class is the aristocracy, the second-class the bourgeoisie, and the people in the 'tween-decks are the proletariat.'

On the lowest rung of the social ladder, there were the 'black gangs' of the firemen and stokers, who worked far below in the depths of the ship in dreadful working conditions, confronted with steam boilers and fires. The firemen humped coal out of the bunkers, whilst the stokers shovelled it into the fires and stoked the fire with long rods. The noise was deafening, the heat was unbearable and the air was heavy with coal dust. The rhythm for the men, stripped to the waist and their faces covered in soot, to swing their shovels, was sounded with a bell. During the crossing, they would toil round the clock in four-hour watches: four hours on duty, four

hours off, four hours on duty and so on. On the *Mauretania*, a 200-strong 'black gang' fed 1,000 tonnes of coal to the 192 fires of the 25 boilers each day. At the beginning of the 1920s, oil-firing then replaced coal-fired boilers, and since then, an air-conditioned engine room is manned by a handful of crew wearing white overalls.

For millennia, you only travelled if you absolutely had to. Then James Watt invented the steam engine, and everything changed. Firstly, industrialisation brought a newly wealthy bourgeoisie, and on the other hand, it made humanity mobile thanks to steam railways and steam ships. Anyone who had any money wanted to travel in luxury, wanted to sleep surrounded by luxury and live like a prince. Designers Johannes Georg Poppe and Charles Mewès converted ships into 'floating palaces' and grand hotels for that reason.

Passenger ships have never been more beautiful and more exquisitely tailored than between the two world wars, never before nor since. It was

79

the golden age of ship travel on the Atlantic, on which seven of the finest luxury liners ever built made their maiden voyages in the space of nine short years: the *Ile de France*, the *Bremen*, the *Europa*, the *Rex* and the *Conte di Savoia*, the *Normandie* and the *Queen Mary*. For the first time, England and Germany were no longer fighting between themselves for passengers' custom, but now they had to compete with France, Italy and the United States. But Poland, Norway and Sweden also began to fly their own flags.

In the post-war years, the social structure of passengers had changed; Europe's nobility was impoverished, and the flow of emigrants to America had been checked by her now-restrictive immigration conditions. The bulk quarters of the 'tween-decks were removed, giving way to cabins for the new tourist class. Now, businessmen and tourists, sportsmen and film stars travelled on board ship. The ball-room ambience of the 'belle époque' was 'out', and the Charleston, bobbed hairstyle and short skirts of the 'Roaring Twenties' were in. At latest after the time of the Paris Exposition des Arts Décoratifs et Industriels (Exhibition of Decorative and Industrial Arts) in 1925, the architectural extravagance of the past was counted irrevocably outmoded, and fashion now embraced clear lines and bright colours, Art Deco and a trace of Bauhaus. France was the trend-setter on the water. At a shareholders' meeting, John dal Piaz, the Chairman of Transat, provocatively asked: 'Why, ladies, with your short skirts and short-cut hair, would you want to sit in Louis XVI-style armchairs?' He recommended that the now-obsolete traditions should be thrown overboard, and coined the saying 'Life does not mean imitating but creating anew' and – in 1926 – revolutionised ship architecture with the *Ile de France* (43,153 GT). From the outside, the appearance of the two-funnel craft with its undisturbed deck lines and low super-structures created a thoroughly elegant effect, whilst inside it was surprising in that its design was achieved without visible pipe-work, but with a stylish ambience and a comfortable functionality. This was the birth of the 'Style Paquebot', in English 'ocean liner style' or in German 'Dampf-Stil'.

The lobby, which extended over three decks, with its boutiques and a branch of 'Au bon marché', one of the very earliest names in department stores, constituted the centre of life on board. Here, people would meet to chat and to shop, and from here stairways and lifts led to cabins and public rooms. And this was a concept which, like Albert Ballin's grill restaurants, had been taken over from the transatlantic ships of the 1880s. There was a bar 9 m long and, for the

COMPAGNIE GENERALE TRANSATLANTIQUE
French Line

Guy Silhouette

"ILE DE FRANCE"
LIGNE LE HAVRE SOUTHAMPTON NEW YORK

The Ile De France *of Compagnie Générale Transatlantique revolutionised ship architecture in 1926: Elegance in the first-class reading room, with no surface pipe-work (above), and sober functionality in second-class cabins (below).*

From the roomy first-class cabins, dominated by 1920s style (below), wide staircases led to the 'Grand Hall' of the Ile De France *(above). 'Steamship Style' had replaced the overloaded 'Bremen Baroque'.*

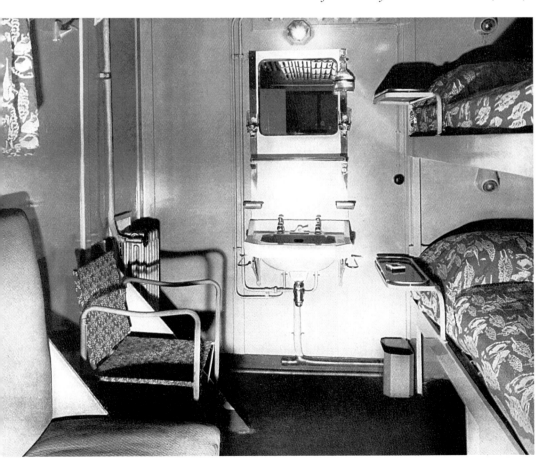

LUXURY LINERS AS FILM STARS

Ocean steamers promised glamour, provided the cure for homesickness and offered a whiff of adventure - the ideal ingredients of the 'dream factories' between Hollywood and Babelsberg. Again and again, scriptwriters would concoct the lives and loves of

people living for a brief spell in a visible microcosm of tragedy and comedy.

In 1942/43, scenes from a German production about the Titanic were filmed on the Cap Arcona, and the French Line's Liberte plays a key part in the Hollywood film 'French Line'. The thriller 'Juggernaut' (18 Hours To Eternity) tells the story of time-bombs on board a fictitious Britannic, the former Hanseatic, what is now the Maxim Gorky. The Constitution was the venue for the melodrama 'An Affair to Remember', with Cary Grant and Deborah Kerr. 'Made for Each Other', with James Stewart, was made on the Normandie, and Erich von Stroheim and Michel Simon were filmed on the "Transatlantico" (Paris - New York). The Queen

Mary features in some scenes of the musical 'Shall We Dance'. Fred Astaire steps out to the music of George Gershwin in the engine-room and sings at the guard-rail with Ginger Rogers. In 'Assault on a Queen', Frank Sinatra and some accomplices with a

In 1957, the Constitution was the stage for the melodrama 'An Affair to Remember', with Cary Grant and Deborah Kerr in the lead roles. - In 1976, 'Voyage Of The Damned' was made on the cruise ship Irpinia with Faye Dunaway (right), Maria Schell, Oskar Werner and Orson Welles. Stars of the German TV series 'Dream Ship' were the cruise ships Vistafjord, Astor and Berlin respectively.

submarine surface in front of the Cunard liner and abduct her.

In 'The Man With The Golden Gun', Roger Moore, alias James Bond, meets his Secret Service boss in a cabin of the Queen Elizabeth (which lies burnt-out and tipped-over at Hong Kong).

Where a funnel is burning on deck in the disaster movie 'The Last Voyage', a steam boiler explodes and water penetrates the engine-room, the effect is extremely realistic. This is no wonder, as the scenes were filmed on the de-commissioned Ile de France. The damage left out by the film crew was then completed by the welding torches of the Japanese scrap company. 'Gentleman Prefer Blondes', with Marilyn Monroe and Jane Russell, was filmed, in Anita Loos' story, on the fictitious Ile de Paris. What viewers see as the ship is only the model of a

liner with the red/black funnels of Transat steaming across the screen, and later the two stars disembark at Cherbourg from a real ocean liner, the Conte de Savoia with her red/white/green funnels.

In 'Gentlemen Prefer Blondes', 1953, Marilyn Monroe and Jane Russell travelled on the fictitious Ile-De-Paris.

first time, a memorial chapel, whilst children could play on a roundabout and dogs could choose between four menus, including a vegetarian one.

The particularly Francophile Americans took the *Ile de France* to their hearts. In the first-class restaurant, it is said that Ernest Hemingway got to know Marlene Dietrich, and Errol Flynn attracted attention by appearing more or less the worse for wear every evening with a fresh beauty on his arm, coming down the large staircase, always ordering nothing but oysters and sporting red socks in the smoking room.

"WHEN DOROTHY AND I ACTUALLY TRAVEL ON A SHIP TO EUROPE, EVERYONE CAN SEE US IF THEY LOOK OUT TO SEA. (....) I LOVE SHIPS AND IN PARTICULAR I LOVE THE MAJESTIC, YOU WOULD NEVER BELIEVE THAT SHE IS A SHIP, YOU'D THINK YOU WERE AT THE RITZ. (....). THE STEWARD HAS JUST TOLD ME THAT IT'S TIME TO EAT, SO I SHALL GO UP NOW, AS THE GENTLEMAN THAT DOROTHY GOT TO KNOW ON THE STAIRS HAS INVITED US TO THE RITZ, WHICH IS A SPECIAL DINING ROOM WHERE YOU CAN SPEND LOTS OF MONEY IN AN ENJOYABLE WAY, BECAUSE IN THE OTHER DINING-ROOM THE SERVICE IS REALLY NOT UP TO SCRATCH."

ANITA LOOS, IN "GENTLEMEN PREFER BLONDES", 1925

Even before the First World War, passengers had their photographs taken as a souvenir of their voyage on the Bremen.

With the 'Style Paquebot', ship constructors had finally developed an independent style. No longer were they imitating, now the design code ran 'form follows function'.

'In order to regain some of our previous status on the New York run, we have decided to commission two passenger steamers which will comply in every respect with the heightened requirements for international passenger traffic.' This sentence from the trading report of Norddeutscher Lloyd in March 1927 heralded the construction of the high-speed steamers *Bremen* and *Europa* and reflected the beginnings of Germany's resurgence to become one of the leading nations on the North Atlantic.

The *Bremen* and the *Europa*, which in 1930 – together with the *Columbus* – had once again enabled weekly high-speed travel on the pre-war route of Bremerhaven – Southampton – Cherbourg – New York, constantly hit the headlines. Once the *Bremen* had won the 'Blue Riband' on its maiden voyage in July 1929, the

THE BREMEN AND THE EUROPA – PIONEERS OF A NEW GENERATION OF SHIPS

When the *Bremen* reached New York at the end of July 1929 after only 4 days, 17 hours and 42 minutes, she had broken the record set by the *Mauretania* in 1909 by all of 7 hours, and won the 'Blue Riband'.

The *Bremen*, which was already the fourth ship of Norddeutscher Lloyd to bear that name and was disproportionately more popular than the *Europa*, her younger sister by 8 months, was the pioneer of a new generation of ocean-going giants, the interior being functional and largely committed to the new discipline, whilst on the outside her streamlined profile, two extremely low funnels and bulbous bow exhibited an uncompromising design for speed. In other respects, too, the *Bremen* offered many innovations. Between her funnels, she stowed a Lufthansa mail plane, which would be catapulted into the air while the ship was still out at sea, and one day's journey from port. This made it possible to reduce the delivery time for mail between Berlin and New York to five days and

11 hours. The swimming pool was heated, the lifeboats had engines, the cabins were equipped with fire-warning devices. Rolling was reduced by the Frahm anti-roll tanks, the predecessors of stabilisers.

The *Bremen*, working in conjunction with the other ships in her team – the *Europa* and the *Columbus* – as welcome messengers of the Third Reich, crossed the Atlantic 186 times, without incident. The brown-shirted Nazi rulers were not worried by the fact that she was getting further and further into the red. On 28 August 1939, the ship moored in New York after her last peacetime voyage, and two days later she set sail for the last time from jetty 86 flying the swastika from her stern and carrying no passengers. With all lights out and her port-holes covered, she forged eastwards across the Atlantic, and was nowhere to be seen by the time of the outbreak of war on 1 September. The luxury steamer had become a ghost ship which bore camouflage paint and reached her home port on 13 December, by

Norddeutscher Lloyd's Bremen, *which in this photograph is already equipped with the funnels raised by five metres. The previously aerodynamic funnels had been raised in order to reduce nuisance to passengers from exhaust gases, smoke and soot.*

The high-speed steamer Europa (right) won the 'Blue Riband' in March 1930 for the quickest Atlantic crossing, and lost it three years later to the Italian Rex. – Each of the four 4-bladed screws weighed 17 tonnes (below).

circuitous routes. The *Bremen* and her sister ship the *Europa*, which was lying at Bremerhaven upon the outbreak of war, first became quarters for the German Navy and then were equipped as transporters for the planned invasion of England. Whilst the *Europa* survived the war and then flew the French flag until 1961, as the *Liberté*, the *Bremen* was lost through arson in March 1941, was salvaged and supplied Hitler's armament industry with 9000 tons of scrap which was valuable to the Nazi war effort.

NORDDEUTSCHER LLOYD BREMEN

EUROPA

BREMEN

SCHNELLSTER WEG NACH NEW YORK

Alex Kircher, in his painting of 1934, captured the hectic atmosphere of preparations for casting off the Bremen *(left).*

With the three liners the Bremen, *the* Europa *and the* Columbus, *the shipping line advertised its express service to New York (above). In 1929, the first catapult launch of a sea-plane (below) was performed from on-board the Bremen.*

Bremer Nachrichten newspaper, on the front page, boasted: 'Upon arrival of the *Bremen* in New York, she was dubbed the 'New German Queen of the Sea' by the Americans. Her speed on the last day of cruising, when the ship covered 713 nautical miles in 24 hours, equating to an hourly speed of 29.7 nautical miles, is regarded as a glittering achievement'. It was the *Bremen*, even more than the *Europa*, which became the darling of the Germans and Americans.

The streamlined profile of the 286 metres-long ship was emphasised by two funnels which were longer than they were high, but passengers were irritated by exhaust gases, smoke and soot. The height of the funnels was raised by five metres, which reduced the nuisance, but put aesthetes in a fury: they considered that the elegance of the ship's profile was impeded.

Externally, the new 'Queen Of The Seas' was uncompromisingly trimmed for aerodynamics, whilst inside she exhibited a German approach to ocean-liner ship style: on the one hand functional and committed to the new discipline, but on the other hand taking account of customers' desire for prestige and comfort. As well as the excessive 'Bremen baroque' of the former house architect Poppe and some

incorporation of younger-generation style, the interior cabins were configured by six designers according to the principle of 'Functionality combined with aesthetics'.

The first class dining-room was adorned with figures with sporting motifs, and the sun-deck had an intimate à-la-carte restaurant, whilst the crew ate in the 'Crew cafeteria'. The semi-circular conservatory gave an unobstructed view over the bow of the ship and the sea, whilst the indoor pool had its own bar. There were also a bowling alley, children's rooms, a firing range, a travel agents', tobacconist and flower-stall.

According to the brochure of Bremen Lloyd, "All cabins are equipped such as to avoid superfluous luxury whilst taking account of the needs of comfort and the usual layout of furni-

89

Here we see a new liner in process of construction before the First World War at the Blohm & Voss Yard in Hamburg, which had a long tradition of shipbuilding. Then, hulls and decks were riveted together from sheets (above). – The high-speed steamer Europa *(right) and the* Bremen, *belonging to Norddeutscher Lloyd, sported a revolutionary bulbous bow. Towing tests with models had indicated that the new underwater form of the bow produced improved flow characteristics, reduced dipping in heavy seas, increased speed and reduced fuel consumption.*

ture. A large number of first-class cabins are equipped with bath and WC or with shower and WC, or with WC only. Bedrooms and adjacent bathrooms contain washing facilities.'

In 1932, just 20% of all passengers crossing the Atlantic had used a Norddeutscher Lloyd ship for their voyage. When Hitler came to power, the kosher kitchens were closed, the swastika flew from the stern and booking figures dropped alarmingly. But the reason was not just Nazi rule, but also the global economic crisis of the 1930s: passenger figures rapidly dropped from 1.1 million (1929) to 685,000 (1931). However, new ships had long been ordered and were about to be completed.

In 1927, Charles Lindbergh crossed the Atlantic in the *Spirit of St. Louis* in 33 hours and 29 minutes. In the same year, Benito Mussolini informed the politically conformist Press that Italy was to 'Construct two ships which the whole world has been waiting for'. The *Rex* was announced as the largest luxury liner since the 1st World War, and the *Conte de Savoia* as a ship on which it was guaranteed that nobody would be sea-sick. These promises proved to be ambitious – at 51,062 GT, the *Rex* was smaller than the *Bremen*, and in rough seas the *Conte de Savoia* would roll despite the gyro stabilisers introduced by American inventor Elmer A. Sperry. On the other hand, the 'near sister ships' constructed at Genoa and at Trieste had contributed another innovation to shipbuilding: on their generously sized sun-decks, they had proper pool landscaping with loungers, tables and sun-shades.

Since the Italian 'Bellezze' (beauties) did not use

the windy, stormy North Atlantic route but travelled by the more calm and sunny southern route, life on-board moved into the open. The *Rex* and the *Conte de Savoia* were no longer 'floating grand hotels' but the first holiday hotels on the sea. The shipping line Italia, which in the United States went by the name of the Italian Line, for the first time did not emphasise – in its advertising – the size or speed of its new ships, but rather referred to the 'Lido Crossing' and a 'new concept of luxury on the sea'. The illustrations showed sporting, tanned people who lay about on loungers all day in their bathing costumes and promenaded around the pool in the evening, wearing evening dress, beneath a starry sky. Promotional texts enthused: 'Life in the open, under the Sun and its ultraviolet rays, is beneficial to health.' This set an entirely new standard of illustration and a new tone in writing. For decades, Italy's interior designers had depicted 'La Grande Opera' on the sea with grotesquely overdone rooms, but now

The Saturnia of the Italian Cosulich line, which crossed the Atlantic by the southern route, was one of the first passenger ships to have verandah suites, at the end of the 1920s.

they provided a surprise with their elegance, expertise and new ideas: on the covered promenade, which was 27 metres long, the windows went down to floor level, all public cabins were refreshed by air-conditioning, whilst a handful of luxury cabins even had private verandahs. Even the third class had a sports deck, a conservatory and a dining-room with windows.

On 28 October 1932, the tenth anniversary of Mussolini's 'March on Rome' and his seizure of power in Italy, the *Rex* set sail for her maiden voyage. This streamlined giant with her black hull, white superstructure and two funnels located well astern, and sporting the national colours of red/white/green, steamed westwards through the Mediterranean. Off Malaga, the lights went out, the lifts stopped and the water supply failed – there had been turbine damage due to penetration of sea-water. The repair time was three days, and 700 angry passengers left the ship and booked crossings on other steamers. Italy's prestige liners reached New York with three days' delay.

In August 1933, the *Rex* sailed across the Atlantic at an average speed of just 29 knots, making her 1 knot faster than the *Europa*'s time recorded one and a half months previously. Thus the 'Blue Riband' went to Italy for the first and only time. Benito Mussolini's transport minister Costanzo Ciano interpreted this success as proof that fascist Italy had 'Regained its rightful position on the seas of the world thanks to discipline, technology and the spirit of enterprise.'

After the *Conte de Savoia* had been baptised in the presence of Guglielmo Marconi, the inventor of wireless telegraphy, she set out on her maiden voyage three weeks after her slightly larger 'near sister ship'. Unfortunately for the passengers, the sea remained calm, so that the gyro stabilisers, 'one of the greatest innovations in shipbuilding since the change from sail to steam', could not function. The 'Sperry gyro

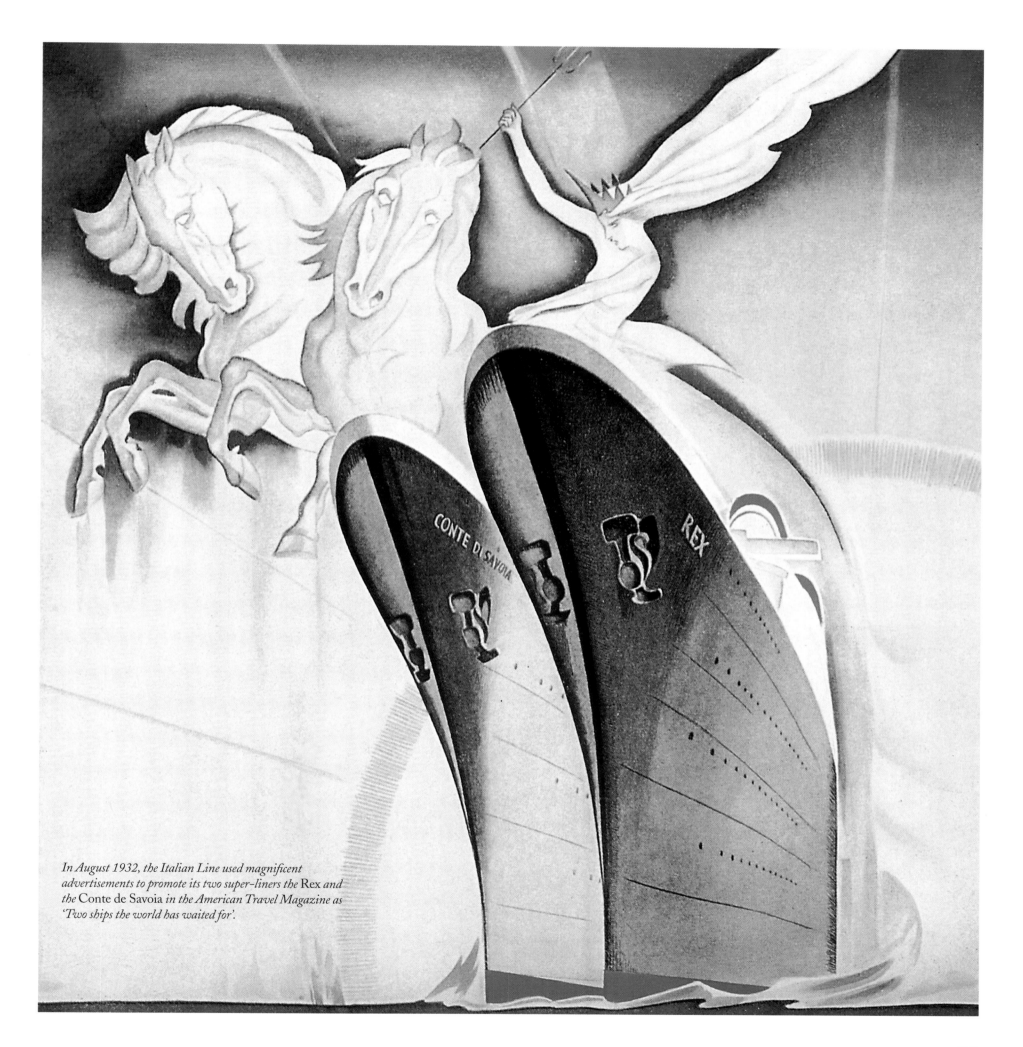

In August 1932, the Italian Line used magnificent advertisements to promote its two super-liners the Rex *and the* Conte de Savoia *in the American Travel Magazine as 'Two ships the world has waited for'.*

stabilisers', costing 1 million dollars, were installed in the front section of the ship. Their three independently rotating flywheels, each weighing 100 tonnes, measuring 5 metres in diameter and rotating at 800 rpm, were intended to counteract the ship's rolling motion, keeping her stable and preventing sea-sickness. But the invention proved to be inadequately developed. It was only after the Second World War that Denny Brown stabilisers, floats that could be extended below the waterline, brought passengers noticeable relief. The two Italians were amongst the most beautiful and innovative ships ever to have taken to the sea. With their Lido decks and swimming-pools, they were far ahead of their time, and it was not until the cruise ships of the 1970s that similar sunbathing and open-air sports facilities were offered. Sadly, they were permitted only a short life, and were de-commissioned shortly after the outbreak of the Second World War.

Joan Of Arc, *Napoleon*, *Maurice Chevalier*? For a long time, guesses were made as to what France's new 'super-liner' would be called; she had been in the process of planning since 1928 and was to be launched at the end of 1932. Finally, Compagnie Générale Transatlantique decided on the name of *Normandie*. France's intention with the new 'super liner' was to follow up the *Ile De France*, the trend-setter of the 'Roaring Twenties' with a forward-looking ship for the

The Normandie *of Compagnie Générale Transatlantique was the ultimate luxury liner – she embodied what was almost the ideal combination of innovative technology and high speed with beauty and luxury.*

'Swinging Thirties'. The periodical *L'Illustration* announced the Normandie as a wonder ship and a 'floating embassy' which would prove to the world that 'France was not only the land of the arts and of luxury, fashion and perfume, but also the land of science and technology'. The exiled Russian marine architect Vladimir Yourkevitch, who had designed battleships for the Czars before the revolution, and the French engineers and designers, had succeeded in something much greater: virtually the perfect ship, the almost ideal combination of innovative technology and high speed with aesthetics and luxury. Connoisseurs of ships the world over still regard the *Normandie* as the ultimate luxury liner: beautiful but not snobbish, elegant whilst still powerful.

Three imposing red/black funnels, which were inclined 10 degrees to aft, and between which there was located a tennis court, soared 44 metres into the sky and dominated the well-proportioned profile of the ship. The stern-deck was so huge that a Royal Air Force aircraft was able to perform an emergency landing on it in June 1936. Safety was writ large, the bridge had an echo sounder and an early form of what is now known as radar, and all public rooms were equipped with fire-warning devices and fire safety systems, which made the *Normandi*e 60 tons heavier and placed her 25 centimetres lower in the water than the shipbuilders had envisaged. At the end of May 1935,

95

France's floating bastion of national pride set out on her first transatlantic voyage. She carried with her a film team from the French 'Pathé' weekly review, so that later on the whole nation could participate audio-visually, and to the accompaniment of sentimental music, in this event. 'In the evening, passengers attend the gala dinner in evening dress, with a gala theatre show and a gala ball. Some tireless night birds stay up until dawn, whilst high up on the bridge of the ship, which glides over the waves of the night, a dedicated sailor watches over the sleeping city below the star-studded sky.'

There were two sources of excitement: firstly, the ship was plunged into darkness when the lights were put out by a short-circuit, then one of the four propellers failed and the ship continued across the Atlantic, sometimes at reduced speed. Nonetheless the *Normandie* reached New York in a new best time, and on her arrival a banner 29.98 metres long – 1 metre for each knot of the record speed – fluttered from the stern mast. The *Normandie* was thus the fastest, longest (314 metres) and largest (83,324 GT) passenger ship on the Atlantic. These superlatives were soon excelled, but nothing came close to the luxurious opulence of the first class. The fact

Class	Passengers	Proportion	Area of decks	m² per Passenger
First	864	44 %	4140 m²	4.79 m²
Tourist	654	33 %	2610 m²	3.99 m²
Third	454	23 %	1260 m²	2.77 m²

that the *Normandie* carried almost as many first-class passengers as those in the two other classes put together is an index of her exclusiveness: the privileged few in the first class entered the ship through a 3-storey entrance hall, from which access to cabins and suites was provided by wide staircases and four lifts. Each of the 431 cabins was furnished and decorated in a different way, but even on this, the most luxurious of all luxury liners, there were 30 cabins without a bath. The 10 'de luxe apartments' and the four 'grand-luxe apartments' having seven rooms and their own kitchens were all the more sumptuous.

Three-quarters of the space allotted to promenades, saloons and other public rooms were reserved for the 'top drawer'. The central point was naturally the great dining-room: below a gilded dummy ceiling, and surrounded by wall lights, column lights and 157 tables, there was an army of stewards and wine-waiters. Passengers could choose between 75 courses,

prepared in the kitchen by 30 cooks at a cooking system 17 metres long and equipped with 56 electric plates. Anyone wishing to treat themselves to greater intimacy could book – for themselves and a few friends – one of the eight smaller sections on either side of the large dining-room or climb via a wide staircase to the 'Café Grille' on the after boat deck. Whilst the other rooms were kept in Art Deco style, here the ambience was dominated by a sober discipline of chrome and glass. The view astern from the entrance to the Café Grille must have been magnificent: over almost 120 metres length of ship, an evenly divided succession of saloons and galleries, some larger, some smaller, some higher, some lower. This was an expanse of opulence that could only be dreamed about by the passengers in the lower two classes.

The word 'luxury' is relative and has to be seen in the context of its time, but nonetheless the *Normandie* is definitive as a

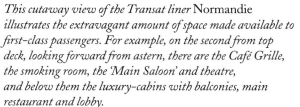

luxury liner. American writer Harvey Ardman, in his ship biography *Life and Times of the Normandie* set out to illustrate in numerical terms the exceptional status of the French ocean-going giant. A passenger on a 'floating luxury hotel' would expect excellence of food with attentive service in elegant surroundings: large numbers of helpful stewards and a sumptuous allowance of space. The second of these is easier to gauge than the first. Ardman calculated the passenger/crew and passenger/space ratios, using this as the basis for an authoritative 'luxury index' and by this means arrived at a 'hit parade' of the most luxurious pre-Second World War liners. Anyone wishing to belong to the 'creme de la creme' of the 'ship set' had to cross the Atlantic on the *Normandie*, on which 1,345 crew members took care of 1,972 passengers – in July 1938, her passengers included Hollywood stars Gloria Swanson, David Niven, Johnny Weissmuller, and Fred Astaire. Even blind passengers

This cutaway view of the Transat liner Normandie *illustrates the extravagant amount of space made available to first-class passengers. For example, on the second from top deck, looking forward from astern, there are the Café Grille, the smoking room, the 'Main Saloon' and theatre, and below them the luxury-cabins with balconies, main restaurant and lobby.*

Ship	Luxury-Index
Normandie	2945
Empress of Britain	2211
Queen Mary	1918
Europa	1240
Majestic, previously Bismarck	1226
Bremen	1172
IledeFrance	1083
Berengaria	834
Conte di Savoia	825
Leviathan, ex Vaterland	774
Rex	755

Continued on page 104

Passengers entered the first class dining-room through an archway 6 metres high, extending up through three decks and spanned by a gilt dummy ceiling.
The French Press raved about this floating restaurant:
'Such light! Such beauty! Such freshness!'

THE NORMANDIE, ALMOST THE PERFECT SHIP

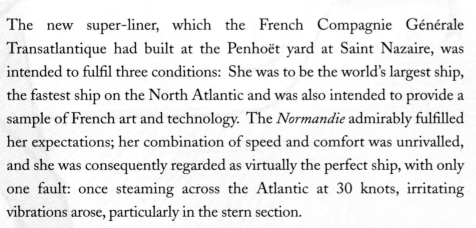

The Normandie offered first-class passengers a degree of luxury hitherto unknown at sea. From left to right: bedroom in a luxury apartment, view over the stern-deck, concert in the theatre and lounge in a luxury apartment.

The new super-liner, which the French Compagnie Générale Transatlantique had built at the Penhoët yard at Saint Nazaire, was intended to fulfil three conditions: She was to be the world's largest ship, the fastest ship on the North Atlantic and was also intended to provide a sample of French art and technology. The *Normandie* admirably fulfilled her expectations; her combination of speed and comfort was unrivalled, and she was consequently regarded as virtually the perfect ship, with only one fault: once steaming across the Atlantic at 30 knots, irritating vibrations arose, particularly in the stern section.

The *Normandie*, at 313.8 m, was the first liner to be longer than 100 ft, and was also to be the largest, at 79,000 GT. When the French found out that Cunard's *Queen Mary*, whose launch had been set for the end of 1934, would have more tonnage, they got into a panic. The *Normandie* was placed in dry dock, received an additional lounge aft of the "Café Grille" and was re-surveyed at 83,423 GT, all of 2,649 more than the *Queen Mary*. The most beautiful and most luxurious liner ever to sail reached New York in a time of 4 days, 3 hours and 2 minutes on her maiden voyage at the end of May 1935, and as such was 11 hours faster than the previous record holder *Rex* of the previous year, and once again secured the "Blue Riband" for France. On the return voyage, the *Normandie* excelled the record of the Bremen from 1929, also by 11 hours. The "giant of France's renown" was finely cut at the bows, waisted in her centre section and well rounded at the

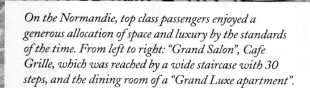

On the Normandie, top class passengers enjoyed a generous allocation of space and luxury by the standards of the time. From left to right: "Grand Salon", Cafe Grille, which was reached by a wide staircase with 30 steps, and the dining room of a "Grand Luxe apartment".

stern, she had three chimneys, the after-most being a dummy, wide-open decks with no disruptive vent shafts, and stepped terraces in the after section. Below deck, the travelling radio reporter Léonce Peillard found that "everything was wonderful": the pictures, the lamps, the luxurious suites, the extravagant allocation of space, and particularly the 86 m long first-class dining-room which extended over three decks, was the only room to be air-conditioned and was reached by a show staircase, ideal for making a grand entry.

By the time of the outbreak of Second World War, the *Normandie* had crossed the Atlantic 139 times and had transported all the celebrities of the 1930s; Maurice Chevalier and Douglas Fairbanks Jnr, Thomas Mann and Antoine de Saint-Exupéry, and Arturo Toscanini.

When war broke out, the ship was in New York, where she lay at anchor, inactive, for the next few months. In February 1942, the luxury liner was destroyed by fire when she was due to have been converted into an American troop transporter. For more than 21 months, the ruined hulk dominated jetty 88, and only in November 1943 was she once again floated at a cost of $20 million and sold - three years later - to a salvage company for $161,680.

The 'Grand Salon' with its columns and mirrors constituted the central point of social life on the Normandie. *Here, 'ship society' would meet in grand evening dress for concerts and balls.*

made her their favourite, and in August 1938 she was found to be carrying 14 blind people on just one crossing: an unbroken record.

The 'dream boat' amongst luxury liners was burnt-out, tipped over and plundered, but some works of art survived. The New York Museum of Modern Art has some engraved glass panels from the 'Grand Salon', whilst the Miami Fontainebleau Hilton has the bronze statue 'La Normandie' which used to stand before the 'Café Grille'. A fragment of the *Normandie* even survives in the transatlantic ships of the

The tennis court between the first and second of the three red/black funnels, which soared 44 metres into the sky, was the favourite position on the Normandie *to pose for that souvenir photo.*

Sovereign of the Seas class, which were constructed at the same yard in Saint Nazaire, half a century later. They have incorporated the elegantly formed stern of the speed queen, a homage to the legendary ship. The *Normandie* imparted an atmosphere of French 'savoir faire' and was technically pioneering. The *Queen Mary* gave out an aura of being 'very British' and embodied traditional ship-building skills. Both 'super liners' were of almost the same age, with the construction of the French ship dating from 26 January 1931, and that of the English

THE CLUB FOR HIGH-SPEED SHIPS

When the Normandie *arrived early in the afternoon of 3 June 1935 in New York, a blue banner just 30 metres long fluttered from her stern mast. This was the only time that a passenger ship carried the 'Blue Riband', the symbol for the highest average speed on an Atlantic crossing. The contest for speed records, which brought national prestige, publicity and passengers to shipping lines and countries alike, is as well established as the tradition of transporting passengers on the 'Big Pond'. The quickest passages were painstakingly recorded since the times of the first steamships, going back to the* Sirius *in April 1838* (6.7 knots) *and extending to the figure set by the* United States *in July 1952 (34.51 knots).*

But it was not until 1900 that the term 'Blue Riband' was created. This symbolic distinction rapidly became an established concept and, in parlance at least, was retrospectively used to honour previous record holders. In 1935, Englishman Harold Hales donated a 120 centimetres high trophy for the winner of the 'Blue Riband'. At the base of this gilt monstrosity, the sea god Poseidon can be seen seated with his wife Amphitrite, and a goddess of victory bears aloft a globe of the world with a Blue Riband and two Titans battling over an ocean steamer. There were neither established rules nor any jury in the duels for the imaginary Riband, but only a gentlemen's agreement.

Steamers forged across the race track extending over approx 3,000 nautical miles between Europe and America, and the starting line for English ships was at first Queenstown and later the Bishop Rock lighthouse on one of the Isles of Scilly at the western exit of the English Channel; for German ships it was at Cherbourg, whilst Italian ships were deemed to start at Gibraltar. The destination was a succession of New York ports, the Sandy Hook peninsula and the Ambrose light-ship off New York. The costs of these prestige voyages to win the 'Blue Riband' were astronomical because of the immense fuel consumption, but the advertising effect transcended cost considerations.

The United States *is the unbeaten 'Speed Queen of the Atlantic' (above). – A grouping of top transatlantic giants in New York in March 1937. The jetties on the Hudson river, where most liners would moor, was also called 'Luxury Liner Row'. From top to bottom: the* Europa, *the* Rex, *the* Normandie, *the* Georgic *and the* Berengaria, *previously* Imperator. *– Overleaf, see – in June 1951 – the* Britanic, *the* Queen Mary *and the* Mauretania *(from left to right).*

ship dating from 1 December 1930. However, the 'progressive' *Normandie* never got out of the red, while the 'conventional' *Queen Mary* enriched her owners.

Round the clock, at John Brown & Company in Clydebank, 3,640 yard employees laboured in three shifts in order to assemble the new ship, which was known only as No. 534. The company was disabled by the economic crisis, and the shipping line ran out of money, and work was suspended for 39 months. The *Daily Telegraph* lamented: 'This decision is a blow to our national pride.'

The government declared its willingness to subsidise No. 534 with countless millions of pounds and No. 552, which was to become the *Queen Elizabeth*, the largest luxury liner ever built, at 83,673 GT. However, the government imposed one condition: the rival shipping lines of Cunard and White Star must combine to form the Cunard White Star Line. After the merger, the money flowed, dock workers were able once again to enter the yard site, filing in behind Scottish pipers. After they had scraped off 130 tons of rust, production continued smoothly.

In May 1936, the *Queen Mary*, praised by the poet laureate John Masefield as being 'as long as a street and as high as a building', set sail from Southampton for her maiden voyage. Although

Cunard's ships the Queen Mary *and the* Berengaria, *anchoring in mid-April 1936, at Southampton (left). – At the end of December 1951, Winston Churchill (on the left in the photo) crossing the Atlantic on the* Queen Mary, *in eminent political company.*

she had not set any new speed record, four days later the 'Big Apple' honoured her by naming a railway station after her. Fire-fighting ships, ferry ships, sailing yachts and destroyers provided her with an escort. An Eastern Airlines DC3 scattered flowers over the ship, and the English National Anthem was played on board an excursion steamer, by a band. 6,000 New Yorkers paid one dollar in order to be allowed on board the ship for a visit. They recouped their entrance fee by pilfering large quantities of ashtrays and cutlery as souvenirs.

The *Queen Mary* was a floating city with 3,000 people and a gigantic food depot: 25 tons of vegetables, 15 tons of fruit, 10 tons of sugar and 8 tons of fish, 50,000 eggs, 25,000 packs of cigarettes and 5,000 cigars, 20,000 bottles of beer and 14,500 bottles of wine. The social centre of the ship was formed by the "main lounge" which extended over three floors and had its own funnel: in the morning it was the site

THE QUEEN MARY – A SHIP WITH "CHARACTER AND PERSONALITY"

The 'supermarket' of the Queen Mary *carried all of the minor essentials of day-to-day needs (below).*

If the wind was not too strong, then tennis was played on the stern decks (below)

The *Normandie* was more elegant, the *United States* faster and the *Queen Elizabeth* was larger – but no ship enjoyed more popularity than the Cunard liner *Queen Mary*. In the course of her 31-year career, the *Queen Mary* covered 3,794,017 nautical miles in 1,001 voyages and transported 2,224,000 paying passengers, 810,730 soldiers, 19,000 war brides and their 4,000 children. The '*Mary*' no longer travelled over the seas merely in the role of a luxury liner but also as a troop transporter and floating hospital, and transported England's Prime Minister Winston Churchill to his historic meeting with US President Roosevelt.

When Cunard boss Sir Percy Bates commissioned two ships at the beginning of the 1930s, they were to be the 'smallest and slowest ships which would just guarantee economic operation', but at the same time be 'very large and very fast' – the *Queen Mary* and the *Queen Elizabeth*. The *Queen Mary*, which set off for her maiden voyage in 1936, was the last three-chimney ship and the first liner to steam from West to East across the North Atlantic in less than four days. Her character was thoroughly British, with tea at five o'clock, and bridge. The English architectural journal *Architect and Business News*, gave a gruff verdict: 'The overall impression is one of moderate but expensive vulgarity'. However, she was popular with passengers, and the passenger list read like a 'Who's Who' of nobility, finance and show business. In the bar, the stewards often came from families that had worked for Cunard for generations and were given strict instructions on how to deal with their 'betters'.

After their wartime service, the *Queen Mary* and the *Queen Elizabeth* returned to civilian life, to continue scheduled voyages between Southampton and New York. The *Queen Elizabeth* was four years younger, 3.65 m longer and, with her gross tonnage of 83,673, she was – until 1996 – the largest passenger ship ever built, but she never obtained the same popularity as '*The Mary*'.

For one and a half decades, the two Cunarders constituted a successful team, and they were the most profitable of all liners, earning annual profits of $50 million. Then the competition from air travel became more tough, and cabins became increasingly vacant, the 'money makers' became 'money losers' and were finally sold in 1967: the *Queen Mary* to be used as a hotel and conference centre in Long Beach, California; whilst *Queen Elizabeth* went to Hong Kong, where she was destroyed by fire in 1972. Geoffrey Marr, her last captain, was convinced: 'If there is a Valhalla for ships, the Queens must be there.'

The Queen Mary, *shown here at the jetty in New York, crossed the North Atlantic in just four days.*

A senior officer would inspect the bellboys before they entered into service, not only for an impeccable fit of uniform, but also for their haircut and cleanness of fingernails.

The Californian municipal authority of Long Beach, near Los Angeles, bought the de-commissioned Queen Mary *(right) for $3.4 million, in 1967. Up to 1.4 million visitors each year take a look behind the scenes on the legendary liner.*

The Queen Mary *not only became a floating museum providing a record of the age of Atlantic liners – at left the telephone system, at right the bridge – but also a conference centre and hotel with 800 beds.*

of organ concerts, in the afternoon tea and bridge, and in the evening there was dancing; and a religious service on Sundays. For the first time, the smoking room was also open to women, and passengers were transported between the 12 decks by 21 lifts, and there was a floating shopping centre with 24 businesses. Nourishment was supervised by a French chef, and this aroused the anger of patriotically inclined English people: 'This is an English ship, so why must there be a French menu?'

In the summer of 1936, the *Queen Mary* deprived her rival the *Normandie* of the 'Blue Riband' and was the first to cross the Atlantic from West to East in less than four days. The next three years held a recurrent succession of record best times for the two 'super liners' and ultimately the winner was the *Queen Mary*. Her record voyage in 1938, when she steamed to New York at 31 knots and reached it in three days, 21 hours and 48 minutes, was not excelled until 1952, when the record was broken by the *United States*.

The largest passenger steamer which was ever operated under an American flag, was "made in Germany": Hapag's *Vaterland* was moored at New York when the First World War broke out, she remained there for three years, and was requisitioned by the Americans in 1917, converted into a troop transporter and renamed

The Vaterland, *at the time of its launch in April 1913, was the world's largest ship (right). – In 1927, an aircraft took off from the* Leviathan, *a record operation from a passenger ship (above).*

"Vaterland" grösstes Schiff der Welt — Vergleich mit dem Dampfer — "Victoria Luise" 16500 Brutto Registertons, Länge 202 m, Breite 20,5 m, Höhe 13,5, 600 Passagiere, 470 Mann Besatzung
56 000 Brutto Registertons, Länge 276 m, Breite 30,5 m, Höhe 20 m, 4450 Passagiere, 1200 Mann Besatzung

the *Leviathan*. After the war, the United States Lines, formed in 1921, took over the giant ship and made it the flag ship of their cheerfully haphazard fleet of 'second-hand ships'. The 'palm garden' became a night club, whilst in the 'great saloon', where once the bust of the Kaiser had stood, people danced the Charleston, whilst mineral water was dispensed in the bars – the *Leviathan* was 'dry' as there was the Prohibition in the USA, until 1933. America's 'high society',

which now had its first 'floating palace', preferred English, German or French ships, because there they did not have to get by without their martinis and bourbons. The French Line stewards received a crash course in English and the first words were the answers to the question 'Where is the bar?'

The passenger ships of the Holland America Line, whose names traditionally ended in the letters 'dam', such as *Maasdam*, *Statendam* or *Rotterdam*, had been crossing the North Atlantic since the 1870s with great commercial success. They were extremely popular and were known, because of their cleanliness, as the 'spotless fleet'. Because the Dutch were never the largest or the fastest and never displayed ambitions for the 'Blue Riband', these ships, with their green/white/green stripes on yellow funnels,

After the First World War, the Vaterland *was given to the USA as part of reparations. She was converted by William Francis Gibbs and then operated as the* Leviathan *for the United States Lines. Here she is shown in dry dock in Boston (photo from 1930).*

HOLLAND-AMERIKA LIJN

were not concerned with a sophisticated image. This changed in 1938, when the *Nieuw Amsterdam* began her line service on the Rotterdam-New York route. She was one of the most modern ships of her time, with a very trim cut to her hull, and very roomy on the inside. The Holland-Amerika Lijn, which within one year was carrying 25% more passengers thanks to the newly-constructed craft, referred to the 'ship of tomorrow'. The world-wide economic crisis after 'Black Friday' in October 1929, had caused passenger figures to slump, in 1928 they had been more than 1 million whilst in 1938 they were still as low as one half of that figure. Nonetheless, the shrunken market was still the target of not only the large lines but also an increasing number of small ones. Hence in the 1920s the *Gripsholm* and *Kungsholm* of Svenska Amerika Linien had been travelling to New York, and in the 1930s Poland's Gdynia-America Line had been operating a transatlantic service with the *Batory* and *Pilsudski*, whilst in 1938 the Den Norske Amerika Linje added the *Oslofjord* to its fleet.

On 6 August 1939, the *New York Herald Tribune* published, as it did in each of its Sunday editions, a map with the positions of all passenger ships on the Atlantic. On that day, 49 liners were travelling between Europe and America, including giants such as the *Europa*, the *Ile de France*, the *Normandie*, the *Queen*

The liners of the Holland-Amerika Lijn: in 1938, the Nieuw Amsterdam *began line service on the Rotterdam-New York route. The* Rotterdam, *date of construction 1959, is shown in the foreground. She was de-commissioned at the end of 1997.*

Mary, the *Rex* and the *Conte di Savoia*. A few weeks later, the golden age of luxury liners was terminated by the onset of the Second World War.

Travelling in wide-bodied jet aircraft over the Atlantic has long been a matter of routine today. Passengers check in unceremoniously, patiently endure security checks and delays, spend the entire journey eating, sleeping and reading in one and the same seat, inundated with videos and tapes, and climb stiffly out of the jet eight hours later to battle with 'jet lag'. Before the Second World War, transatlantic voyages across the 'big pond' still held a whiff of adventure. Passengers – provided they had booked first-

class – were ushered to their cabins and suites by boys in livery uniform. Champagne corks popped at 'bon voyage' parties with well-wishing friends, whilst cabins resounded to the music of their owners' gramophones, or there was dancing to live music in the lounge, until stewards asked the visitors to leave the ship. When the ship was cast off, everyone would stand at the railings, wave to those who had remained behind and throw countless paper chains.

The next day, the everyday routine of shipboard life would begin. You could take endless turns around the deck, or recline in armchairs and

Even in the 1920s, sporting activities were highly favoured on the Cunard liner the Aquitania; *this photo dates from 1926.*

read, wrapped up in woollen blankets, indulge in clay-pigeon shooting, play golf, ride 'electric camels', play innumerable games of poker, bridge and bingo, shovel board, tennis and mini-golf, and there was plenty of time for flirting, and you could be seduced by lady passengers of 'easy virtue' or fleeced by professional gamblers. You could hang about in bars, or luxuriate in the on-board restaurants, but you always adhered to

on-board etiquette: evening dress had to be worn after 6 pm, apart from the first and last day of travelling, because at such times your luggage would either not be unpacked or would have been packed up again. Add to this the round of theatre, ballet, film screenings, concerts and dance events.

The glamour of first-class with its evening dress and culture of smoking, champagne and caviar

This is how passengers spent their days at sea, in the old days: they would have sack races (photo from 1900), or take each other on at various on-board games, as shown in the photograph below, taken on the Bremen *in 1930.*

"BECAUSE YOU HAVE TO HAVE SOME MOVEMENT AND THE CONTINUAL CIRCULATION AROUND THE PROMENADE DECK IS STUPEFYING, WE TURNED TO DECK GAMES AND SPENT MANY HOURS ON THEM BOTH MORNING AND AFTERNOON. WE PLAYED SHOVEL-BOARD, WHOSE RED NUMBERED SQUARES ARE PAINTED EVERYWHERE ON THE DECK PLANKING, A STIMULATING AND WELL-THOUGHT-OUT GAME, IN THE COMPANY OF A YOUNG DUTCHMAN WHO HAD ADOPTED US."

THOMAS MANN, IN "MEERFAHRT MIT DON QUIJOTE" (SEA CROSSING WITH DON QUIXOTE), WRITTEN IN 1934 ON THE VOLENDAM DURING THE CROSSING FROM BOULOGNE TO NEW YORK.

Shuffleboard on the Queen of Bermuda *in 1961 (top picture), miniature golf on the* Bremen *in 1933 (above), and a boxing match with a life-size doll on the* Queen of Bermuda *(right). 'Horse racing', in which both first place and runner-up places are contested, was already a favourite on the* Andora Star *in 1931 (opposite).*

120

122

The other side of life on-board is illustrated by the great German photographer Erich Salomon, who travelled on the Europa *in 1930: people reading a book or writing letters in peace and quiet.*

was what made up the luxury image of sea travel, and still clings to transatlantic crossings. There is no need to remind you that in those days the lower classes remained excluded from the "high life". The only aspect of equality was seasickness, which could afflict all passengers alike. On 9 May 1936, some European passengers reached American soil after a voyage of just 61 hours and 30 minutes. They had crossed the Atlantic on the maiden flight of the airship LZ 129 *Hindenburg*, having set out from Friedrichshafen on Lake Constance, and everyone had had the impression of being 'on-board a small ocean steamer' and, after landing at Lakehurst, near New York, spoke enthusiastically of the peaceful voyage they had spent travelling at 130 km per hour.

The *Hindenburg*, from the German Zeppelin Line, which had been founded in the previous year, appeared to be the means of transport of the future, which could seriously jeopardise the monopoly status of the ocean-going liners.

Prominent figures on board the Albert Ballin: *the conductor Arturo Toscanini (second from left) together with the violinist Adolf Busch and his wife and daughter (left). The actor Emil Jannings with his wife Sussy Holl (above). Below, film actress Lilian Harvey poses with the captain of the* Bremen.

The 245-metre long 'silver cigar' offered its 20 passengers a level of comfort which could hardly be equalled by the *Queen Mary* or the *Normandie*. Then, however, upon the 21st flight of the Zeppelin on 6 May 1937, Lakehurst was the scene of a catastrophe with serious consequences. Upon its landing approach, the *Hindenburg* exploded and 35 passengers and crew members died. Confidence in the Zeppelins was shattered, and the short age of transatlantic airship travel in "floating hotels" was at an end.

In Autumn 1939, liners had to perform military duties, for the second time in this century. Originally painted white, with a green band around their hulls and a red cross amidships, they were converted to 'floating hospitals' painted entirely in grey or, repainted in bizarre

Neville Chamberlain, the English Chancellor of the Exchequer and later the Prime Minister (seated, third from left), shown above on-board the Empress of Britain *in 1932. Below: Albert Einstein as a passenger on the* Deutschland *in 1931, and at right in 1939, the English Royal Family on the* Empress of Britain.

camouflage colours, they were used as ancillary ferries and troop transporters by the military. The tremendous speed and size of the *Queen Mary* and the *Queen Elizabeth* made them ideal for service as transport ships. Their doors were removed, furniture was placed on land and salted away, and bunks at up to six levels were set up in cabins, suites, saloons and swimming pools. This created 8,000 sleeping berths, which was doubled up by sleeping in shifts and camping on deck. The *Queen Mary*'s record was made in July 1943 with 16,683 soldiers, and the log book records: 'This is the largest number of persons ever to have boarded a steamer.'

The 'Queens' in the capacity of 'Grey Ghosts' transported American soldiers to Australia and Australian soldiers to England, English troops to the Near-East and American tanks to West

Africa, and thereafter they concentrated on the Atlantic route – 'East-bound' with soldiers, 'West-bound' with diplomats, businessmen and German POWs.

1,200 military policemen and an extensive set of rules ensured order amongst the tumult of humanity. Each soldier, on boarding, received a veto on bad language, noise, gambling games, radio and alcohol.

Only prime minister Winston Churchill, who had been on board three times in his capacity as the Colonel Warden, received an exception to these rules. By 1945, the *Queen Mary* and the *Queen Elizabeth* had transported exactly

In spring 1940, the Queen Elizabeth *was taken out of range of German bombers. In grey camouflage, she steamed across the Atlantic to New York (above).*
- For Hitler's planned invasion of England, the Bremen *was painted in military colours: white/grey/black/green (above).*
- In the Second World War, the Queen Mary *and the* Queen Elizabeth *(right) transported 1,622,054 soldiers and diplomats.*

coloured card informing him of the area he was to use: Red for the fo'c'sle, white for amidships, blue for the after-deck. It was forbidden to leave the allotted colour zone. A one-way system prevented collisions: on the starboard side of the ship you had to be walking towards the bow, on the port side you had to be making for the stern. Mealtimes were organised in six sittings each lasting 45 minutes; and for each breakfast, 30,000 eggs had to be cooked. Life jackets had to be worn round the clock, whilst there was a

1,622,054 soldiers and diplomats. 'Without their help', Churchill records, 'the day of eventual victory would no doubt have had to be deferred.' One third of the passenger ships did not survive the Second World War. The *Normandie* was burnt in New York, the *Bremen* suffered a similar fate in Bremerhaven, and the *Rex* and the *Conte di Savoia* were sunk by British and German bombers respectively. Transat lost 4 of its 10 ships, whilst the Cunard giants survived. Hapag and Norddeutscher Lloyd now

127

THE UNITED STATES – THE FASTEST OCEAN-GOING GIANT OF ALL TIME

William Francis Gibbs, the American marine architect, had changed the *Vaterland* into the *Leviathan* after the First World War, and in 1939 he had constructed the *America*. However, his pièce de résistance remains the *United States*, the largest passenger ship constructed in the USA, at 53,329 GT, and the fastest ocean-going giant of all time (officially 35, but probably 42 knots).

In the late 1940s, the American government planned the construction of a superliner which could on the one hand transport 2,000 passengers across the Atlantic and on the other hand could be converted into a troop transporter for 14,000 soldiers at short notice.

William Francis Gibbs completed the designs, Washington paid 70% of the 78 million dollars construction costs, and the United States Lines leased out and operated the 'Yankee super liner'. The *United States*, which was 301 m long, and was also affectionately known as the 'Big U', had two over-sized funnels 17 m high, and was practically 'impossible to burn'.

For the interior cabins, Gibbs made exclusive use of fire-resistant material, wood was taboo, and was only – reluctantly – permitted for the meat-chopping block in the kitchen and for the Steinway grand piano in the saloon. The atmosphere on board ship was almost ascetic; on the other hand, each of the cabins was equipped with air-conditioning and smoke-warning devices. Captain Leroy Alexanderson claimed, 'We are not only the safest but probably also the cleanest ship.'

This cover panel of a menu on-board the United States is firmly dedicated to pleasure.

On her maiden voyage in July 1952, the *United States* forged across the Atlantic in a new record time eastwards at an average of 35.6 knots, westwards at 34.5. This was the first time since the *Baltic* in 1852 that a ship flying the 'Stars and Stripes' was to win the 'Blue Riband'. Initially, the 'Big U' operated extremely successfully and was 90% booked out. Soon, however, she entered stormy waters: competition from jet aircraft became increasingly intense, and trades unions made life difficult for the Line with their wage claims and strikes. Despite massive subsidies, the *United States* got further and further into the red, and when the last holder of the 'Blue Riband' was mothballed in Newport News, Virginia, in 1969, after 400 crossings, she had cost the American taxpayer a total of $118 million.

In 1981, the *United States* was bought by a property dealer in Seattle, who intended to use her for crossings from the west coast of America to Hawaii, but plans were shelved. In 1992, the ship was acquired by the Turkish Marmara Marine Incorporation, and transported to Istanbul for conversion. In 1996, the untouched 'speed queen' was returned to America, rusted up and dilapidated, travelling at only 4 knots, in tow from a deep-sea tug. The fate of the famous oldie since then can only be guessed at.

*The **United States** set off on her maiden voyage on 3 July 1952, from jetty 86 in New York (above). She was not only the largest liner ever constructed at an American yard, but also the quickest passenger ship of all time, and the ship with the best fire safety system.*

"...getting more than our money's worth
...and having a Wonderful Time!"

Colorfully tiled throughout, the swimming pools of the MANHATTAN and WASHINGTON are two of the largest afloat.

HOW perfectly this excerpt from a recent letter summarizes a crossing on the MANHATTAN or WASHINGTON—a voyage which blends into six brilliant days at sea, the luxury of spacious surroundings, a truly superlative cuisine—sparkling entertainment, American-style, the friendliest of shipboard hospitality. Rates are surprisingly moderate: Cabin, $186 up;

Tourist, $127 up. Weekly sailings to Ireland, England, France, Germany alternating with the popular *Pres. Harding* and *Pres. Roosevelt*, Cabin, $141 up. • COMING IN 1940—another great "American Flagship", the new AMERICA, designed to offer all the features which have made the MANHATTAN and WASHINGTON so well-liked.

Ask your TRAVEL AGENT for complete details

U.S. Lines
ONE BROADWAY, NEW YORK CITY

216 North Michigan Avenue, Chicago • 665 Market Street, San Francisco • 19 King Street, East, Toronto. • Offices in other principal cities.

Shipping lines used colour advertisements to promote their liners in magazines such as Harper's Bazaar, as shown here in 1939: a happy life on-board ship around the swimming pool, travel to exotic holiday destinations such as Hawaii, and the friendly and ever-helpful crew (right).

MAKING HER BOW AS A
HAPAG-LLOYD TRANS-ATLANTIC COMMUTER

existed only on paper, since what they had not lost in the war had to be handed over to the allies.

In Autumn 1945, Pan American opened a regular passenger route across the Atlantic, but aircraft did not yet constitute a serious competitive threat. Although they could cross the Atlantic in just 16 hours, they were on the other hand noisy, narrow, uncomfortable, expensive and liable to shake passengers up with turbulence. The sea was still the most important traffic link between Europe and America, and over the next 12 months, the luxury liners experienced a final period of glory (see table).

Transat was operating the *Ile de France* and *Liberté*, and the former *Europa*, Cunard provided weekly sailings with *Aquitania*, the *Queen Mary* and the *Queen Elizabeth*. The *Nieuw Amsterdam* sailed for the Holland-Amerika Lijn, the *America* sailed for the United States Lines, and was launched two days before the outbreak of war in 1939. It was not until the

Year	Passengers by ship	%	Passengers by aircraft	%	Total No. of passengers
1948	620,000	63.9	350,000	36.1	970,000
1952	840,000	66.0	433,000	34.0	1,275,000
1953	892,000	69.4	522,000	37.0	1,414,000
1954	938,000	61.8	578,000	38.1	1,516,000
1955	964,000	58.2	692,000	41.8	1,656,000

middle of the 1950s that occupied Germany was able to fly its flag on the Atlantic with 'second-hand ships': the *Berlin* and *Bremen* of Norddeutscher Lloyd, the *Hanseatic* of the newly founded Hamburg-Atlantik Linie. Gradually, the liners of the 1930s began to show their age, and they were replaced by newly-constructed ships which complied with the increased demands for comfort in the post-war period.

On 2 May 1952, a De Havilland Comet 1 took off from London Heathrow airport with a full complement of 36 passengers, for its maiden flight, and after 23 hours and 30 minutes, the 4-engined jet aircraft landed at Johannesburg. The 'jet age' had begun. On 3 July of the same year, the *United States* set out from New York for her maiden voyage and reached Southampton 3 days, 10 hours and 40 minutes later – a new and unbroken world record for an Atlantic crossing by a passenger ship.

However, the largest funnels ever constructed for a passenger ship acted as gigantic sails and thus affected her stability. On the other hand, America's 'speed queen' only arrived late four times in her 400 voyages over the next 17 years and became the darling of the 'celebrities'. The passenger list records included Senator John F Kennedy with his wife Jacqueline, Germany's Chancellor Konrad Adenauer and the Emperor Haile Selassie of Ethiopia, Yehudi Menuhin, Leonard Bernstein, the Vienna Boys' Choir and half of Hollywood. The Duke and Duchess of Windsor were regular passengers, and Prince Rainier of Monaco travelled to America on the *United States* to seek the hand of Grace Kelly in marriage.

In 1957, a record year, 1,036,000 passengers crossed the Atlantic on one of the fleet of approximately 70 liners: the highest figure since 1945. 1958 was a turning point as the first jet airliner, a Pan American Boeing 707, flew from

The Italian liners crossed the Atlantic on the calm, sunny southern route, which meant that life on board could move into the open air. Illustrated here from top to bottom: the Cristoforo Colombo *(1954), the* Michelangelo *(1965) and the* Conte Grande *(1928).*

New York to London on 26 October 1958. Passengers enjoyed more comfort, and the flight time had been better than halved; in future, anyone who was in a hurry would use jets. And the statistics at the end of the year were correspondingly impressive – for the first time, aircraft had transported more passengers than ships had: 957,000 passengers travelled by sea, 1,280,000 by air. In the same year, employees of the Chantiers de l'Atlantique yard at Saint Nazaire had constructed the *France*. In 1962, the last luxury liner designed exclusively for the Atlantic began crossings to New York. The Compagnie Générale Transatlantique promoted her as being 'modern, comfortable and elegant' whilst in the meantime speed had become secondary. On the other hand, the *France*, which is still known of today, albeit by the name of *Norway*, is the longest passenger ship of all time at 315.5m length. For one last time, *France* wished to shine at sea with 'joie de vivre' and 'haute cuisine'. However, times and public tastes had changed, and the *France*

THE MICHELANGELO AND THE RAFFAELLO – THE BEAUTIFUL ITALIANS

The Michelangelo *and the* Raffaello *(right above) would ply the southern route to New York from Genoa via Cannes and Naples (very top) until 1975. Passengers could sun themselves in deck chairs (above) or dive into swimming pools.*

They were trimly cut ships of capricious design: entirely painted in white and with green decorative strips, with both chimneys far astern, surrounded by a grid of pipe-work, and finished off at the top with a horizontal panel which protruded far astern. For just 10 years, from 1965 to 1975, the *Michelangelo* and *Raffaello*, 45,900 GT, and 276 m long with cabins for 1,775 passengers, travelled the southern route from Genoa and Naples across the Atlantic to New York, and also on the standard transatlantic routes. They offered cool elegance, 'Italian grandeur', 50 types of pasta, six swimming pools and a steward specifically for pets.

The first twinned ships since the *Bremen* and the *Europa* were beautiful and elegant, but were also the wrong ships at the wrong time. They were too old-fashioned in the 'jet age', too big for the new transatlantic market and too expensive to maintain. The trades unions insisted on a doubled-up crew: whilst 720 crew were resting on land, a further 720 crew on board often had only 400 passengers to serve. The trades unions caused continual delays with lightning strikes, and on one occasion even walked out when waiting for a purchaser, and then the 'white giants' – which had cost $45 million – were sold to Persia for $4 million as accommodation for officers. In February 1983 the *Raffaello* was sunk after a bomb attack from the Iraqi air force. In summer 1991, the *Michelangelo* was sold off to a Pakistani salvage company and ferried to the Gadani Beach not far from Karachi. Here, where thousands of ships met their end, specialists dismantled the flag ship (which had in the meantime become completely dilapidated) of the Italian passenger fleet. For two further years, Karachi's street traders were selling off all kinds of kitchen equipment, water taps and toilet bowls which came from the vanished *Michelangelo*.

The two Italian beauties had capriciously styled gridded funnels and a stern deck that was set out in terraces – top for the first class (lower picture), bottom for the tourist class.

the crew was served tap water instead of mineral water. In vain, the Line attempted to control costs by cost-cutting measures: they reduced the cruise speed and saved costs on provisions, whilst the trades unions rigidly refused to accept any reduction in the number of employees and imposed further wage rise claims. The superliners entered further and further into the red, and finally the government was subsidising each passenger to the extent of $700. Italy's taxpayers began to complain, and the newspaper *Epoca* called for the sinking of 'This floating memorial to a bygone era'.

In April 1975 the *Raffaello* was de-commissioned, followed by the *Michelangelo* three months later. For two years, they lay idle off La Spezia

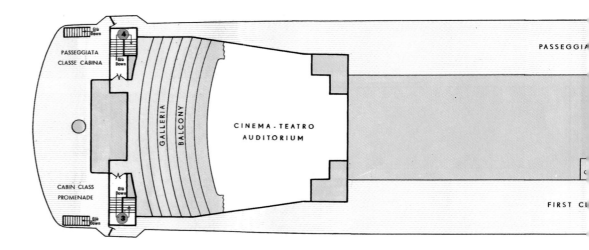

RAFFAELLO, DATE OF CONSTRUCTION 1965

The deck plans of twin ships the Michelangelo *and the* Raffaello *illustrate three of the top four decks, which were reserved for first-class passengers.*

Lido deck: well to the right on the starboard side, situated immediately below the bridge, the Captain's suite, and on the port side the slightly smaller suite of the chief engineer.

Aft of there, we have the solarium, gymnasium and massage room, a swimming pool, changing rooms, dog pens and the 'auditorium' (cinema/theatre) which extends over three decks.

Upper deck: looking towards the bow, the starboard and port sides and some of the first-class cabins. The lifeboats which are drawn in indicate that the view over the sea would have been blocked from these cabins. Moving astern, there follow the 'auditorium', a second gymnasium and the teenager club.

Boat deck: once again, first-class cabins, aft of them the 'auditorium' and the stern-deck swimming-pool. There is a promenade around the deck.

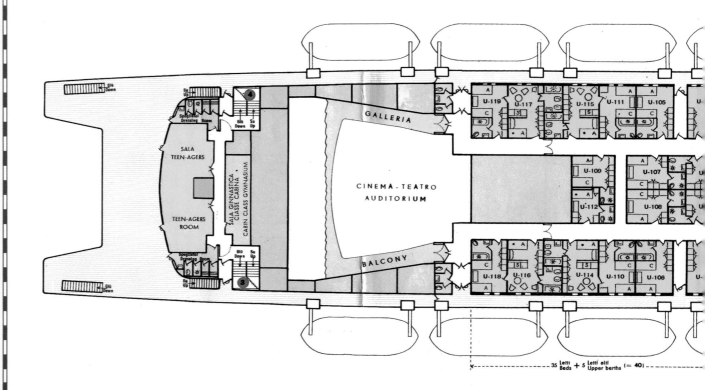

Red: cabins

Blue: common rooms

White: corridors and staircases

Dark blue: lifts

Hatched in blue lines: deck areas

Grey: crew and service

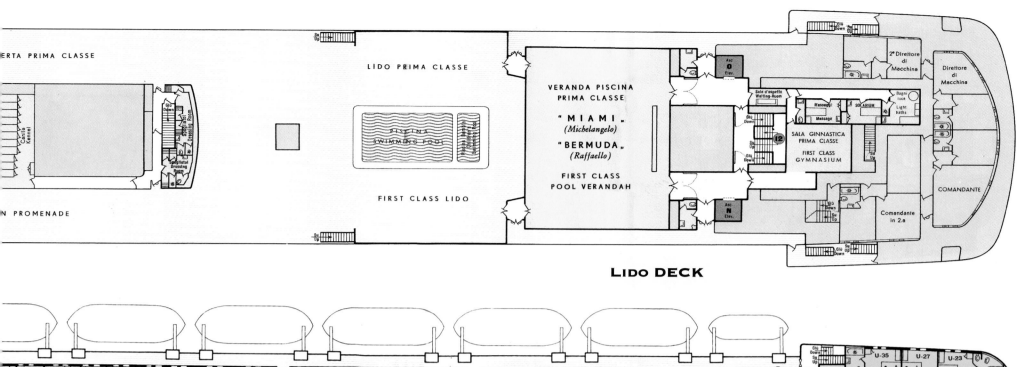

LIDO DECK

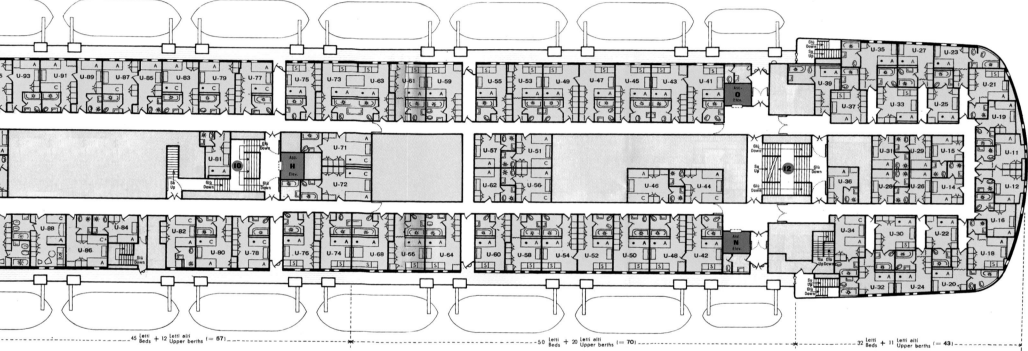

UPPER DECK

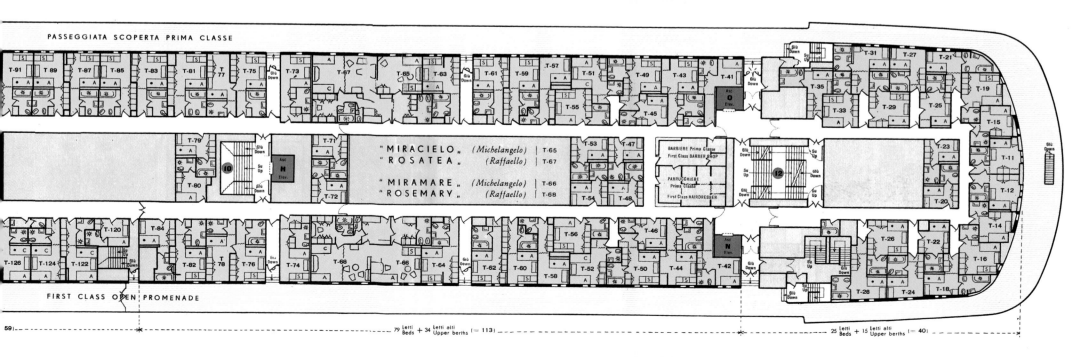

BOAT DECK

never achieved the glamour of a '*Normandie*'.

In Italy, which had lost 31 of its 37 passenger ships at the end of the Second World War, a real fever of construction broke out. Between 1952 and 1965, 9 liners left their yards: beautifully formed and brilliant white ships, named after famous Italians, from *Julius Caesar* to *Guglielmo Marconi*. The *Leonardo da Vinci*, commissioned in 1960, possessed six swimming pools on her over-sized stern decks, three of them being intended for children, and one of them even being infra-red heated. The Italia Line also announced that with effect from 1965 at latest, the new liner would be converted from steam turbines to nuclear power.

In 1965, 4 million people crossed the Atlantic by jet aircraft, and 650,000 on ships. The *Leonardo da Vinci* kept her conventional engines whilst the *Michelangelo* and *Raffaello*, the last and largest liners of the Italia company, were commissioned. Giuseppe Zuccoli, the Chairman of Italia, stated optimistically: 'The future of marine travel, allowing 8 days instead of 8 hours to cross the Atlantic, resides in the height of luxury and the height of quality.' But his prophecy was soon to be contradicted by the figures, and the trading report of Italia exhibited an astronomically high deficit in 1974.

Cunard, undeterred by the rapid increase in air travel, held on to its ship transport operations. On 20 September 1967, two days before the *Queen Mary*, now 31 years of age, left New York for her last regular Atlantic crossing, Queen Elizabeth II baptised the new ship with the name of *Queen Elizabeth 2* (written with an Arabic '2' rather than a Roman 'II'). The new liner had an entirely new profile, just one funnel and only two passenger classes. She was smaller than her predecessors and was designed both as a liner and as a cargo ship.

In 1969, two jet aircraft of entirely different types made their first test flights in America and Europe, and were to revolutionise air travel: in February, a Boeing 747, and in March a Concorde. The advent of wide-body and supersonic aircraft started the countdown to the end of the luxury liners. Two months afterwards, *Queen Elizabeth 2* started her maiden voyage.

The shipping companies, which had reaped rich profits in the 1950s, in the next decade were to be abandoned in droves as customers opted for the services of competing airlines. On one voyage at the end of 1961, the 1,000-strong crew of the *Queen Mary* had just 437 passengers in their charge, and John Malcolm Brinnin, an English passenger, experienced a feeling of isolation at afternoon tea, when 'only a dozen stewards were standing around like so many sentries waiting for a command'.

At the end of the 1960s, 96% of all transatlantic travellers went by air. In the 1970s, the price of oil increased from 35 to 95 dollars per barrel, due to the oil crisis, and at the same time the trades unions imposed higher and higher wage claims and shut the liners down by their strikes. When the crew of the *United States* walked out, the shipping line experienced the painful humiliation of having to book their passengers on aircraft flights. This downturn in fortunes was one that could not be sustained, once luxury liners had played out their role as vehicles for the national image. Governments now looked more to 'high-tech' for prestige than to ocean-going giants which were no longer modern, and decades of generously dispensed subsidies came to a sudden end. This was the final curtain for more than 100 years history of shipping on the Atlantic. One by one, the large steamers died out: the *Liberté* was scrapped in 1962, the *Queen Mary* and the *Queen Elizabeth* were decommissioned in 1967, the *United States*

The Italian artist Raphael shown in relief in the lobby of the Raffaello.

Michelangelo Buonarroti illustrated in relief in the lobby of the Michelangelo.

The twin ships the Michelangelo *and the* Raffaello, *Italy's last super-liners, offered cool elegance and numerous works of art by famous artists. Clockwise from top left: the teenager club and the cinema in the* Michelangelo's *vestibule, teenager club, ballroom and chapel on the* Raffaello.

139

THE FRANCE – YESTERDAY LUXURY, TODAY MASS TOURISM

In the theatre, the first-class passengers sat on the balcony and the tourist class in the stalls.

The first-class library was dominated by cool elegance.

The 518 first-class passengers reached the Chambord restaurant via a staircase.

The French Line promoted the France *with advertisements that emphasised the culinary aspects of voyages on board the new craft.*

COMING EARLY IN 1962

On 11 May 1960, this was the scene, after a construction period of 4 years, 3 months and 28 days: at Chantiers de l'Atlantique in Saint Nazaire, Madame De Gaulle broke a giant bottle of champagne on the bow of the ship and gave her the name of *France*. Then the President, Charles de Gaulle, gave a speech in praise of the new craft: 'It will be the function of the *France* to transport people, and their ideas and activities, science and work, art and wealth from one coast of the Atlantic to the other'.

On 3 February 1962, the third ship named *France* set sail on her maiden voyage to New York from Le Havre in order to fulfil the function bestowed upon her. France's new prestige steamer measured 15 m longer than the height of the Eiffel Tower, her twelve decks reached the height of the Arc de Triomphe and the total deck area was as much as that of the Place de la Concorde. The French superliner was surprisingly slim for her length, and exhibited a revolutionary innovation on her two red/black chimneys: laterally-mounted wings with a span of 19 metres. These were intended to deflect the unwanted smoke upwards. Inside, the 2-class ship varied between luxury and trendiness: expensive elegance for the older generation

Cabins were designed to please American passengers' tastes.

One covered courtyard on the sun-deck was reserved for luxury cabin passengers.

A chapel and children's playrooms were open to both classes on the 2-class ship.

First-class passengers could meet for dancing and cocktails in the 'Fontainebleau' saloon.

of passengers, and a discotheque and teenager club for young people. But there was more: a prison cell, a mortuary, an outlet of 'Galeries Lafayette', 94 car-parking spaces and a carpeted dog enclosure. Naturally the centre-point was the 'cuisine'. Kitchen chef Henri Le Huédé, who had a brigade of 180 under his command, could fulfil every passenger's wish. Only once did he have to admit defeat – when an eccentric oil millionaire from Texas ordered a rattlesnake steak. In just 13 years, the *France* crossed the North Atlantic 377 times and transported 588,024 passengers; she performed 93 crossings with 113,682 passengers and covered a total of 1.8 million nautical miles with no accidents. The most prominent 'passenger' came on-board in December 1962, and had booked cabin M 79; she was guarded around the clock – Leonardo da Vinci's 'Mona Lisa', who was travelling to the USA for an exhibition. However, what the statistics do not show is that the Mona Lisa's hostess, albeit an 'elegant French lady', was a floating anachronism in the age of

booming air traffic, and she ran into further deficits with each voyage, and was only kept afloat thanks to massive government subsidies. In July 1974, however, the French government turned off the credit tap, preferring to finance Air France's no less unprofitable Concorde, which the government considered to hold out the prospect of more prestige for 'La Grande Nation'.

This meant the end for the *France*, and on 18 September 1974, Compagnie Generale Transatlantique de-commissioned their flagship. For five years, France's prestige steamer hung about in Le Havre, until Norwegian shipping line owner Knut Kloster acquired her and converted her into the *Norway*. In that guise, as the world's largest pleasure steamer, she set sail for the first time in 1980.

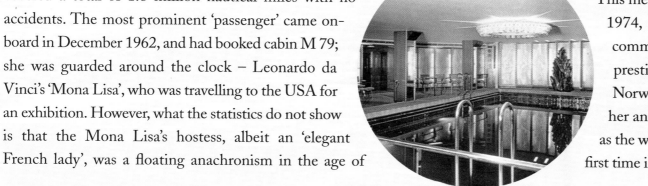

The swimming pool for first-class passengers was deep in the heart of the ship.

was mothballed in 1969, the *Nieuw Amsterdam* was scrapped in 1974, and in the spring of 1975 the *Raffaello* was laid up. The competition for prestige and passengers, size and speed, which had once raged across the Atlantic, became transferred to the air. But Pan American referred to its jet aircraft as 'clippers' whilst American Airlines spoke proudly of its 'luxury liners'.

On 11 September 1974, the *France*, which was the world's largest and longest luxury liner, was expected to arrive from New York and reach Le Havre at around 10 p.m. The three men of the Port Authority had long seen the ship on their radar screen when, to their amazement, it stopped 5 km in front of the harbour mouth.

At the same time, the 1,266 passengers were still sitting in the two on-board restaurants, the 'Chambord' and the 'Versailles'.

Having reached their desserts and coffees, they noticed that the 160,000 PS power engines had stopped. Stewards told the irritated passengers: 'Mutiny on-board!' The crew had relieved captain Christian Pettré of his command and taken over control of the ship, in order to demonstrate against the de-commissioning of the *France* which the government had ordered. They distributed fly sheets printed in French and English, backed up with a public address announcement: 'We regret that your voyage has been brought to such an unexpected end. Please excuse us and accept the fact that we regarded this as our only opportunity to keep the ship alive. We wish you every success and trust that we shall have the opportunity of welcoming you on board the *France* again soon. We thank you for your understanding and your co-operation.'

COMPAGNIE GÉNÉRALE TRANSATLANTIQUE

B

FIRST CLASS

French Line

The France, *now sailing as the* Norway, *is the longest passenger ship ever built. Most first-class passengers had cabins on the three top decks of the total of 11 decks, which also contained common-access rooms, and other cabins and the restaurant and swimming-pool were on the lower decks amidships.*

Hardly anyone seemed to take offence at this incident. Drinks were handed round free of charge, the passengers collected money for the strikers and posed on the bridge with the crew, for souvenir photos. For a day and a half, the events of that night hit the headlines worldwide: 'Crew goes on strike on the luxury liner *France*', 'Mutiny onboard the *France*', 'Doomed to end up onboard the *France*'. The forthcoming end of the high-deficit luxury liner, which the ship's owners Transat had arranged for the end of October, had become a political matter.

Onboard France's prestige steamer, in the meantime, the mutinous crew of around 900 had formed their own government: the 'Prime Minister' was moustachioed cabin steward Marcel Raulin, and he was flanked by six 'ministers', who were responsible for Information, Welfare, Leisure, Safety, Social and Financial affairs.

The situation was grotesque: the effect of the action by France's Communist Party was to use workers' tax to subsidise rich tourists to continue to wallow in luxury. In a radio appearance, Premier Jacques Chirac argued against this, saying that he could not see why the loss-making ocean-going giant should be subsidised merely in order to enable a handful of wealthy people to maintain a form of travel which was now out of date. The crew countered with this argument: 'So what? Even if the *France* is still losing money and is reliant on subsidies, isn't it better to pay taxes for pleasure than for atom bombs?' But Transat stood firm, and on 18 September it de-commissioned the *France* with immediate effect.

On Thursday, 26 June 1975, just before four o'clock in the afternoon in New York. A dull, rainy day. The piers on the bank of the Hudson, where, at the end of the 1940s, up to a dozen

Hundreds of the Norway's *crew members work below deck. When the ship is in port, therefore, they take every opportunity to get a breath of fresh air (following page).*

In order for the superstructure and sides of the ship always to be glittering white, the crew is constantly at work with paint rollers. This picture shows the exemplary Atlantik, which has sailed under the name of Melody since 1997.

Concerned with the physical well-being of passengers: here on the Queen Elizabeth 2 *(below), stewards serve meals in the restaurants and also – if desired – in cabins. On-board the* Horizon, *320 of the 645 crew members work in the kitchen, restaurants and bars (centre, below). The cooks of the* Splendour of the Seas *prepare meals for 1,800 passengers and a crew of 730 each day (bottom picture).*

A glimpse behind the scenes: Bridge of the Horizon, *with Captain Gerassimos Andrianatos (third from right, left-hand photo). Control room of the* Queen Elizabeth 2 *with monitors (below), the engine-room of the* Daphne, *which has sailed as the* Switzerland *since 1997 (bottom picture). Laundry of the* Meridian, *which is staffed by a team of Chinese, as on almost all passenger ships (bottom left).*

liners would have been moored at any given time, are rusty and dilapidated. The *Michelangelo*, Italy's last great luxury liner, is setting off on her last voyage with 1,202 passengers. The ship, which the government is keeping alive for the sum of 100,000 million lire per day, is to be laid up at Genoa when she arrives. The *Michelangelo*'s American passengers wanted to give her a send-off worthy of her status, but her appearance was far from brilliant. The onboard shops did not stay open very long, the cigarettes and schnapps ran out and souvenir hunters were grabbing everything that was not secured. The library and laundry were closed, the first paintings were being taken down. Then the air-conditioning system was switched off.

There was a mood of annoyance. The crew were nervous about losing their jobs as the liner was to be removed from service, and passengers were complaining about the increasingly sloppy service. In the first-class 'Ristorante Monte Carlo', a Hollywood script writer was complaining because there was no Sevruga caviar left on board: 'What a crappy steamer! She should be sunk with a torpedo!' Whilst the same American was incongruously drinking champagne with spaghetti, seasoned stewards lamented the loss of 'savoir vivre' amongst their passengers: 'The first class is not what it used to be. Customers like that were once only to be found in second class.'

Thousands were standing on the pier to greet the *Michelangelo* and wish her well when she arrived at around 3 pm in Genoa harbour after a 9-day voyage. On the port section of the bridge, Captain Claudio Cosulich, resplendent in his white uniform, directed the tug-boats' pushing and pulling operations with a degree of theatricality. When the *Michelangelo* was

The sailor's job is made easier by computers and electronics. But heavy ropes still have to be handled, as in the old days, in order to moor up a ship in port.

moored, there were calls of 'Bravo, Capitano!' In the lounges, passengers were still waiting to disembark, whilst wall decorations were being removed in the dining rooms, cutlery and crockery were being packed in boxes and inventory lists were being written. After 10 years and 121 Atlantic round trips with 245,839 passengers, the flagship of Italia's fleet was taken out of service. The *Michelangelo* was scrapped, the *Queen Elizabeth* was burnt out, the *Queen Mary* became a floating conference centre in California, the *France* became the *Norway* and worked on ferry crossings in the Caribbean. Upon the demise of the liner, not only was a piece of traffic history concluded, but also there was an end to a travel tradition in which 'time' had not yet been 'money' and in which it had been almost better to travel opulently than to

arrive, at least for the 1st-class passengers. Although the millions of emigrants, huddled together on the 'tweendeck for the transatlantic voyage, would have seen it differently.

The 'floating palaces' and Grand Hotels, which had ousted sailing ships from the Atlantic one hundred years before, had now fallen victim, in their turn, to jet aircraft. But not all of them. The *Queen Elizabeth 2* of the Cunard Line, whose paddle steamer *Britannia* had started it all in 1840, still travels between the Old and New Worlds and takes all of six days to complete a journey which Concorde completes in three hours. Instead of speed, what the last liner offers is 'the finest form of leisurely travel', and thus a new form of luxury: time to relax, and the incentive to reflect.

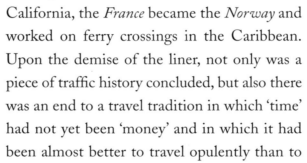

Millions of Europeans emigrated to North America on steamers. The emigrants hoped for a better future in the 'Land of unlimited opportunity'.

4 July 1975, just before noon. On her last voyage, the Michelangelo *has called at Naples for the last time. The ship is moored and the engines are still. While the luggage is being off-loaded, passengers are waiting impatiently to be able to go aboard (following page).*

THE 11 BIGGEST ATLANTIC LINERS

NAME	TONNAGE	CREW	LINE
Queen Elizabeth	83,673	1,940	Cunard
Normandie	83,423	1,935	Transat
Queen Mary	80,774	1,936	Cunard
Queen Elizabeth 2	70,327	1,969	Cunard
France	66,348	1,962	Transat
Bismarck / Majestic	56,551	1,922	Hapag / White Star
Vaterland / Leviathan	54,282	1,914	Hapag / United States Lines
United States	53,329	1,952	United States Lines
Imperator / Berengaria	52,117	1,913	Hapag / Cunard
Bremen	51,656	1,929	Norddeutscher Lloyd
Rex	51,062	1,932	Italia

THE QUEEN ELIZABETH 2 –
THE LAST "QUEEN OF THE SEAS"

The Queen Elizabeth 2 *is the last passenger ship to make scheduled voyages across the Atlantic between Southampton and New York, 6 days out, 6 days back.*

The time is 1 pm, in Southampton harbour. On the pier, looking as solid as a multi-storey block of flats, there is the *Queen Elizabeth 2* with her blue/black hull, red/black chimney and imposing bulk: she is all of 294 metres long, 32 metres wide and 13 decks high. Officers speak into intercom systems, fork lifts manoeuvre their way around, cranes hoist baggage nets on-board, and passengers board the ship by means of the roofed gangway.

5 pm. The floating giant sounds her hooter, and a military band strikes up with marching music. Four tugs draw the *Queen Elizabeth 2*, commonly known as the *QE2*, slowly off the jetty. The ship is at the threshold of a transatlantic crossing of 3,005 nautical miles: six days out and six days back. The *QE2*, referred to by Captain John Burton-Hall as 'the fine old lady', glides over the Atlantic at 28.5 knots.

The sea is as flat as a mill-pond, and there isn't a cloud in the sky. Passengers distribute themselves over five restaurants, sit around on loungers, jog over the boat-deck, work off their excess fat in the fitness centre or check out the goods on sale in the on-board shops.

For days at a time, all that can be seen is the infinite expanse of the ocean! However, you can never be bored, there is simply too much entertainment on offer: clay-pigeon shooting, mini golf

and golf lessons – from teeing-off to putting – on deck and below decks there are courses in computing, flower-arranging classes and photography lectures; in the evening there are two shows with three bands, pounding rhythms in the discotheque, the strains of more melodic music in the piano bar, and roulette and blackjack in the casino.

On the robust Cunard liner, which has been built to withstand heavy seas, the 1,500 passengers experience an emphatically British atmosphere on board, from the keel to the mast-top. There is a bust of Queen Elizabeth 2 in the 'Queen's Room'; it was she who launched the ship in 1967. On the quarter-deck a transcript of the Queen Mother's radio broadcast is posted, dating from when the QE2, serving as a troop carrier, was returning from the Falklands War in 1982, and the Queen Mother was welcomed aboard the ship. And on Sunday morning, the captain continues a tradition of British sea travel by holding a religious service in the theatre.

On the sixth day, shortly after 6 am, the *QE2* steams up the Hudson at half power. On the port side, the Statue of Liberty comes into view, and the buildings of Manhattan can be seen towering into the sky ahead of the bow. These are virtually the same impressions of the 'New World' as have been experienced in their time by millions of hopeful emigrants and experienced visitors to America.

QUEEN ELIZABETH 2

🇺🇸 TRANSATLANTIC VOYAGE 🇬🇧

NEW YORK   THIS CERTIFICATE IS PRESENTED TO   SOUTHAMPTON

ON THE OCCASION OF SAILING ABOARD
QUEEN ELIZABETH 2 ON HER
TRANSATLANTIC VOYAGE No. **457 East**

Bob Arnott
MASTER OF THE QUEEN ELIZABETH 2

CUNARD

*Anyone who travels across the Atlantic on
the Queen Elizabeth 2 is undertaking a
nostalgic voyage in the wake of legendary
liners such as the Normandie or the
Queen Mary; immaculate dining in five
restaurants (above), swimming in the pool
and – in the evening – show–time in the
'Grand Lounge' (left).*

Cruises

FROM ELITE HOLIDAY PLEASURES TO MASS TOURISM

Cruise ships of yesterday: exclusive sea voyages with an educational slant for a few privileged people who, despite their pioneering attitude, did not want to dispense with the level of comfort to which they were accustomed even on board.

Arthur Anderson was editing the first edition of his *Shetland Journal* in 1835, and time was running out. But the hard-pressed editor just could not find enough news to fill his pages. The nearer he got to the deadline, the less fussy he became in terms of accepting advertisements to fill the many blank pages that remained in his paper. And as he not only earned his money as a journalist but also as a ship's broker, he announced under the heading 'To Tourists' a fictitious voyage which was to journey to the Faroe Islands via Iceland and back to the Shetlands in two weeks. Thus the cruise was born, at least on paper.

Nine years later, Anderson was a director of the Peninsula and Oriental Steam Navigation Company (P&O) in London. He was thinking about how he could make better use of his ships and, remembering the fake advertisement, he began planning pleasure trips around the Mediterranean. On these trips, passengers would have the opportunity to get to know the country and its people on organised excursions in and around the various ports of call. To publicise this innovative idea, Anderson invited the author William Makepeace Thackeray to go on the first voyage and to report on it. Thackeray travelled to Gibraltar via Vigo, Lisbon and Cadiz on a wooden paddle steamer, from Gibraltar to Malta and Constantinople on another steamer, and finally to Alexandria on a third one. He became seasick, did not get on with his fellow passengers and was bored in Constantinople, where he happened to be staying during the Islamic fasting month of Ramadan.

Six weeks later, Thackeray returned to England and, writing under the pseudonym Michael Angelo Titmarsh, he described his experiences in a book called *Diary of a Voyage from Cornhill to Grand Cairo*. He saw Athens as a 'a pile of tumble-down huts', and the hubbub in Jerusalem's Church of the Holy Sepulchre 'as a shabby theatre', and at the pyramids he was annoyed by the 'hoards of persistent beggars'. However, Thackeray's overall verdict was positive: 'a wonderful journey,' which he would recommend to anyone who 'had the time and the necessary resources'.

The cruises offered by P&O in the Mediterranean were revolutionary: for the first time, passengers did not use a ship purely as a means of transport to get to their destination quickly and safely. Instead they travelled for relaxation or because of a desire for education, in other words as tourists visiting different ports, going on excursions ashore, returning on board and going on to their next destination. Anderson's pioneering cruises had only one flaw – the passengers travelled on scheduled ships and had to keep changing from one steamer to the next. In February 1867, the American Leary Bros.

Line announced a 'party tour to the Holy Land, Egypt, the Crimea, Greece and other interesting destinations en route'. The *Quaker City*, a 70-metre-long paddle steamer with two funnels and two masts for auxiliary sails, furnished 'with all the necessary comforts including a library and musical instruments', was to leave New York at the beginning of June, 'stop off for one or two days' in every port it sailed to and dock again in New York after five months. The price of the trip was $1,250, and extra costs for excursions ashore were put at '$5 in gold per day'.

Captain Charles Duncan raised the anchors on the morning of 8 June. There were 74 passengers on board, including three clerics, eight doctors and a 32-year-old reporter from the *Daily Alta California* called Samuel Langhorne Clemens. He was to send several despatches en-route to the editors of his newspaper to tell readers about

These days, cruises are offered to suit every pocket and every taste. There are both economical and exclusive ships sailing the world's oceans in much the same way as there are family-oriented bed and breakfast establishments and luxury five-star hotels ashore.

this unusual journey. Two years later, his collected reports were published as *The Innocents Abroad*. The book became a best-seller and thus began the fame of the man who was later to write under the pen-name of Mark Twain.

With as much precision as humour, Twain describes life aboard a pleasure trip at sea during the second half of the 19th century. He and another young man shared a luxury cabin which he described as follows:

'It contained two sleeping bunks, a dismal ceiling light, a drain with a washing bowl and a long, generously-upholstered trunk which is supposed to serve partly as a sofa and partly as

Mark Twain (seated) describes a pleasure trip on the Quaker City *in the Mediterranean in 1867 in his* The Innocents Abroad. – *Unlike liners (right), there were no classes on cruise ships.*

"AT SEVEN BELLS THE FIRST GONG SOUNDED; AT EIGHT THERE WAS BREAKFAST FOR THOSE WHO WERE NOT TOO SEASICK TO TAKE IT. AFTER THAT, ALL THE HEALTHY PEOPLE WANDERED ARM IN ARM UP AND DOWN THE LONG PROMENADE DECK AND ENJOYED THE BEAUTIFUL SUMMER MORNING, AND THOSE WITH SEASICKNESS CREPT OUT, STOOD IN THE LEEWARD SIDE OF THE WHEEL CASES, CONSUMED THEIR PITIFUL TEA WITH TOAST AND LOOKED TERRIBLE."

MARK TWAIN IN "THE INNOCENTS ABROAD".

a hideaway for our things. Despite all these furnishings, there was still plenty of room to turn around in'.

Hardly had the *Quaker City* left New York, when it ran into a storm:

'One could not promenade without risking one's neck; one moment the bow sprit was pointing with deadly accuracy at the sun high in the sky, and the next it was attempting to harpoon a shark in the depths of the ocean.'

Once the sea had calmed down, everyday life

156

on-board in the North Atlantic could begin. After breakfast at 8 o'clock, passengers strolled about on the promenade deck, the gong sounded for lunch at 11, for dinner at 6 o'clock, and

Hapag's Meteor *on a voyage in the North, 1909 (left). – The* Augusta Victoria *on a Mediterranean voyage, 1891 (right).*

between times people 'read a little, smoked a lot and crocheted'. In the evenings the passengers wrote diaries, read descriptions of the countries they were to visit, organised magic lantern shows or danced on the upper deck.

After its ten-day transatlantic crossing, the *Quaker City* anchored off the coast of Horta on the island of Faial in the Azores, it sailed through the Straits of Gibraltar and began its Mediterranean cruise. Passengers went on various excursions ashore, each lasting several days, to Paris, Venice, Florence, Pisa and Rome. 'Home again!' or 'To be back at sea again was worth a king's ransom', noted Mark Twain with relief when he felt the decks of the *Quaker City* underneath his feet once more after an extended educational trip.

Whilst Mark Twain outlines the Old World with irreverence and occasional earthy humour, he enthuses about his sea voyage like someone writing the copy for a cruise brochure: 'Dancing

159

and promenading and smoking and singing and flirting. […] Jumping around on deck, filling the ship with the sound of shouting and laughter, or reading novels and poems in the shade of the funnels during the day.'

The voyage of the paddle steamer *Quaker City* not only made literary history, it also heralded the birth of maritime tourism: for the first time, a ship was sailing across the sea solely for the pleasure of its passengers, following a route which would incorporate as many interesting ports for excursions ashore as possible. In accordance with the spirit of the times, this first cruise had the character of an evening class on occidental culture and history for people with a lot of time and even more money.

A highly solvent public increasingly favoured this new form of holidaying, and when the *British Medical Journal* emphasised the positive effects of sea voyages on health, it went from strength to strength over the decades that followed. More and more shipping lines discovered a new market in pleasure cruises; they were the ideal product to get them get through the quiet winter months when the storm-tossed North Atlantic discouraged passengers from crossing it.

As early as 1891, Hapag sent the Augusta Victoria *on a 58-day pleasure cruise to the Mediterranean (below); the majestic fittings in the salon (above) were impressive. – Nine years later the same shipping line had the world's first cruise ship built, the yacht-like* Prinzessin Victoria Luise *(right).*

"IS IT NOT DELIGHTFUL TO VISIT A WHOLE SERIES OF WONDERFUL COUNTRIES AND
CITIES, TO BE ABLE TO ADMIRE THEIR PICTURESQUE SCENERY AND WONDERFUL
VEGETATION UNDER A SUNNY SKY, WITHOUT HAVING TO CHANGE CARS AND
HOTELS, WITHOUT HAVING TO WORRY ABOUT ONE'S LUGGAGE — THE BASIC EVIL OF
ALL RAIL TRAVEL — AND TO GET TO KNOW NEW PEOPLES, NEW CUSTOMS AND
HABITS WITHOUT HAVING TO SACRIFICE THE CUSTOMS OF ONE'S HOME COUNTRY?"

H. WEITH IN "DIE ORIENTREISE DER AUGUSTA VICTORIA"
(THE ORIENTAL VOYAGE OF THE AUGUSTA VICTORIA)

One stood on ceremony: people embarking on a pleasure cruise on the Augusta Victoria *(below right) did not yet know about the casual look. As a token gesture to the unusual situation, people wore "Prince Heinrich" caps in addition to their usual clothing. He was, after all, the brother of the emperor and the Admiral of the Fleet.*

In 1862, eleven years before Jules Verne published his adventure novel *Around the World in Eighty Days,* Thomas Cook organised the first round-the-world trip, for which he had to use four different liners and during which passengers had to be taken from New York to San Francisco by rail. In the summer of 1875, Cook chartered the *President Christie* in Norway for a cruise from Bergen to the North Cape. The journey to the land of the fjords and the midnight sun was so successful that it was repeated the following year and in 1877 needed a total of four ships.

From then on, Norwegian coastal steamers lived a double life: from autumn to spring they ran scheduled services for passengers and cargo along the west coast with their hulls painted black. The ships would then go into dry-dock to be re-fitted for the summer season: the hull was given a coat of white paint, the deck was fitted with canopies to protect from the sun. In this more friendly outfit, which cruise ships still use to this day, the ships travelled to the North Cape in the summer. In 1886 a small shipping company with the complicated name of North of Scotland & Orkney & Shetland Steam Navigation Company, ran pleasure trips from Scotland to the Orkney Islands, Shetland and

Before World War I, strict dress codes were observed. Even in tropical waters, long robes and blouses buttoned up to the neck were the order of the day for the ladies.

the Norwegian fjords for the first time. Thus Arthur Anderson's advertisement in the *Shetland Journal* had become a reality – albeit after some considerable delay.

In 1889, the Orient Line in England used its ship the *Chimborazo*, which made regular scheduled voyages to Australia, for pleasure trips first to Norway and later to the Mediterranean. Then in 1890, Norddeutscher Lloyd's high-speed steamer *Kaiser Wilhelm II* left Bremerhaven for the first time on a three-week cruise to the

Norwegian fjords. A shipping line brochure guaranteed conveniences 'as only a first-class hotel may offer', and underlined the benefits of a sea voyage: 'The passenger is free of all the drudgery associated with hotels, railways and shipping luggage.' The Hamburg-Amerikanische Packetfahrt-Aktien-Gesellschaft (Hapag), the arch rivals of Bremer Lloyd, came into the cruise business a year later. They sent their *Augusta Victoria* from Cuxhaven on a 58-day 'pleasure trip' to the Mediterranean. Thus as early as

163

Thanks to Hapag director Albert Ballin's (right) innovative ideas and their lavishly furnished passenger ships, Germany was the world's leading nation in maritime tourism.

the late 19th century, ships used to cruise in areas where holiday fleets still voyage today – the Caribbean, the Mediterranean and Northern Europe. However, these ships were designed as liners, and their facilities only met the requirements of a pleasure-seeking market to a limited extent. Albert Ballin, the far-sighted general manager of Hapag, was the first person to recognise that pleasure trips could be a second pillar of business for shipping lines in addition to traditional scheduled voyages, but that this new form of travel also needed ships built specifically for that purpose. He ordered the world's first cruise ship, the *Prinzessin Victoria Luise*, a ship 124 m long and with 120 cabins, from Blohm & Voss in Hamburg in 1900. Named after Emperor Wilhelm II's daughter, the ship had a narrow white hull, a streamlined clipper-like bow, an elegantly-shaped stern and two slim funnels. Thus the silhouette was exactly the same as those of the luxury yachts on which millionaires and royalty would sail on pleasure trips at the end of the 19th century. When Emperor Wilhelm II inspected the *Prinzessin Victoria Luise*, he found to his disapproval that it was 8 metres longer than his *Hohenzollern*. Albert Ballin's cruise ship was exactly to the taste of a small well-to-do group of the upper crust who wanted to be pampered on long cruises lasting many weeks. The accommodation was luxurious, the service excellent, the food superb. And of course there was only one class – first class. But unfortunately the first cruise ship was destined to have only a short life, as it ran aground in 1906 and had to be abandoned.

The four-funnel *Deutschland* won the Blue Riband for Germany in 1900 and defended the title successfully for two years. However, Hapag had trouble with its record-breaking steamer: on the one hand the 16 steamer boilers devoured 3,000 tonnes of coal on every five-day transatlantic crossing, which ate up profits. On the other hand, the 38,000 hp engine made the ship vibrate heavily, which caused the passengers to complain.

In 1910 Alfred Ballin converted his troubled *Deutschland* into the cruise ship *Victoria Luise*, reduced the number of passengers from 2,050 to 487 and cut the power of the engines by half, in the correct assumption that a travelling speed of a comfortable 17 knots would be sufficient for pleasure voyages. The Hapag boss also had bathrooms installed in some of the cabins, provided amateur photographers with a dark room and equipped a gym for the fitness-conscious. When the *Victoria Luise* left the shipyard the following year, it was barely recognisable: the hull and superstructures were now painted brilliant white, there were still four mighty funnels, although the only the front ones billowed smoke and the two rear ones were simply decorative. The former high-speed steamer had been transformed into the largest and most luxurious cruise ship in the world (16,700 GT).

Faded black-and-white photographs taken during the winter of 1913/14 during some of the *Victoria Luise*'s many four-week Caribbean cruises record the atmosphere on board and on

Many of the big high-speed steamers led a double life. They ran on scheduled routes and also occasionally undertook 'pleasure trips on sea' to the Caribbean, the Mediterranean or even round the world.

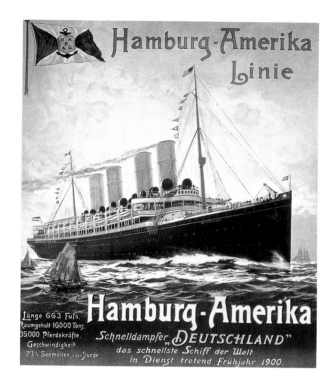

Food on board was always of major significance. Even the menus – here from the "yacht" Prinzessin Victoria Luise – were a feast for the eyes with their decorative designs.

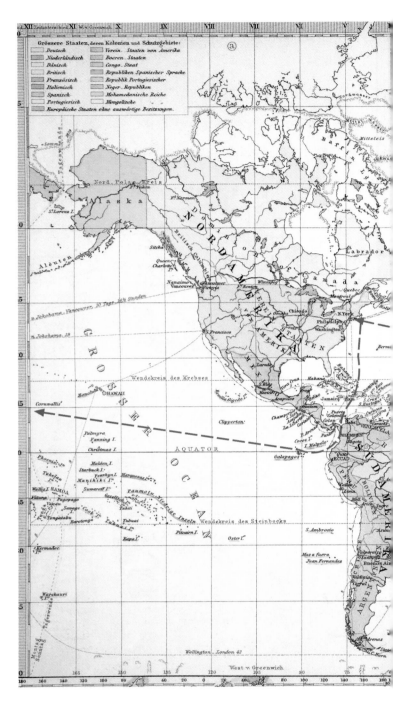

the many excursions ashore on the eve of the First World War. Even in the intense Caribbean heat the women wore long dresses, covered their arms with white gloves and preferred to stay in the shade. A parasol was an indispensable prerequisite for ensuring that they would return to Europe with the same elegant pale skin they had when they set out. Hats, jackets and ties were the order of the day for men, even in temperatures of 30°C. Entertainment on board was restricted largely to sack races and similar games. Anyone who went on land avoided the beaches. Baedekers were packed instead of bathing costumes, and visits were made to the few cultural attractions the Caribbean had to offer. On Martinique, for example, there was La Pagerie, the birthplace of the French Empress Joséphine Bonaparte, and the ruined town of Saint-Pierre, which had become famous as a 'Caribbean Pompeii' after a volcanic eruption and became a tourist attraction.

A few months later the first shots were fired at Sarajevo. World War I broke out, and the 'Belle Epoque' came to an end. Between the two World Wars, the 'floating towns' competed bitterly against one another for the Blue Riband, and at the same time the maritime tourism business was establishing itself. France's *Normandie*, Italy's *Rex* and England's *Mauritania* – they all went on

"THE FOOD IS PLENTIFUL, IT IS REALLY SOMETHING TO BE APPRECIATED ON ANY LEVEL. PATRONS DO NOT CHOOSE FROM A LIMITED MENU. THE ENTIRE, CLOSELY-PRINTED MENU, WHICH IS ALWAYS DIFFERENT, IS AVAILABLE; ONE CAN PUT TOGETHER ONE'S MEALS COMPLETELY TO ONE'S OWN TASTE, AND, IF ONE SO DESIRED, EVEN TAKE THE SAME MEAL THREE TIMES A DAY – FROM THE HORS D'OEUVRES TO THE ICE CREAMS. BUT HOW SOON ONE MEETS ONE'S OWN LIMITS!"

THOMAS MANN IN "MEERFAHRT MIT DON QUIJOTE"
(SEA VOYAGE WITH DON QUIXOTE)

Canal, traversed the Pacific Ocean and stayed in Japan for ten days. The Cunard liner then anchored in Shanghai, where passengers had the opportunity to go on an overland trip to Peking lasting several days and then to re-embark in Hong Kong. The voyage continued via Manila, Batavia, Singapore and Colombo to Calcutta, where a train was waiting to take the passengers across India to Bombay. From Bombay the ship continued westwards and through the Suez Canal. The third excursion, lasting several days, began in Suez; this time it went to Cairo, Luxor and Aswan. After more stop-overs in Naples, Monaco and Gibraltar, the *Laconia* steamed across the North Atlantic and docked again in New York on 13 March 1923.

The journey was such a success that other shipping lines followed suit. The Red Star Line's *Belgenland* left New York at the end of 1925 on a 132-day round-the-world voyage during which the ship docked at 60 ports in 14 different countries. The Canadian Pacific Company's *Empress of Britain* went on a round-the-world voyage almost every winter from 1930 until the beginning of World War Two. In 1936, newspaper advertisements announcing a four-month voyage not only spoke of exotic travel destinations ('Wake up one morning in Bali!') but also emphasised the many activities available on board: 'In between foreign ports, play tennis on an original-sized court, swim in a spacious pool and enjoy the wide variety of entertainments that only a ship like the *Empress of Britain* can offer.' The cheapest cabin cost $2,000, the most expensive suite $16,000, albeit including all excursions ashore. Accommodation for servants accompanying their masters and mistresses cost an additional $1,000.

The elite image of cruising as a form of travel for

cruises with well-to-do passengers on board. During the summer the liners cruised in the Caribbean or around northern Europe, and during the winter they went on round-the-world voyages.

Fifty years after Thomas Cook had organised the first round-the-world voyage which entailed having to change ships three times, American Express ran the first real round-the-world cruise on the *Laconia* in 1922. The steamer, which was chartered from Cunard, set sail from New York on 21 November, travelled through the Panama

the rich and super-rich changed in America when a law was passed which was in fact designed to serve public health and had nothing to do with tourism at all. On 17 January 1920, the National Prohibition Act came into force, making half the continent dry overnight. Over the next 14 years anyone who wanted to drink alcohol had to do so illegally. Whilst Al Capone rose to become the uncrowned king of Chicago through alcohol smuggling and speakeasies, shipping lines made money from the Prohibition in a completely legal manner: their ships left the ports for a couple of hours, anchored in international waters, where the alcohol forbidden ashore flowed freely, and then returned a few hours later. The Americans called these 'Booze Cruises', the shipping lines preferred to call them 'Cruises to Nowhere'.

Now, travelling on the sea was no longer just a dream. And once the initial alcoholic euphoria had settled down, people began to discover the charm of cruising. Demand increased, more and more liners set out in winter from New York to Cuba, Haiti, Bermuda and the Bahamas in search of the sun. Thanks to short voyages at

"CRUISES ARE A DEVELOPMENT OF THE LAST 20 YEARS. BEFORE THAT, ONLY THE VERY RICH WHO HAD THEIR OWN YACHT COULD AFFORD IDLY TO WANDER FROM PORT TO PORT."

EVELYN WAUGH IN
"LABELS. A MEDITERRANEAN JOURNAL"

rock-bottom prices, Caribbean cruises in the 1930s became holidays for (almost) everyone; what had previously been a holiday for the rich became democratised – at least in the USA. Thus maritime tourism attracted two different customer groups: on the one hand low-cost one-week cruises for the middle classes and on the other expensive cruises lasting several weeks for the well-heeled upper classes.

In the winter of 1938/39, three luxury liners left New York for a round-the-world voyage, but it was the voyage of the *Normandie* to the carnival in Rio in February 1939 that was regarded as the event of the season. The passenger list read like a 'Who's Who' of American high society, the Press spoke of a 'million dollar cruise' and noted with awe that two tonnes of caviar and 150,000 bottles of champagne had been

The Columbus *travelled between Bremerhaven and New York in the summer, and in winter it went on cruises.*

taken aboard for the 975 passengers.

Europe also extended its offer of cruises during the Roaring Twenties and Swinging Thirties. Whilst Holland and Italy were content to send their liners on only the occasional pleasure trip, Germany developed innovative ideas for tourism on the high seas. In 1928 Norddeutscher Lloyd advertised in American newspapers a 'Cruise as never before', the 'First Air Cruise in History'. At the beginning of September, the high-speed steamer *Columbus* crossed the Atlantic from New

THE "SEA CLOUD" – A LADY ALL IN WHITE

Marjorie Merriweather Post was given the Hussar *as a divorce settlement in 1935 and renamed it the* Sea Cloud.

Captain Ed Cassidy gives the order to set sail. Thirty crew members climb up the shrouds, balance along the yards at dizzying heights and untie the heavy sails.

The *Sea Cloud* sets off under full sail – with its four mighty masts up to 58 metres in height, 3,000 square metres of sail, a golden eagle as the figurehead, creating a majestic and nostalgic picture. You can hear the wind in the shrouds, the creaking of the rigging, the lapping of the waves. The passengers laze around on the aft sun deck, on the foredeck the crew sew sails, splice ropes and polish brass.

The first owners of the ship were the millionaire American couple Marjorie Merriweather Post and Edward F. Hutton. They had the *Hussar*, a superlative yacht, built at the Friedrich Krupp Germania shipyard in Kiel at a cost of $900,000, some $30 million at today's rates. Only the very best and the very finest was good enough for the cabins below deck: Carrara marble fireplaces, Venetian glass mirrors, stuccoed ceilings and gold-plated taps.

When the *Hussar* set sail for the first time in 1931, it was the biggest private yacht in the world. The Huttons sailed around the world in the company of the rich and the beautiful with champagne flowing freely, cared for by a 72-man crew. However, four years later all this splendour came to an end. Marjorie got a divorce, was given the yacht as settlement, renamed it the *Sea Cloud* and a little later married the lawyer Joseph E. Davies.

Thus began the filmworthy history of a ship with changing fortunes and a belated happy ending. Davies became the American ambassador to Moscow and had the *Sea Cloud* moored in Leningrad, where he spent weekends with diplomatic colleagues – a veritable showpiece of capitalist decadence as far as the staunch communists were concerned.

During the Second World War the US Navy chartered the ship to use as a floating weather station. After its military service, the *Sea Cloud* once more reverted to its role as a grand hotel under sail; anyone with rank and renown came for the sumptuous parties on board: famous names like the

Windsors, the moneyed like the Vanderbilts and monarchs like Queen Maud of Norway. The latter remarked in amazement: 'Marjorie, you live here exactly how people imagine kings live!'

During the 1950s, the costly toy became too expensive even for an eccentric multimillionairess. She sold the ship to Dominican dictator Rafael Leonidas Trujillo, who renamed it the *Angelita*. Trujillo was assassinated in 1961, after which the four-master rusted away in the port of Colón, Panama, until it was discovered in 1978 by Captain Hartmut Paschburg from Hamburg.

He fell victim to its charm and bought the windjammer. The *Angelita* became the *Sea Cloud* once more. Since then she has been sailing around the oceans of the world, a lady all in white - completely renovated and with all the glamour she had in the past, providing well-to-do passengers with a little bit of the nautical romance of yesteryear.

The bridge of the Sea Cloud *has retained the charm of a luxury yacht with lots of wood and brass. – Also nostalgia, but of the brawny type: the crew climb the shrouds to set the sails (top).*

The jewel in the crown of the 39 cabins is the luxury suite with its marble fireplace which the ship's first owner had furnished as her private refuge. – The on-board restaurant offers the traditional atmosphere of an English gentleman's club.

The Cap Arcona, *the 'Queen of the South Atlantic', travelled on cruises to South America, the prices of which included overnight excursions ashore and hotel accommodation.*

The Hamburg–Amerika Line sold tickets for flights from Germany to Brazil on the Zeppelin.

York to Bremen, the passengers transferred to a Lufthansa plane which flew them right across Europe via Berlin, Vienna and Munich to Zurich, via Cologne, Paris, Berlin and Amsterdam to London. The *Columbus* then took the 'sea/air cruisers' from Southampton back to New York. This pioneering journey cost $1290 – 'all expenses on land, water and in the air included' – and was decades ahead of its time: this was the very first collaboration between airlines and shipping lines. The 'Fly and Cruise' travel formula had been born.

The Hamburg-Südamerikanische Dampfschiffahrts-Gesellschaft's *Cap Arcona*, built in 1926 by Blohm & Voss in Hamburg, was a luxurious three-funnel ship with a heated saltwater swimming pool and a large sports deck. Advertised as the 'Queen of the South Atlantic', it transferred the glamour and glitz of the North Atlantic liner to the South American route. Travel journalist Albert Köhler noted: 'Naturally the high class ladies on this ship change their clothing at least three times a day and have matching shoes and hats for every frock.'

When passenger numbers fell dramatically during the second half of the 1930s, Hamburg-Süd tried to make up for losses with tourist programmes. In 1937 it offered 35-day voyages to South America, costing 1525 reichsmarks including sea passage, excursions ashore, hotel accommodation and food. Holidaymakers travelled from Hamburg to Rio de Janiero via Madeira, where they disembarked and stayed in the town for four days. They took part in a wide range of guided tours, and on the sixth day travelled onwards to Sao Paulo and then by rail to Santos two days later. On the tenth day they boarded the *Cap Arcona* once more for the return journey to Hamburg. By combining travel by ship with a stay on land, they invented a type of holiday which was taken up again after World War Two under the fashionable appellation 'Cruise and Stay'.

In the America of the Prohibition, booze cruises had popularised cruising, whilst in Germany the Nazis invented mass maritime tourism in order to exploit it for propaganda purposes. 'It is the Führer's will that every worker and every employee should be able to take part in a cheap 'KdF trip' at least once a year. In doing so he should not only be able to experience the most beautiful German holiday regions but also travel abroad by sea', Robert Ley declared in November 1933. Ley headed the *'NS-Gemeinschaft Kraft durch Freude*' ('National Socialist Community of Power through Pleasure') abbreviated to 'KdF', the recreational division of the state *Gewerkschaft Deutsche Arbeitsfront* (German Labour Front Union).

'*Kraft durch Freude*' chartered and purchased ten passenger ships, commissioned new ships *Robert Ley* and *Wilhelm Gustloff* and sent them off on cruises. They started with five-day trips to the English south coast and to the Isle of Wight, followed by journeys to Norway, Portugal and Madeira, the Baltic Sea and the Mediterranean. The cruises were a complete success: in 1934, there were 54 cruises carrying 80,000 passengers, and in 1936, a record year, an impressive 144,000 passengers went on 108 trips.

The KdF ships, described in Nazi propaganda as 'the fleet of peace', only appeared to be intended for leisure purposes on the surface; the idea was to lull the 'national comrades' with games and fun, convince them of the regime's achievements and train them to become loyal Nazis. Members of the Gestapo who went along as 'auxiliary tour guides' kept a watchful eye on the passengers. Hitler's speeches blasted out from the numerous loudspeakers – there were 158 on the *Wilhelm Gustloff* alone. The daily agenda on a round-Italy trip on the *Wilhelm Gustloff* in the winter of 1938/39 documents the military discipline on board: '6:20: wake up, 6:30: early morning sport, 9:00: talk: "Our former colonies", 13:30-15:30: general rest period, 20:30: grand fancy dress and hat party in all rooms, 0:30: bar closes, 0:45: music ends, 1:00: quiet in the ship'. For all that, the trips were cheap: a 5-day journey to the Norwegian fjords cost less than 60 reichsmarks,

including the train journey to and from the home port. At the end of August 1939, one week before the outbreak of World War Two, the 'fleet of peace' received coded radio messages ordering them to return immediately to Germany. By this time, the two KdF units *Berlin* and *Stuttgart* had already been refitted as hospitals and were lying ready for action at the East Prussian town of Pillau, now Baltijsk in Russia, just 46 nautical miles east of Danzig (now Gdansk).

At 4:45 a.m. on 1 September, the German cruiser *Schleswig-Holstein* fired its first salvo at the *Westerplatte* just outside Danzig harbour. World War Two had begun.

When the guns were once again silent in Europe five years and eight months later, no one was thinking of 'pleasure trips' but hundreds of thousands wanted to leave the old continent to start a new life abroad. And thus the first wave of emigration to the USA which had petered out in the 1920s was followed by a second consisting primarily of refugees from eastern bloc countries to Canada, Australia, New Zealand and North and South America. The International Refugee Organisation in Geneva, set up specifically to deal with this situation and financed by the UNO, entered into long-term transport agreements with European shipping lines and guaranteed generous subsidies for the emigrants' passages.

The shipping lines expanded their fleets with second-hand ships bought at low prices, installed additional beds and sent them overseas laden with emigrants. Accommodation was primitive, frequently consisting of cabins with no washing facilities, some of them even with dormitories containing up to 200 bunks; and in the tropics

The Nazi version of early mass tourism: hundreds of thousands of meritorious national comrades took part in strictly organised holidays on cruises such as the Wilhelm Gustloff.

The Wilhelm Gustloff: *'Kraft durch Freude'* (Power through Pleasure) *were the magic words for holiday trips at sea which generally offered passengers only a basic level of comfort.*

A Hapag brochure advertising cruises on the Milwaukee *with its hull painted white, which was used solely as a cruise ship after 1936 – showing brightly coloured pictures of on-board scenes and destinations.*

many preferred to bivouac on deck rather than having to lie dripping with sweat in the cabins with no air conditioning. The return journeys carried tourists who had booked passages to Europe at very low cost.

In Piraeus in 1915, John Demitrios Chandris had set up a shipping company which bore his name, and acquired a cargo sailing ship, the *Demitrios*, which he used to transport olive oil, feta cheese and other goods between the Greek islands. Sixty years later, the Chandris Shipping Line, now managed by Anthony, the founder's younger son, not only had the largest passenger fleet in the western world with its thirteen ships, but it also owned sixteen tankers, thirteen cargo ships, five holiday hotels and a shipyard. The

transformation of a small family-run operation into a maritime 'multi' is typical of the gold-rush spirit prevalent after the Second World War. Chandris sent his liners laden with emigrants to Australia, New Zealand and South America. The *Australis*, formerly the United States Lines' *America*, carried up to 2,258 passengers in one standard class, whilst under the American flag it had carried up to a maximum of 1,046 passengers in three different classes. In their best years, Chandris ran five ships simultaneously which took a total of 50,000 emigrants a year down under.

When the emigration market dried up in the 1960s, the small southern European shipping lines had to look for other uses for their fleets.

Their ageing tubs had no chance in the North Atlantic, where liners were struggling for survival against the impact of the aircraft. An alternative was to offer cheap cruises.

At the end of 1960, the telephone rang in Chandris's Athens office: the director of a London travel agency was looking for a ship 'for about 200 people' to run cruises to the Greek islands. By chance the shipping boss had recently seen a newspaper advertisement: King Ibn Saud's 221-berth yacht, the *Mansour*, was for sale. The 99-metre long *Mansour*, built in 1936, seemed to be just what the British travel agency was looking for. He bought the royal yacht for $150,000, re-christened it *Romantica*, and in 1961 started to run 2- to 5-day cruises from Piraeus to Mykonos, Delos and Santorini. Chandris had thus discovered the Aegean as a cruise destination. This was the first time since the ideologically-tainted KdF trips that a European shipping company was offering short cruises at low prices – a two-day trip cost all of $19.

The Chandris veterans with the white X (the Greek letter 'Chi') on their blue funnels also departed on cruises from North America and Australia. For two decades the little *Romanza* was the most popular ship in the Mediterranean; the big two-funnel *Britanis*, built in 1932, was the oldest 'showboat' around in the 1990s. In 1990 Chandris became been a Greek-American company and changed its name to Celebrity

Celebrity Cruises' Meridian, the refitted Lloyd Triestino liner Galileo Galilei, in the Mexican Playa del Carmen.
– The Costa Victoria, built in 1996, is characterised by its unusual funnels.

Cruises. With five new German-built ships, the company these days positions itself at the top end of the market.

The history of Costa Crociere began in 1860 with oil, or more specifically cooking oil, which Giacomo Costa produced in Genoa and which his sons shipped in small cargo ships in the Mediterranean for the first time in 1924. The dramatic ascent of this Genoese family-run shipping line began after World War Two, and by the end of the 1970s, with its 18 ships, most of which had been taken over from other companies and re-fitted, it was one of the biggest providers of scheduled voyages and cruises in the world. Costa ships, which were characterised by

a blue C on their yellow funnels, cruised the Mediterranean, the Caribbean, the Antarctic and the Amazons, sometimes running scheduled services to South America as well.

The tradition of the Lauro fleet is characterised by one single man, Achille Lauro from Sorrento in the Gulf of Naples. As a young man he had inherited a small shipping company from his father, which he was able to expand into an empire of 90 passenger and cargo ships thanks to the emigration runs to Australia at the end of the 1950s. Italians always spoke of the *Achille Lauro* respectfully as '*La grande nave blu*' – the big blue ship.

With its blue hull, two blue funnels and lifeboats

"THE WORD TOURIST IS INEVITABLY ASSOCIATED WITH THE IDEA OF RUSHING ABOUT AND HECTIC ACTIVITY. NONE OF THAT IS TRUE OF A CRUISE. THE MOST REMARKABLE THING ABOUT THIS FORM OF TRAVEL SEEMS TO ME TO BE COMFORT AND LAZINESS."

EVELYN WAUGH IN "LABELS. A MEDITERRANEAN JOURNAL"

positioned unusually low down, the flagship of the Lauro fleet was a well-known sight on the world's oceans for 28 years. Although the funnels bore the shipping line's logo, a five-pointed white star, the *Achille Lauro* was an unlucky star right from the start.

In August 1938, Koninklijke Rotterdamsche Lloyd commissioned a liner from De Scheide Werft in Vlissingen in Holland, which was to be launched in the spring of 1940 and set out on its maiden voyage in the summer of 1942. The construction work was all but complete when German troops occupied the Netherlands in May 1940 and the shipyard had to stop work. The ship was named the *Willem Ruys* in July

1946 (Willem Ruys was the founder of Rotterdam Lloyd); 5 years late, it started its scheduled services to Indonesia in 1947, was bought by Achille Lauro in 1964, re-named the *Achille Lauro* and beset by terrible bad luck thereafter: it caught fire in Palermo during modernisation work (three fatalities) again in Genoa during overhaul work and again off the coast of Las Palmas during a cruise (two fatalities), it rammed an Italian fishing boat (one fatality), collided with a Lebanese cargo ship (four fatalities) and was arrested in the port of Santa Cruz in Tenerife for unpaid bills. However, the worst was yet to come.

In October 1985, the Achille Lauro was en-route

The Achille Lauro *from the Italian Lauro fleet – here seen off the coast of Genoa (following page).*

Princess Cruises' Royal Princess, *built in 1984, here seen off the coast of Alaska, popularised cabins with balconies (page 182).*

HOW SAFE ARE CRUISE SHIPS?

'Love boat in trouble!', 'Trawler rams luxury cruise ship!', 'Luxury liner stranded!' Every misadventure to befall a cruise ship provides headlines which inevitably puts safety at sea in a bad light. And wrongly, as the statistics prove. Over the last ten years, the fleet of holiday ships has grown to more than 230 units worldwide and more than 50 million people take holidays at sea. There have indeed been many minor collisions and at least 20 accidents, some of which have involved considerable damage, but only 18 fatalities and 4 total losses. However, these optimistic sounding statistics not only exclude ferries, freighters and tankers but also all cruise ships that do not fly under a western flag. In order to avoid a repeat of the Titanic disaster, the International Convention for the Safety of Life at Sea (SOLAS) was set up in 1913 to lay down binding safety regulations for the first time: radio stations manned 24 hours a day, life-jackets that were safe for unconscious people, lifeboat drill within 24 hours of departure and enough rescue devices – motor lifeboats, life-rafts – both for the passengers and the crew. Today the International Maritime Organisation (IMO), a UN agency based in London, monitors the observance of these regulations worldwide. IMO regulations for tenders and lifeboats have been in place for new ships since 1986. At the end of 1997 more stringent safety and environmental protection regulations came into force which, amongst other things, prescribed sprinkler systems and automatically-illuminated escape route markers.

A report by the American National Transportation Safety Board concluded that cruise ships were safe, albeit with the proviso that there is room for improvement in some areas. An analysis of shipping accidents over the last ten years confirms that fire on board continues to be the number one danger, followed by collision and grounding.

Germanischer Lloyd has also established that 99.9% of all accidents are the result of human error and only 0.1% are caused by technical failure. A visit to the bridge of a modern cruise ship reveals a mass of electronics and a generally high level of safety. There is no bearded John Maynard turning an oversized wheel with a nervous hand as in Theodore Fontane's ballad; an almost imperceptible movement of the joy-stick and even a giant like the Carnival Destiny will change course. The Voyage Management System takes the ship to its destination fully automatically once the speed, changes of direction and destination have been entered. The latest version of the GPS (Global Positioning System) gives the ship's position accurately down to three metres. Refined navigational instruments

An icon of Saint Nicholas always hangs on the bridge of Greek ships

automatically sound the alarm in case of danger of collision, thrusters at the bow and stern increase mobility, a complex system of bulkheads protects against fire and taking in water. Fire alarms and TV monitors monitor potential danger spots. The Dynamic Positioning System (DPS) at least theoretically makes an anchor obsolete: the computer which is in contact with a navigation satellite calculates the current and the wind and keeps the ship stationary.

However, Greek captains appear not to trust modern technology entirely. They always have an icon of Saint Nicholas, the patron saint of Greek sailors, hanging on the bridge or in the chartroom.

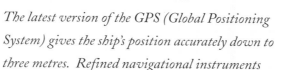

Lifeboat drill is compulsory on cruise ships within 24 hours of leaving port.

Lobbies which extend over several decks, like this one on the Costa Marina, have been popular since the 1980s. – Nowadays, ships are no longer designed on the drawing board but with the aid of computers.

A ship is put together from pre-fabricated sections.

TV monitors on the bridge are used for surveillance; this one is keeping an eye on the ship's entrance.

from Genoa for a cruise of the eastern Mediterranean when four Palestinian terrorists hijacked the ship and took the passengers hostage in order to force Israel to release fifty political prisoners. They murdered Leon Klinghoffer, a New York Jew who was wheelchair-bound after two strokes, in cold blood and threw his body into the sea. The hijackers left the ship after three days when Egypt promised them safe passage out of the country. In 1994, the *Achille Lauro* had passed through the Suez Canal on a cruise from Genoa to Durban and was off the coast of East Africa when a fire broke out in the engine room. The fire quickly got out of control and burned its way through the passenger decks. Captain Giuseppe Orsi radioed SOS, and an extensive rescue operation was put into action. Ten ships took 577 passengers and 402 crew members to the African mainland, from where they were flown home. Three passengers died, one was missing. The death throes of the *Achille Lauro* continued and it was three days after the outbreak of the fire that the waves of

the Indian Ocean finally closed in over the stern of '*La grande nave blu*'.

In the 1950s, which saw the rise of Greek and Italian shipping lines, landlocked Switzerland also tried for a short time to establish itself in passenger voyages on the world's oceans. In Geneva, Nicolò Rizzi, who liked to spend his winter holidays in Arosa, set up the Arosa Line. He acquired four floating veterans, the oldest of which was 32 years old, and re-named them the *Arosa Sun*, the *Arosa Sky*, the *Arosa Kulm* and the *Arosa Star*. The quartet crossed the North Atlantic between Bremerhaven and Canada – taking emigrants on its outward journey and students and returning immigrants on its return journey. They also occasionally sailed to Australia and Venezuela.

Once the flow of emigrants had dried up to a trickle, Rizzi tried his luck with cruises from Bremerhaven to Norway, and from New York or Miami to the Caribbean. Passengers came across a complete mishmash of crew on the Swiss ships, which for legal reasons sailed under the Panamanian flag: the *Arosa Sun* had an Italian captain and a former German U-boat officer as the purser; the chefs for the first-class passengers were Italians while Germans cooked for the tourist class. Although the Geneva-based shipping line was in financial difficulties, Rizzi believed in the future of low-cost pleasure trips on sea: 'The young people of today want to see and get to know the world. We can help them do so with our cruises.' Unfortunately, Rizzi's idea came just at the wrong time: it was too late for scheduled services in the North Atlantic, and too early for cruises; the Arosa Line went bankrupt in 1959.

In the 1960s, the Soviet fleet made life difficult for western shipping lines who were offering cheap cruises. Accommodation was spartan, the food hearty, and it was not always easy to make oneself understood by the crew. However, there were plenty of Lenin pamphlets lying around, the vodka flowed and tipping was unknown.

In the 1970s, the Soviet Union expanded its fleet of cruise ships with five new ships built in

Right: Celebrity Cruises' Horizon *under construction at the Meyer Shipyard in Papenburg in north Germany, with its pear-shaped bulbous bow in the foreground.*
– Above: cruising in the Caribbean.

BRITANIS, BUILT IN 1932

The Britanis – *formerly the* Monterey/Matsonia, *18,655 GT, 1,655 passengers* – *is a typical first-generation cruise ship: previously used as a liner in the Pacific, taken over by Chandris Cruises in 1970, converted into a cruise ship and used for low-cost cruises until 1994. The deck plans with the bow at the top and the stern at the bottom, show the nine decks from bottom (D deck) to top (sun deck). The empty areas are service, engine and storage rooms, the crew's quarters, shops or open decks. The cabins, drawn in great detail, are distributed over eight decks, are primarily on the inside, and are of different sizes. Some of the cheap cabins on C deck have communal toilets near the stern. The two dining rooms are down on B deck and have no portholes. There are very few communal rooms.*

The bridge as it used to be: the helmsman at the giant wheel.

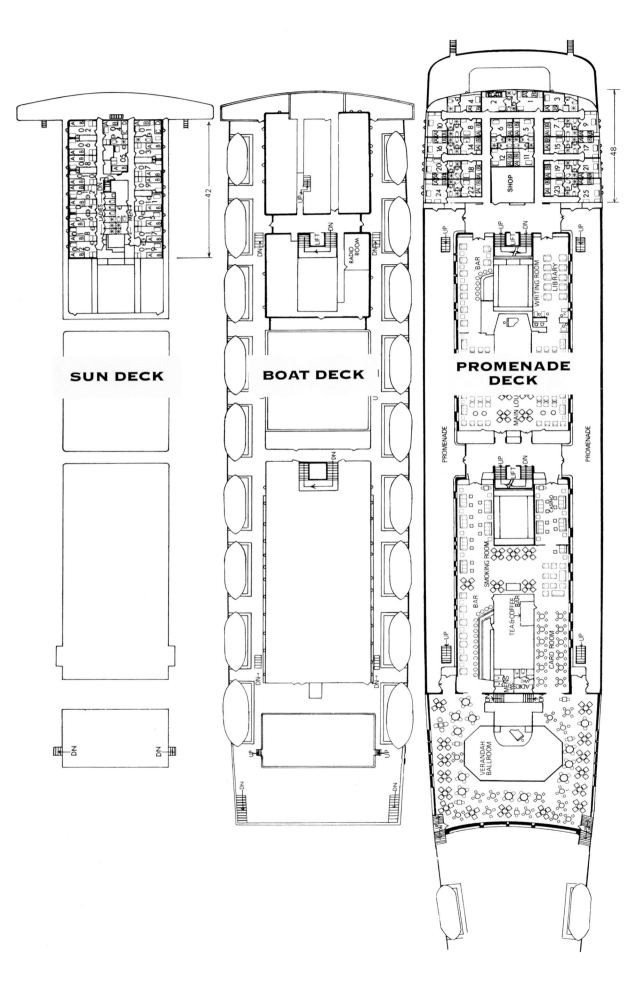

SUN DECK

BOAT DECK

PROMENADE DECK

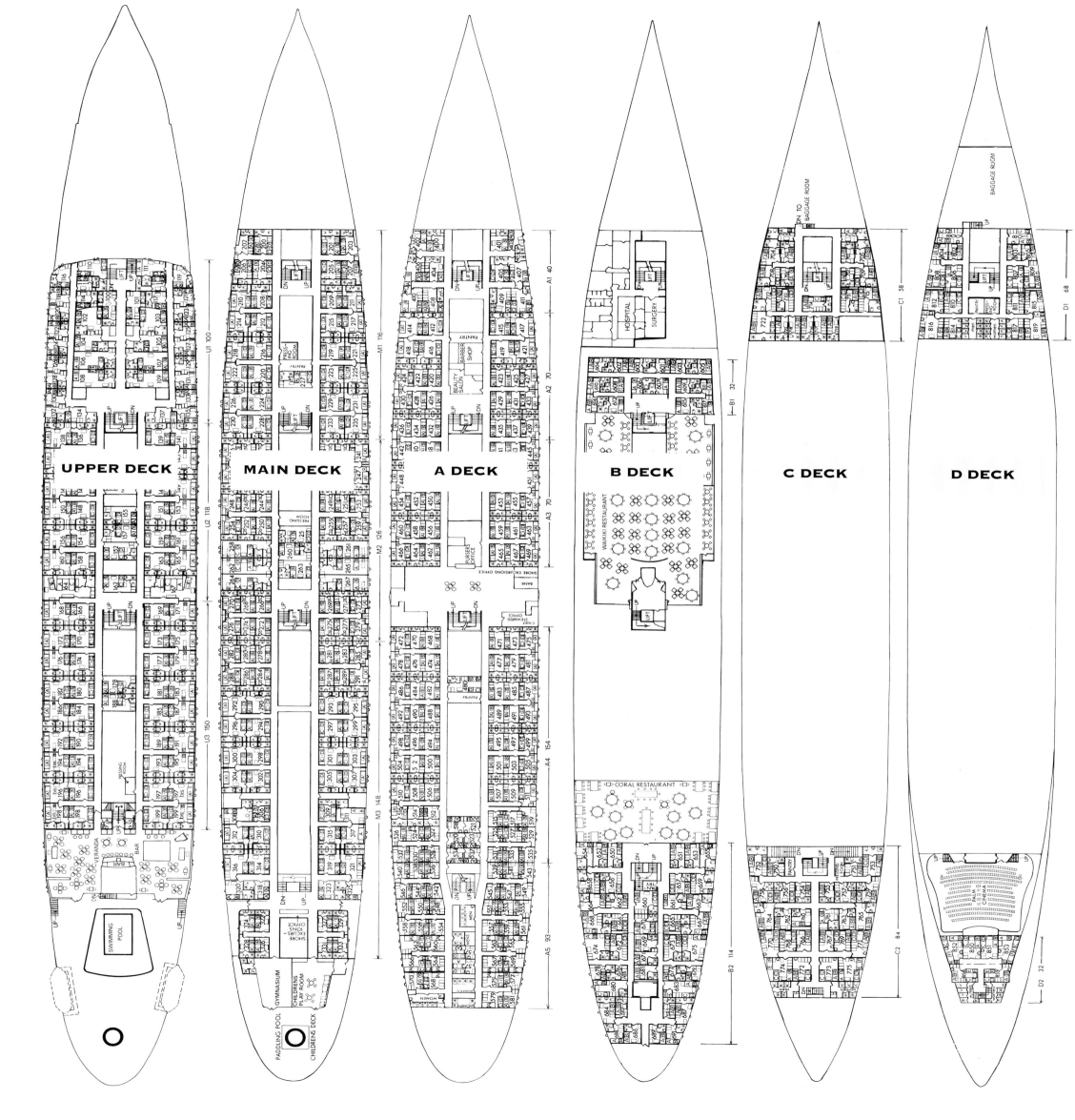

UPPER DECK

MAIN DECK

A DECK

B DECK

C DECK

D DECK

VISTAFJORD – A CLASSIC ON THE WORLD'S SEAS

The elegant Vistafjord – *with its traditional silhouette – used to be a transatlantic liner. It now sails under the Cunard banner as a cruise ship with Norwegian officers and an international crew. – Right: the aft Lido Deck with pool and lido bar.*

'Well,' says Captain Terje Sörensen, when he is asked about the features on his *Vistafjord*. Then he reels off in his laid-back Norwegian way: 'We have good food, good entertainment and good routes. Also the *Vistafjord* is not a floating hotel but a proper ship – stable and safe.' With regret he adds: 'Ships like these are no longer built today.'

Launched at an English shipyard, the *Vistafjord* has elegant lines, a sleek bow, a promenade deck running all the way around the ship and terraced decks at the back. A swimming pool, a mighty funnel amidships, lots of cabins with portholes and what used to be a typical feature of ships' architecture: the hull line lifts slightly to the fore and aft.

It is an elegant ship in the style of the ocean-going giants of yesteryear and is one of the later styles of these ships. It made its first scheduled voyage for the Norwegian American Line from Oslo to New York in May 1973. Transatlantic business collapsed, and the shipping line sent the 'beautiful Norwegian' on cruises. In 1983 the *Vistafjord*, along with its sister ship the *Sagafjord*, was purchased by Cunard. Two face lifts have filled out the *Vistafjord*'s balanced silhouette somewhat, but passengers will now find all the conveniences of today combined with the charm of yesterday. Although the Bahamian flag flies at the stern, a picture of the Norwegian

King Harald V. still hangs in the stairwell. The Garden Lounge and the North Cape Bar radiate maritime nostalgia. And just as in the good old days, male 'hosts' look after female passengers who are travelling alone. On the other hand, there are new cabins with balconies, two double-storey penthouses, a business centre with computers and a CD-ROM library, an intimate Italian restaurant in addition to the main dining room, along with

a casino, a disco and a fitness studio. Anyone expecting a spectacular lobby, noisy hustle and bustle or even Las Vegas style shows is on the wrong ship. The 'old lady' may be modern but she is not a fashion victim. She prefers quiet

elegance, refined cuisine and discreet service in a cosmopolitan atmosphere. The *Vistafjord* also has a thoroughly loyal community of fans. The record is held by an 82-year-old American woman who has clocked up well over 1,800 cruising days. After

The Vistafjord *and its older sister ship the* Sagafjord *have been re-fitted several times. The shuffleboard areas on the promenade deck have had to give way to new luxury cabins. However the elegance, the library (left) and the red and black funnel have been retained.*

the last $15 million re-fit, the many regular guests found to their relief that despite all the innovations the atmosphere has remained unchanged: 'The ship has retained its soul'. And full of hope they listen to Captain Sörensen's promise that the *Vistafjord*, now of mature age, will continue to sail forever if it is looked after carefully …

Finland and originally designed as ocean-going ferries – ships such as the *Azerbaydzhan*, *Kareliya* and the *Belorussiya* (today the *Kazakhstan II*). These offered neither luxury nor elegance, but the service and food improved greatly over time. In 1974 the Soviet Union bought the *Hanseatic*, renamed it the *Maxim Gorki* and chartered it to a German travel company. Thus the then proletarian state, feared by its western rivals as the 'cheapjack of the world's oceans', owned its very first elegant four-star cruise ship.

Established shipping companies had for some time been continuing the traditions of the pre-war period. They once more ran regular cross-ings over the Atlantic and continued to organ-ise cruises for a well-heeled clientele: the Italian Line with the *Michelangelo* and the *Raffaello*, the Compagnie Générale Transatlantique with the *Ile-de-France* and the *France*, the Holland America Line with the *Rotterdam*, the Swedish American Line with the *Gripsholm* and the *Kungsholm*, Norddeutscher Lloyd with the *Berlin* (formerly the *Gripsholm*), the *Bremen* (formerly the *Pasteur*) and the *Europa* (formerly the *Kungsholm*), the Norwegian America Line with the *Sagafjord* and the *Vistafjord*, P&O with the *Oriana* and the *Canberra*, Cunard with the *Caronia*, the *Queen*

Princess Cruises' Pacific Princess was the first 'Love Boat' to appear on our TV screens (small picture); eight years later the Royal Princess started running cruises to Alaska and the Caribbean (left).

191

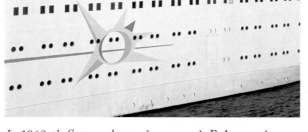

In 1968, the Starward, *now known as the* Bolero *and owned by Festival Cruises, was the first new ship used by Norwegian Caribbean Lines (NCL) for cruises from Miami to the Caribbean.*

Mary and the *Queen Elizabeth*.

The 1950s and the early 1960s were dominated by European shipping lines whose vision of sea voyages characterised the cruise scene. Then along came the Americans and everything changed.

On 19 December 1966, the *Sunward* set sail from Miami, passed through the Suez Canal into the open sea and set a course for the Bahamas. It was not a beautiful ship, more like a car ferry which also carried 540 passengers on two decks. But the ship, with its square stern and the two funnels projecting up on the sides, marked the beginning of the age of the Caribbean cruise.

Knut Utstein Kloster, owner of the Klosters Rederi shipping line in Oslo, had been running the cruise-ferry *Sunward* on the Southampton/Lisbon/Gibraltar route in the spring. When this stopped being a commercial success, he docked the new ship in Gibraltar harbour. At the same time, Ted Arison in Miami also had a problem to solve. This immigrant businessman from Israel who occasionally organised cruises was looking for a charter ship after his business partners went bankrupt. His son Nicky recalls: 'Ted had heard that the *Sunward* was in Gibraltar, he phoned Knut Kloster and said: you have a ship, I have the passengers, let's get together and create a cruise company.' The Norwegian with no passengers and the American with no ship founded the Norwegian Caribbean Lines (NCL, known as the Norwegian Cruise Line since 1987) and made cruising history.

The team complemented each other ideally: Kloster provided maritime expertise and Scandinavian seafaring tradition, and Arison provided American marketing and management skills. They offered regular three- to seven-day Caribbean cruises from Miami at low prices. Dress codes were

unknown, a relaxed atmosphere guaranteed – the motto was 'bikinis not Baedeker'. The Americans took to it instantly, and soon NCL had to deploy ever more and ever bigger ships. The Caribbean islands, once the exclusive holiday destination of the few, became a

"CONQUERING A NEW WORLD ON THE SEA, THAT'S MORE THAN A JOURNEY!"

HEINZ G. KONSALIK IN "PROMENADEN-DECK"

popular playground for hundreds of thousands of people. Kloster and Arison parted on bad terms in 1973; Knut Kloster continued to run the company on his own, and his ground-breaking ideas turned NCL into one of the leading cruise operators in the 1970s, as he was the first one to recognise that 'a ship is no longer simply a means of transport taking people to their destination. It is the destination itself'. In July 1979 he bought the super-liner *France* for $18 million and had it converted into the first mega-cruise ship for a further $110 million. When the *Norway* left

The Arosa Line's Arosa Sky was also used for cruises in the 1950s.

A beautiful ship with two funnels and different names: the Gripsholm *in 1957 (Swedish American Line), the* Navarino *in 1975 (Karageorgis Cruises), the* Regent Sea *in 1984 (Regency Cruises) – and finally taken out of service in 1996.*

Miami in July 1980 on its first Caribbean cruise with 1,864 passengers on board, France's floating flagship of yore had become the world's biggest pleasure steamer: the afterdecks had been enlarged, another swimming pool built in between the two funnels, and two tenders, *Little Norway* 1 and 2, which each carried 400 passengers, were housed on the foredeck. Whilst the *France* had once raced across the rough Atlantic at 31 knots, the *Norway* now trundled around the Caribbean at a leisurely 16 knots.

Reverentially, Kloster left the inside largely untouched, at least in the early stages. Both dining rooms retained their elegance, the smoking salon kept its dignity, the nursery its decorative trompe-l'oeil wallpaper. Passengers were able to experience something of the glamour of the long-gone transatlantic tradition. Yet the cabins had televisions and the covered promenades had shops and cafes. Kloster's biggest innovation was with regard to evening entertainment, which at that time was still pretty sparse on cruise ships. Now there

193

194

Among the most attractive cruise destinations is northern Europe, the land of the midnight sun, with its deep fjords and the rocks of the North Cape.

was a Las Vegas-style show every evening with resounding big-band sounds and entertaining revues.

In the meantime, Ted Arison had become the owner of his own company, Carnival Cruise Lines. He chartered the ageing *Empress of Canada*, re-named it the *Mardi Gras* and suffered a spectacular false start: on its first journey in March 1972, the ship, carrying 300 journalists and invited guests from the

IS SEA-SICKNESS A THING OF THE PAST?

If we can believe the cruise brochures, the sky is always cloudless and the sea is always as smooth as glass. If only. When the wind freshens and the waves grow ever higher, Neptune inevitably demands his tribute – and sea-sickness prevails.

Sea-sickness is a motion sickness which occurs when the eyes, nerve cells and the organs of balance in the inner ears send information to the brain which it cannot reconcile with what it has established for itself. When the ground moves and the horizon dances, it therefore sets the alarm bells ringing – the result is nausea, dizziness and vomiting, and in extreme cases apathy, mental confusion and lassitude.

In 6 BC, the Greek philosopher Anarcharis divided people into three categories: the living, the dead and the sea-sick. Since then we have found out that between 10% and 30% of people are immune to sea-sickness, that young children are less susceptible to it, women more susceptible, and that anticipation plays a major role. Anyone boarding a ship with the

negative attitude, 'I'm bound to be sea-sick', undoubtedly will be.

Sea-sickness can be effectively relieved or cured with acupressure bands, lozenges, tablets and capsules. Stabilisers, which are time and again advertised as guarantees of a calm voyage, do reduce the rolling of the ship (movement along its length) but not the just-as-annoying pitching (movement along its width). There are certain things one can do to prevent sea-sickness: the best place to be is amidships in the open air – here the ship movements are less noticeable – if possible, you should keep your eyes on land or on the horizon, and try to avoid alcohol and nicotine. Some people do autogenic training, drink fennel tea, chew dry black bread, wear a bunch of parsley under their shirt, or rely on the calming effect of soft music – anything as long as it helps. The only ship you are guaranteed not to be sea-sick on is the Queen Mary *– this legendary transatlantic liner is now a hotel tied up in Long Beach harbour, Los Angeles.*

Robust gebaute Expeditionsschiffe wie Explorer vermitteln einen Hauch von Abenteuer – aber ohne Risiko. – Hier vor Paulet Island mit einer Kolonie von Adélieping-Pinguinen. Kehlstreif-Pinguine sind an der Westküste der Antarktischen Halbinsel zu finden (rechts).

travel industry, ran aground shortly after setting sail from Miami; it was stuck for 24 hours and had to be towed free by a tug. Arison hovered on the edge of bankruptcy for two years; the rumour that he used to empty the one-armed bandits in the *Mardi Gras*'s casino every evening in order to be able to pay his ongoing bills stubbornly persisted. After two years better times finally arrived, and the concept of 'fun' instead of 'high life', T-shirts

instead of dinner jackets, hot-dogs instead of caviar attracted more and more eager young travellers. Carnival Cruise Lines went for mass instead of class – more successfully than any other company in the past. Bob Dickinson, the then marketing chief, now president of Carnival, explains: "Our customers are not

"THIS ILLUSORY WORLD HAS NOTHING MORE TO DO WITH SHIPPING AS I USED TO KNOW IT. AN EPOCH HAS ENDED."

LOTHAR-GÜNTHER BUCHHEIM IN "DER LUXUSLINER" (THE LUXURY LINER)

197

Explorer – En-Route to the White Continent

The Explorer, *formerly the* Society Explorer, *in the Antarctic: the passengers round the notorious Cape Horn (right), go ashore in sturdy rubber dinghies, make a stop-over at Deception Island with its ruined and deserted whaling station, and marvel at the giant penguin colonies.*

The wind blows at 100 kilometres an hour, the waves are 12 metres high, spray beats against the bridge from all directions. The *Explorer*, a chunky ship just 73 metres in length with a red hull and white superstructures, bounces like a cork through the peaks and valleys of the waves. But Captain Karl-Ulrich Lampe is unimpressed: 'Last time it was worse', he says.

Between Cape Horn and the Antarctic, the ship traverses the infamous Furious Fifties – 1,000 kilometres of open, wind-whipped sea. Twenty-four hours later the sea-sick passengers can breathe out when at a latitude of 64º south Paulet Island comes into view: not a tree, not a shrub, not a blade of grass in sight. Instead, there are snow-covered mountains, their tops in the clouds. Mighty glaciers project right into the sea, ice floes float around in the water. Anyone travelling to the Antarctic on the *Explorer* is partly going on a pleasure trip with an adventurous aspect to it, and is partly

attending an adult education course on the high seas. Scientists travelling on the ship hold daily lectures, accompany the excursions ashore and ensure that the code of the Antarctic is strictly observed: 'Keep a distance of at least 6 metres away from animals! Bring your rubbish back on board! Do not smoke ashore!' Rubber dinghies bobbing alarmingly up and down wait at the bottom of the gangway for the 100 identically dressed passengers preparing to disembark: red parkas, orange lifejackets, woolly

hats over their ears, and knee-length boots. The 40 hp outboard motors roar, the robust boats speed off towards the beach. The sight is breathtaking: hundreds of thousands of penguins! Some breed in giant, cramped colonies, others waddle around comically, having fun sliding down snow slides or plopping clumsily into the sea. As these flightless birds have no enemies on land, they tolerate the visitors without fear. The next day the destination is Whalers Bay on Deception Island. An abandoned whaling station corrects the illusion that this is an unspoiled region. 'Kodak, Kodak! Fuji, Fuji!' Captain Lampe calls the passengers from their beds through the loudspeakers. Half asleep and cameras at the ready, they stand marvelling on deck: in the warm light of the midnight sun, the sea is peppered with innumerable icebergs as far as the eye can see – some as smooth as glass, some projecting steeply upwards like Gothic cathedrals, and some are reminiscent of Emmenthal cheeses, worn away by the seawater. The *Explorer* skirts round these icy giants, some 30 metres high, keeping a respectful distance. She then takes a northerly course, rounds Cape Horn in superbly calm seas and docks in the Chilean port of Puerto Williams. Trees and shrubs for the first time after 3 weeks of ice and snow.

Cadillac drivers but average Americans who work 50 weeks a year and who want to have a bit of fun on holiday".

the coast of Los Angeles anyway, it was the obvious thing to do to transform the Princess Cruise cruise ship into the 'Love Boat'.

In 1964, two years before Knut Kloster and Ted Arison started their Caribbean cruises from Miami, the entrepreneur Stanley McDonald chartered the *Princess Patricia,* a late-1940s vintage steamer, in Seattle to run cruises to Alaska and along the Mexican Riviera to Acapulco. McDonald founded Princess Cruises, and chartered and bought more ships. In 1974 he sold his company to the P&O Group.

The new owners who had brought British officers, the British flag and Italian cuisine on board, had no idea that they had drawn the winning ticket. The same year, the Californian Jeraldine Saunders who had jobbed as a photographic model and a cruise director, wrote a book about her experience on different cruise ships, entitled 'The Love Boats'. It fell into the hands of television producer Henry Coleman, who saw its excellent potential as material for a popular soap opera.

As the *Pacific Princess* had been described by the author as the finest of all the cruise ships – 'no other ship offers better food, finer service or more fun' – and was regularly anchored off

On 17 September 1976 the first pilot episode appeared on our screens, to indifferent reviews. The second was more successful, and the third was a hit. From then on, the Love Boat became a constituent part of the television schedules first in the USA and then

France's last transatlantic liner, the France, now a cruise ship called the Norway, has been cruising in the Caribbean under the Norwegian flag since 1980.

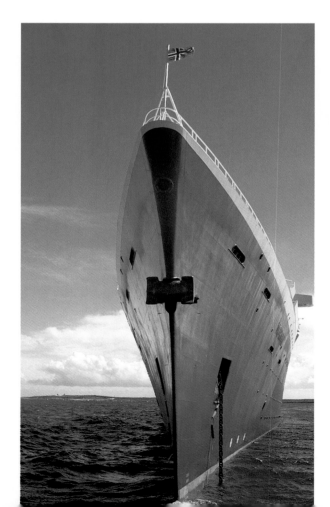

200

"THE UNIQUE THING ABOUT SEA JOURNEYS IS THAT AFTER A FEW
DAYS YOU THINK YOU HAVE BEEN TRAVELLING FOR GOD KNOWS HOW
LONG, AND YOU THINK YOU HAVE KNOWN THE PEOPLE TRAVELLING
WITH YOU FOR AN ETERNITY."

THE CHRONICLER ORLANDO IN FEDERICO FELLINI'S FILM
"E LA NAVE VA" (AND THE SHIP SAILS ON)

201

FITNESS + WELLBEING = HAPPINESS

Older passengers wrapped snugly in woollen blankets lie on the promenade deck in deck chairs dozing and reading. Occasionally a steward passes amongst them serving consommé. Moustachioed men in ties play harmless games like sack races or tug-of-war on the aft deck. In the swimming pool deep down in the belly of the ship, men and women bathe separately,  their bodies modestly covered from head to toe. Or at least that's how it used to be. Today there is a new generation going on cruises, particularly in the Caribbean, who do not want to go without sports, dieting and health farms even on board. Even older ships now have small, modestly-equipped gyms, although  they are usually deep down in the belly. New ships boast light, sunny fitness centres right at the top, with floor-to-ceiling windows offering an uninterrupted view of the sea. The passengers sweat and pant, push and stretch on high-tech equipment  with names like Skywalker, Butterfly or Muscle-Booster. Next door there is a sauna, a solarium and massage rooms, aerobics and stretching classes, with rap and hip-hop coming out of the loudspeakers. Some cruise companies offer the body-conscious fitness regimes called 'Ship Shape', 'Passport to Fitness' or 'Motion on the Ocean', which are worked out right down to the last detail. Anyone who perseveres is rewarded with T-shirts and towels. The Norwegian Cruise Line runs sports cruises with professional football, baseball and basketball players as trainers. The ships of the Holland America Line have a volleyball field, the Monterey has a tennis court, and the Azur a squash court. Aquatic sports are particularly popular on mini-cruise ships with their extendible platforms at the stern. The Holland America 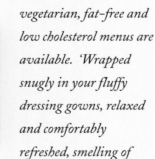 Line, the Majesty Cruise Line, the Norwegian Cruise Line, the Royal Caribbean and Star Clippers all offer diving courses. The Deutsche Seetouristik's Aida specifically targets an 'athletic, dynamic and travel-hungry' clientele. The health theme is continued in the on-board restaurants, where 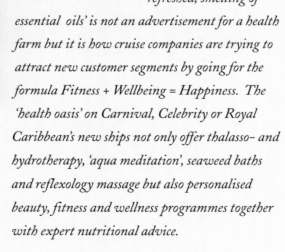 vegetarian, fat-free and low cholesterol menus are available. 'Wrapped snugly in your fluffy dressing gowns, relaxed and comfortably refreshed, smelling of essential oils' is not an advertisement for a health farm but it is how cruise companies are trying to attract new customer segments by going for the formula Fitness + Wellbeing = Happiness. The 'health oasis' on Carnival, Celebrity or Royal Caribbean's new ships not only offer thalasso- and hydrotherapy, 'aqua meditation', seaweed baths and reflexology massage but also personalised beauty, fitness and wellness programmes together with expert nutritional advice.

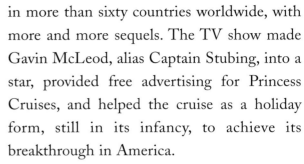

in more than sixty countries worldwide, with more and more sequels. The TV show made Gavin McLeod, alias Captain Stubing, into a star, provided free advertising for Princess Cruises, and helped the cruise as a holiday form, still in its infancy, to achieve its breakthrough in America.

German television producer Wolfgang Rademann adapted the American recipe for success under the title Das Traumschiff (The Dream Ship). Norwegian American Cruises' Vistafjord set sail for the German television station ZDF for the first time on 22 November 1980. The critics were appalled, but audiences loved it. The ratings for Das Traumschiff reached the hitherto unheard-of levels of up to 57%, and by 1987 it was the most-watched German television series ever, with as many as 24 million viewers per episode. Filmed in turn on the Vistafjord, the Astor and the Berlin, the soap opera did not, however, succeed in making cruising really popular in Germany.

Edwin Stephan, an American from Wisconsin who had managed hotels and cruise companies in Miami, had an idea that holidays on the high seas in refitted ships had no future in the long-term: pleasure cruises needed a type of ship that was different from liners. At the end of the 1960s, he had the idea of creating a fleet of three identical new

The Norway, *a 'floating beach hotel', anchors off a private island on every Caribbean cruise. There the 2,000 passengers have the opportunity to participate in aquatic sports.*

Mega-cruisers like the Royal Caribbean's Splendour of the Seas *have dining rooms encompassing two decks and serving that culinary delight Baked Alaska to round off the farewell dinner.*

ships. These would be specifically designed for voyages in southern waters and would cruise the Caribbean islands carrying sun-seeking holiday-makers the whole year round from Miami.

Stephan travelled to Oslo and convinced three Norwegian shipping line bosses with his idea. Together they looked for a catchy name for the new company. They rejected the 'Pleasure Cruise Line' and the 'Crown Cruise Line' and finally agreed on the 'Royal Caribbean Cruise Line', which became known as the 'Royal Caribbean' for short.

In 1969 they ordered the three ships from the Finnish Wärtsilä shipyard, and on 7 November 1970 the first new ship, the *Song of Norway*, set sail on its maiden voyage from pier 5 at the Dodge Island Passenger Terminal in Miami. The snow-white ship with the Norwegian post flag on its stern revolutionised marine architecture. On the funnel, which is set far back, and which is barely recognisable as such, is the Viking Crown Lounge with its huge floor-to-ceiling windows, accessed via a staircase from the deck. The swimming pool is no longer astern but amidships, protected from the wind. The superstructures are higher and stretch from the bridge almost to the stern. Only the open promenade deck all the way round the ship and the streamlined clipper-style bow are reminiscent of traditional ship design.

On the lower three decks there are two corridors running in a straight line from the bow to the stern, with identical cabins. There are only a few cabins on the inside, and most of the outside cabins have windows instead of portholes. There is room enough for 720 passengers to sunbathe on the two upper decks, something previously unheard-of.

The *Song of Norway* was joined shortly thereafter by its sister ships, for the *Nordic*

As the cruise ships grow in size, so too do the public areas. The panoramic lounge directly below the bridge on the Costa Victoria *is the height of four decks and is equipped with balconies and lifts.*

"ON THE GANGWAY OF EACH OF THESE SHIPS THERE IS A HUGE RECEPTACLE WITH A SIGN IN BIG LETTERS. WHEN YOU GO ABOARD, YOU CANNOT SEE EITHER THE RECEPTACLE OR READ THE WRITING ON IT, BUT THEY ARE THERE NONETHELESS. THE SIGN SAYS: 'DEPOSIT ALL INHIBITIONS HERE. THEY WILL BE AUTOMATICALLY RETURNED TO YOU WHEN YOU DISEMBARK'."

JERALDINE SAUNDERS IN "THE LOVE BOAT"

Even experienced cruisers wax lyrical when they sit in the Calypso Bar on the after-deck of the Aida and watch the sun going down.

'Showboats' between Hammerfest and Hawaii

Cruise ships can be found all over the world, as long as there is a little water under the hull. They travel to the Arctic and the Antarctic, cruise to Bermuda, sail round Hawaii and even anchor off the most remote islands in the Pacific Ocean. They travel through the Panama Canal, go on round-the-world voyages, and they are now increasingly frequently to be found in the Far East. However, most of the ships travel in the Caribbean. Miami, from where 30,000 passengers leave every weekend on cruises of usually a week in length, now calls itself the 'cruise capital of the world'. The white fleet of mega-cruisers sails from island to island – yesterday Dominica, today Antigua, tomorrow St. Lucia. Passengers enjoy the relaxed life on board, have fun in the bars, casinos and pools, and go ashore almost every day. 'Have fun' and 'let's do some shopping' are the holidays' watchwords. But when as many as six ships lie off the coast of St. Thomas and thousands of people crowd into the little town of Charlotte Amalie to do their duty-free shopping, the Caribbean dream becomes a nightmare. So the big cruise lines like Carnival, Princess and Royal Caribbean have leased entire islands, planted palms

and shipped in sand to offer their passengers an artificial paradise with all the romance of the Caribbean.

Sun, sand and shopping form the three cornerstones of a Caribbean cruise. In the Mediterranean, on the other hand, so much history and culture come

It's the same now as it was then: travelling in company is so much nicer.

together that a sea voyage inevitably becomes an educational trip. Europeans who like to cruise in the western and eastern Mediterranean from Genoa and Venice, want to climb the Acropolis in Athens, visit Knossos Palace in Crete, and go on a pilgrimage to the pyramids in Egypt. The journey there is cheap, and the ships, which are usually slightly smaller, are child-friendly. Europe's north with the warm light of the midnight sun is fascinating. Ships sail to the Norwegian fjords, the North Cape and up to Spitzbergen or to the Baltic metropolises.

A cruise through the sheltered 'inside passage' along Alaska's west coast enables the passengers to encounter unspoiled landscapes, mighty glaciers and former gold-rush towns. The Mexican Riviera, with such seaside resorts as Acapulco, Puerto Vallarta, Mazatlán and Zihuatanejo has established itself as a summer alternative to the sunny Caribbean. For all intents and purposes, the dollar has become the second currency alongside the Peso, and tour leaders promise their passengers: 'You do not have to understand Spanish. English is spoken everywhere.'

Prince and then the *Sun Viking*, and the Royal Caribbean fleet now ran one- and two-week Caribbean cruises all the year round. These were prototypes for a second generation of cruise ships. 'Floating holiday hotels', designed exclusively for pleasure trips in sunny waters, gradually replaced converted liners. Royal Caribbean ordered more ships and in 1978 increased its passenger capacity in a highly unorthodox way: the *Song of Norway* was put into dry dock and cut in half across its middle, a 26 metre section with 164 cabins was inserted

and the whole thing was then welded together again. Two years later, the same was done to the *Nordic Prince*.

Like NCL, Royal Caribbean had given new impetus to the cruising business thanks to the combination of American management and Scandinavian marine technology. The two companies dominated the Caribbean market during the 1970s, and it was not until 1982 that competition arrived in the form of the *Tropicale* and other new ships belonging to Carnival Cruise Lines. Carnival also ordered its 'fun

The Royal Viking Sky *berthed in Amsterdam bedecked with festive lighting and ready to depart.* – *The Caribbean deck party on Celebrity Cruises'* Century *featuring calypso, reggae, salsa and limbo dancing goes on into the early hours of the morning (left).*

ships' from Scandinavian shipyards and adopted the concept of a fleet of fine-weather ships with a standard, unmistakable image.

The silhouette of these ships, however, was becoming more clumsy-looking, and the focal point was a red, white and blue funnel with stubs on the sides which inevitably reminded one of the jet engines on a Boeing 727. In 1970, when the Royal Caribbean Cruise Line opened up a new era in the Caribbean with the *Song of Norway*, three Norwegian shipping magnates and an American called Warren Titus founded the Oslo-based Royal Viking Line. The company's objective was to offer an alternative to maritime tourism Caribbean-style with world-wide cruises on new, luxurious ships. Like Royal Caribbean before them, they had three identical ships built at the Wärtsilä shipyard in Finland to a similar design: The *Royal Viking Star* (1972), the *Royal Viking Sky* and the *Royal Viking Sea* (both in 1973). The elegant trio, together with the Norwegian American Line's *Sagafjord* and the *Vistafjord*, were the crème de la crème on the world's oceans: impeccable service and excellent cuisine in an elegant ambience. In Douglas Ward's Complete Handbook to Cruising, a Michelin Guide to cruising, these five ships occupied the top five positions for several years – sometimes the Royal Viking Line was ahead of the Norwegian American Line, sometimes it was vice versa.

When the expansion of airline flights caused massive losses on transatlantic traffic during the 1970s, traditional shipping lines such as the French Line and the Italian Line disappeared

The Song of Norway was put into dry dock and cut in half in 1978 and extended with a 26-metre middle section (top left). This not only provided additional cabins but also more space round the swimming pool (right).

The prototype of a new generation of ships: the Song of Norway in 1970 was the first cruise ship to belong to Royal Caribbean, the first cruise ship to have a lounge around the funnel and the first "skyscraper in the Caribbean".

whilst others quickly changed direction and had to struggle against the competition provided by newly-established cruise companies. At the same time, cruises were becoming more and more popular. In Germany, the *Berlin* (1980), the *Astor* (1981, now called the *Arkona*) and the fifth *Europa* (1982) were launched. Carnival Cruise Lines brought in four new units, the Holland America Line three, Royal Viking Line, Princess Cruises and Norwegian Cruise Line one new ship each.

The 1980s, however, were characterised by two opposing trends: on the one hand ever more and ever bigger ships for all-in maritime tourism, and on the other hand, luxury 'yacht cruisers' for an exclusive clientele – the first with the slogan

Continued on page 218

THE SOVEREIGN OF THE SEAS –
A SHIP SETS NEW STANDARDS

The Seabourn Legend *and its two sister ships form a trio of exclusive, yacht-like cruise ships. The food and service are exquisite, the cabins huge. A spiral staircase leads down through five decks.*

15.20 hours. The *Seabourn Legend*, which has reached the eastern entrance to the Corinth Canal from Athens, shuts down its engines. The dead straight canal, 6 kilometres long and just 25 metres wide, lies immediately ahead of the bow.

The 134 metre long, yacht-like cruiser with its streamlined bow and the Norwegian flag flying on the stern is one of the most exclusive and most expensive ships sailing the world's seas – a day on board, including drinks and tips, costs about $1,000. For that money, the 204 passengers are pampered by a 106-member crew, the cabins are enormous, the service and food exquisite. 'I haven't even eaten better on the *France*,' enthuses Bill, a stockbroker from New York. On the inside, bright marble, subtle colours and deep-pile wall-to-wall carpets create an elegant atmosphere.

Paintings of nautical scenes from the 1920s decorate the circular lobby, an elegant sweeping staircase leads outdoors to the whirlpools and swimming pools. An extendible, lowerable marina at the stern offers water sports, and the two tenders parked in the garage in the stern are the very finest with mahogany fittings and air conditioning.

15.27 hours. A boat comes alongside, pilots climb aboard, sailors throw a thick cable to the waiting tug. The cruise ship cautiously sails into the canal at just 6 knots. The captain, four officers and three pilots gather on the bridge – one at the wheel, the others to the left and right of the bridge with walkie-talkies.

The Panama Canal is more famous historically, the Suez Canal older and more impressive. But a trip through the narrow Corinth Canal guarantees

A matter of centimetres: When the Seabourn Legend *sails through the Corinth Canal, there is just 3 metres clearance on either side. Three pilots with walkie-talkies guide the ship carefully from the Ionian to the Aegean Sea.*

a tingle of excitement: the rock walls, which rise vertically up to 80 metres on either side, are within reach of an outstretched hand. The ship lurches to the starboard and threatens to touch the side. '10° to port!' calls the pilot. A slight adjustment at the wheel, and the *Seabourn Legend*, formerly the *Royal Viking Queen*, returns to its ideal course.

Crossing the Isthmus of Corinth saves having to circle the Peloponnese, and shortens the journey between Athens and Venice by 130 nautical miles (240 kilometres). The first plan for a canal came to fruition under Emperor Nero, who is supposed to have cut the first sod with a golden shovel in 67 BC. 6,000 prisoners and slaves set to work, but the project was halted. It was not until 1881/82 that a French company started building the present canal, which cost 78 million gold francs and which was opened in 1893.

16.00 hours. The *Seabourn Legend* glides under the railway bridge, a train thunders by 58 metres above. It issues a muffled hoot, but the echo on the narrow walls of the canal is deafening. The ship reaches the western end of the canal half an hour later. The pilots disembark, the cables to the tug boat are retrieved, the *Seabourn Legend* sets a course for Venice.

ROYAL VIKING SUN, BUILT IN 1988

The Royal Viking Sun – 37,845 GT, 740 passengers, used by the Royal Viking Line for luxury cruises all over the world, taken over by Cunard in 1994 – is representative of the modern design style of 5-plus-star ships. It is twice as big as the Britanis (pages 186 – 187), but accommodates only half as many passengers.

The deck plans are drawn in a more schematic way, the cabins are largely identical, almost exclusively on the outside of the ship, and more than one third of them have balconies. There are 19 suites on the two top decks; the 'owner's suite' is a massive 67 square metres in area. The lobby, with its sweeping staircase, stretches over five decks, the main restaurant takes up almost the entire promenade deck, and the smaller Venezia restaurant is four decks above that. The public rooms – a wine bar, the Casino Royale, and two lounges – are concentrated on the Norway Deck, and aft on the Scandinavia deck is a fitness and wellness centre. The open decks with a whirlpool, two swimming pools, a jogging path and a putting green are generously proportioned.

The bridge today: lots of electronics and high-tech instruments.

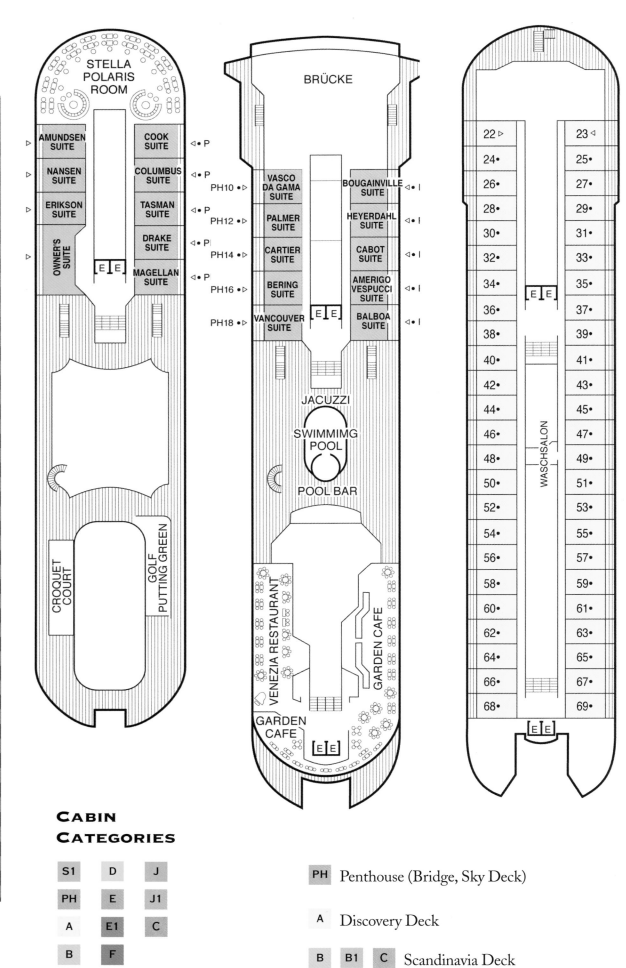

CABIN CATEGORIES

S1	D	J
PH	E	J1
A	E1	C
B	F	
B1	F1	

PH Penthouse (Bridge, Sky Deck)

A Discovery Deck

B **B1** **C** Scandinavia Deck

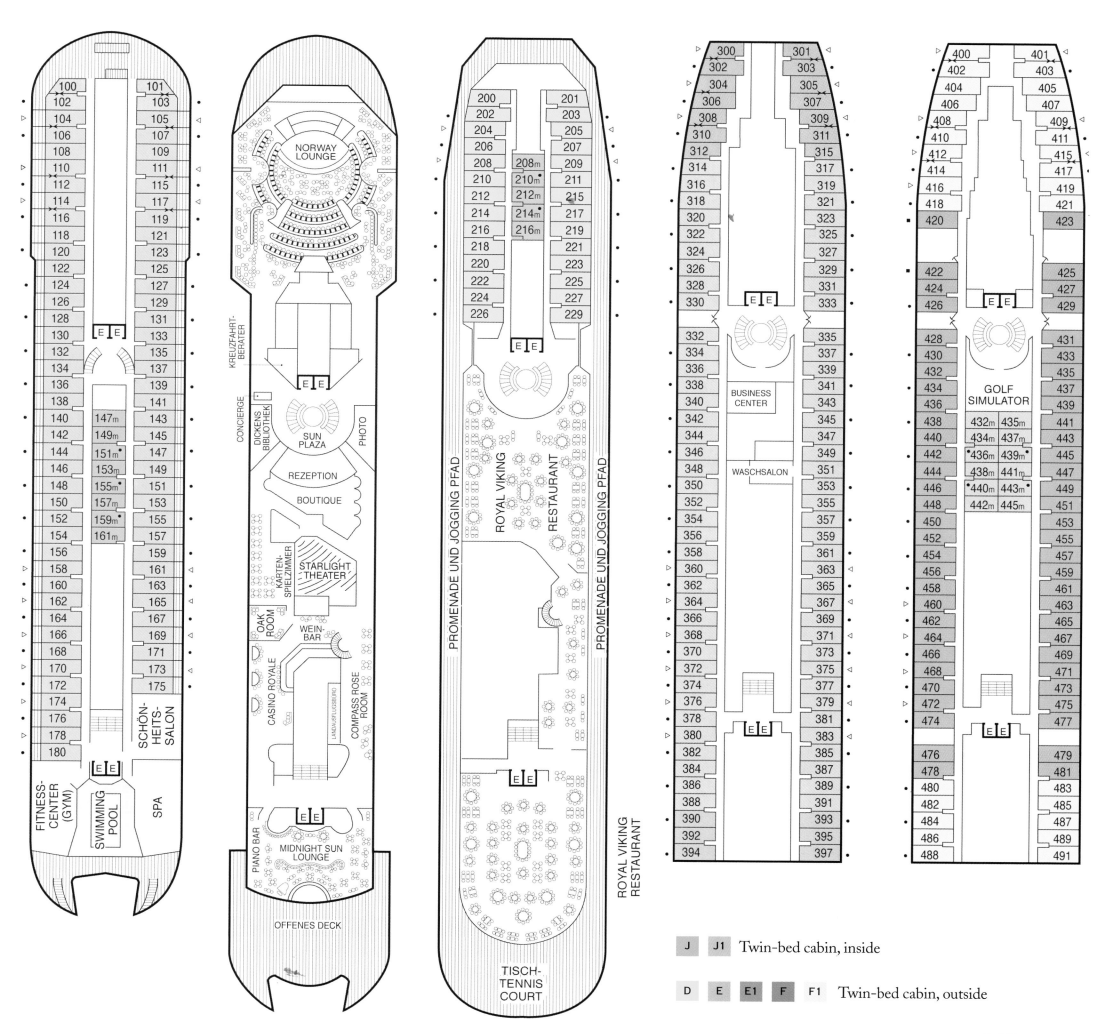

Deck 1

100	101
102	103
104	105
106	107
108	109
110	111
112	115
114	117
116	119
118	121
120	123
122	125
124	127
126	129
128	131
130	133
132	135
134	137
136	139
138	141
140	147m	143
142	149m	145
144	151m	147
146	153m	149
148	155m	151
150	157m	153
152	159m	155
154	161m	157
156	159
158	161
160	163
162	165
164	167
166	169
168	171
170	173
172	175
174	
176	
178	
180	

FITNESS-CENTER (GYM)
SWIMMING POOL
SPA
SCHÖN-HEITS-SALON

NORWAY LOUNGE

KREUZFAHRT-BERATER
CONCIERGE
DICKENS BIBLIOTHEK
SUN PLAZA
REZEPTION
BOUTIQUE
PHOTO
KARTEN-SPIELZIMMER
STARLIGHT THEATER
OAK ROOM
WEIN-BAR
CASINO ROYALE
LANDAUSFLUGSBÜRO
COMPASS ROSE ROOM
PIANO BAR
MIDNIGHT SUN LOUNGE
OFFENES DECK

200	201
202	203
204	205
206	207
208	208m	209
210	210m	211
212	212m	215
214	214m	217
216	216m	219
218	221
220	223
222	225
224	227
226	229

PROMENADE UND JOGGING PFAD
ROYAL VIKING RESTAURANT
PROMENADE UND JOGGING PFAD
ROYAL VIKING RESTAURANT
TISCH-TENNIS COURT

300	301
302	303
304	305
306	307
308	309
310	311
312	315
314	317
316	319
318	321
320	323
322	325
324	327
326	329
328	331
330	333
332	335
334	337
336	339
338	341
340	343
342	345
344	347
346	349
348	351
350	353
352	355
354	357
356	359
358	361
360	363
362	365
364	367
366	369
368	371
370	373
372	375
374	377
376	379
378	381
380	383
382	385
384	387
386	389
388	391
390	393
392	395
394	397

BUSINESS CENTER
WASCHSALON

400	401
402	403
404	405
406	407
408	409
410	411
412	415
414	417
416	419
418	421
420	423
422	425
424	427
426	429
428	431
430	433
432	435
434	437
436	439
438	432m	435m	441
440	434m	437m	443
442	436m	439m	445
444	438m	441m	447
446	440m	443m	449
448	442m	445m	451
450	453
452	455
454	457
456	459
458	461
460	463
462	465
464	467
466	469
468	471
470	473
472	475
474	477
476	479
478	481
480	483
482	485
484	487
486	489
488	491

GOLF SIMULATOR

J	J1	Twin-bed cabin, inside

D	E	E1	F	F1	Twin-bed cabin, outside

'Bigger is better', and the latter claiming 'Small is beautiful'.

'From the beaches of breathtaking dream islands to the elegant meeting places of high society, this ship opens up completely new dimensions in holidaymaking. It is equipped for the elite of seafarers, for the one passenger in ten thousand who appreciates luxury and who can also afford it'. This was the copy in the first brochure of Sea Goddess Cruises, founded by Norwegian Helge Naarstad in 1984. The then 39-year-old former manager of Norwegian Caribbean Lines was aiming for a gap in the market in the top price range and was not overstating.

The *Sea Goddess I* and *Sea Goddess II*, both built at Wärtsilä in Finland, are just 105 metres long, 45 metres shorter than Saudi Arabian King Fahd's motor yacht. They guarantee their 116 guests, who are looked after by a crew of 90, the feeling of really being on holiday on a private yacht. All spirits are included in the daily rate of $650, as are wine, cigars and stamps. Caviar for breakfast? Lobster at 3 a.m.? Nothing is impossible on the *Sea Goddesses* – they offer sheer luxury at sea. There

The Splendour of the Seas *offers all facilities – breakfast in the* Windjammer Café, *mini-golf on the* Compass Deck, *and relaxing in the whirlpool in the* Roman Solarium.

are no organised activities to irritate the guests and no deck games to spoil their tranquillity. Every guest can do just as he or she pleases. Only the safety drill is compulsory.

These luxurious ships travel on unusual routes and because of their shallow draught of just four metres they can enter even the smallest ports. They also have platforms at the stern which can be lowered and from which guests can snorkel, dive or surf. A 14-man kitchen brigade takes care of the guests' physical well-being – the word 'passenger' is taboo in this company, guests can wine and dine in the elegant restaurant in the

MARITIME TOURISM'S BIG THREE

In the 1970s, two European family-run shipping lines, the Costa line and the Chandris line, owned the world's biggest private holiday fleets, consisting of second-hand ships they had bought up. In the late 1990s, cruisers had become a highly competitive multi-million dollar business, and new ships cost figures running into hundreds of millions – Royal Caribbean alone has invested $2 billion in just 4 years to launch six mega-cruise ships for more than 12,000 passengers.

The lines fight a bitter battle for market share. After mergers, joint ventures and take-overs, both friendly and hostile, three large shipping lines dominate maritime tourism: the Carnival Corporation, Royal Caribbean, which took over Celebrity Cruises for $1.3 billion, and the P&O Group. These own one third of the 'show boats' and almost half of all the 200,000 'seaborne beds', they also commission two-thirds of all new ships.

THE CARNIVAL CORPORATION

Based in Miami and run by Mickey Arison, the son of the founder, the Carnival Corporation is a tourism 'multi' whose passenger ships, coaches, railway trains, aircraft and hotels earn profits of $500 million for the company every year. Carnival Cruise Lines' fleet consists of 13 'fun ships' (as at end 1998), of which 9 are mega-cruise ships. The Carnival Corporation has gradually taken over the Holland America Line, Windstar Cruises and Seabourn Cruises (50% shareholding). Arison likes to describe his heterogeneous fleet, which covers almost all market segments, in a graphic manner: 'I have several VW Beetles, a handful of Volvos, three Porsches and three BMWs.' Since he bought out Costa Crociere in 1997, he now also has eight Fiats. With 40 ships and 47,000 beds, Carnival Corporation is the undisputed number one in sea tourism.

ROYAL CARIBBEAN

with its 17 ships and 31,000 beds is the number two company. This Scandinavian-American company is a listed public company, as is Carnival, and is controlled by two Norwegian shipping magnates and the Pritzker family, who own Hyatt Hotels. Its headquarters are in Miami. Its market is mass tourism, split between fun ships and exclusive sea voyages, and despite its Caribbean name, the fleet also travels to Alaska, Bermuda, Mexico, Europe and the Far East.

P&O CRUISES/PRINCESS CRUISES

is the number three, with 14 ships and 21,000 beds. The parent company P&O Group owns more than 100 companies, and in addition to cruise ships also owns freighters and ferries, construction companies and shopping centres.

evening without the usual seating arrangements and enjoy a delicate lunch under parasols on deck.

Just four years after Helge Naarstad launched his business, his fellow countryman Atle Brynestad adopted the concept of offering exclusive cruises on yacht-like ships. He set up the Seabourn Cruise Line and took on former Royal Viking Line manager Warren Titus as president. Titus promised to 'offer only the very best of the best' with cruises which are 'oriented exclusively to the travel experience of individual personalities'. The former child star Shirley Temple launched the *Seabourn Pride* in San Francisco in mid-December 1988. When the mayor of San Francisco, Art Agnos, inspected the ship afterwards, he was thoroughly impressed: 'If the Pilgrim Fathers had crossed the Atlantic on the *Seabourn Pride* and not on the *Mayflower*, they would never have landed.'

The Sea Goddess II *anchored off Portofino (left). – The passengers can participate in aquatic sports from the lowered stern platform (above).*

The *Seabourn Pride*, its sister ship the *Seabourn Spirit*, which was put into service one year later, and the Seabourn Legend, which was added to the duo by a roundabout route in 1996, are 29 metres longer than the Sea Goddesses, but have twice the tonnage and take just under twice as many passengers. Naturally the *Seabourn* ships also have platforms for water sports, and there is even a garage for two elegant mahogany water taxis in the stern.

The luxury cruise ships, both large and small, brought their owners prestige, but hardly any profits. Their operating costs were far too high for companies with just two or three ships but with no powerful marketing or solid financial background. The small, loss-making shipping lines were taken over one after the other by the large cruise companies with a view to rounding off their own range of services: Cunard bought Norwegian American Cruises and Sea Goddess Cruises, Royal Viking Line went first to Knut Kloster and Cunard subsequently bought the *Royal Viking Sun* and the rights to the Royal Viking Line name; Carnival has had a controlling interest in the Seabourn Cruise Line since 1996.

Karl Andren, a passionate sailor who had emigrated to New York from Finland, made a fortune with the barges, container ships and tourist boats of the Circle Line. He wanted to become involved in the cruise business and soon found a gap in the market: 'Sailing boat cruises which combine the romanticism of yesterday with the luxury of today.' For $30 million apiece, of which the French government paid a third, the Société Nouvelle de Ateliers et Chantiers du Havre built three four-masters with 1,400 kilowatt diesel motors and exclusive cabins for 148 passengers: the *Wind Star* (1986),

THE MAN WITH THE FOUR GOLD STRIPES

'I'm supposed to be as fearless as Horatio Hornblower on the bridge, and as charming as Cary Grant when dealing with passengers.' This is how David Hannah, captain of the Noordam, describes the requirement profile of his profession with typical dry humour.

He is 'mayor' of a town with roads (corridors) and squares (lobbies), with residential areas, a theatre, restaurants, bars, a church, shops, sports facilities, a hospital and service companies. But here there is

Captain David Hannah.

no democratically elected administration; the management style is military, emphasised by the uniforms and the rank designations. The captain, the man with the four gold stripes, is the 'master next to God' at the top of a strictly hierarchical pyramid of command.

Leif Rodahl, the Norwegian captain of the Vistafjord, regards his working day in a sober light without glamour; 'I spend a lot of time on the bridge navigating, manoeuvring into berths and working out new timetables. I spend a lot of time sitting at my desk - I have to do that too. I meet the staff captain, who is responsible for safety and discipline, the chief engineer and the hotel manager every day. A captain also has numerous social obligations; there is no shortage of cocktail

parties. I am on board for eight months of the year and on leave for four. During these eight months I have to meet each of the passengers on all the cruises once personally. So that comes to between 320,000 and 345,000 handshakes a year.'

There are other men and women with four gold stripes on the second level of command: the staff captain, the second-in-command and the captain's deputy, the chief engineer, usually known as 'Chief' and responsible for the technical side of the ship, and the hotel manager, formerly known as the purser. Thanks to automation and computerisation, a ship employs fewer and fewer sailors, but more and more staff in the hotel and entertainment sector. A medium-sized ship such as the Horizon has a crew of 645. Of these, only 75 are traditional sailors; all the others work on the hotel side.

The captain (far right) with three officers on the bridge. He is not only a sailor but also a host and a manager. But he cannot legally marry people.

the *Wind Song* (1987) and the *Wind Spirit* (1988).

At 134 metres, they are just as long as the *Seabourns*, and on these ships too, the motto is 'Enjoy yourself!' So when the three ships belonging to Wind Star Cruises cruise in the Mediterranean, the Caribbean or off the coast of Costa Rica there are no cocktails with the captain and no deck games. The much-admired main attractions are the 52-metre-high aluminium masts, although their 1,996 sq.m. computer-controlled sails act more as an eye-catcher and a subject for photographs than as a means of propulsion. Karl Andren's concept, 'Sailing yes, but with comfort please' was soon copied by others offering sailing nostalgia sometimes with more high-tech and some-times less: The *Club Med I* (re-named the *Wind Surf* in 1998), the *Star Flyer*, *Le Ponant*, the *Club Med II*, the *Star Clipper* and the *Lili Marleen*. However neither exclusive motor yachts nor comfortable sailing yachts travelling the world make big money in the cruise business. It is instead the huge medium-class ships which cruise from Miami, Fort Lauderdale and San Juan on the standard Caribbean routes year-in, year-out which make the big bucks, because a ship which carries 1,800 passengers is far more profitable than two ships carrying 900 passengers each. Construction costs are lower and the bigger ship is cheaper to run, as there is no duplication of manpower.

Once again, Royal Caribbean had its ear to the

ground. On 16 January 1988, the *Sovereign of the Seas* left Miami on its first Caribbean cruise: at an imposing 73,192 tonnes, it was the largest ship ever built specifically for cruises. After converted liners and 'floating holiday hotels', it gave the impetus for the third generation of cruise ships, the 'floating holiday islands'. This mega-ship introduced mass tourism on the water, just as the Boeing 747 had done in the air 18 years previously. It became increasingly irrelevant where the journey went. What counted was the experience of the ship with its wide range of sports and the entertainment on offer. And thus began the crazy competition for ever increasing tonnage. Knut Kloster could not cope with the fact that his *Norway* was now only the second biggest 'music steamer'. He sent it to dry dock in Hamburg and had two additional decks installed. In 1990, the flagship of the Norwegian Cruise Line won back the world record with a gross tonnage of 76,049. In 1995,

The romance of the sail instead of high-technology on the Sea Cloud: *a gilded eagle as its figurehead. A crew which sews sails, splices ropes and polishes brass.*

Princess Cruises' *Sun Princess* (77,000 GT) was celebrated as the biggest cruise ship, and in 1996 the Carnival Cruise Lines' *Carnival Destiny* (101,353 GT) won itself the title 'biggest ship in the world'.

Just 18 months later, Princess Cruises' *Grand Princess* (109,000 GT) was the world's biggest ship, and in the autumn of 1999 or in 2000, Royal Caribbean will be beating this record with not one but two 136,000 tonners.

The 1980s motto 'small is beautiful' had been forgotten, everything was now aiming towards 'bigger is better' and fanning the fire of 'gigantomania' at sea. As recently as 1975, the 20,000 tonne cruise ships which carried 750 passengers were regarded as ideal cruise ships. The average tonnage of the approximately 40 new ships built between 1995 and the end of the century, at a total cost of about $11 billion, is around 65,000 and 80 per cent of these can accommodate more than 1,500 passengers. The big cruise companies believe that investing their money in new ships for a new market was a good move: no other branch of tourism has grown

The Royal Princess *stops at a respectful distance in front of the mighty Columbia glacier which flows along Alaska's west coast into the Prince William Sound.*

more rapidly over the last few years than has cruising, where growth rates of 10 per cent and more are the rule rather than an exception. In 1970 just 500,000 travellers spent their holidays on the high seas, by 1996 the figure had reached 7.2 million, and by the year 2000 the most pessimistic forecasts estimate that there will be 8 million passengers and the most optimistic a massive 10 million. In order to be equipped for this deluge, shipping lines are making sure that they set up modern fleets of pleasure steamers in ample time.

A meeting of 'music steamers' in Nassau in the Bahamas, from right to left: the Fantasy *(Carnival Cruise Lines), the* Nordic Empress *(Royal Caribbean), the* Star/Ship Atlantic *(Premier Cruise Lines), since 1997 the* Melody *(Mediterranean Shipping Cruises), and the front of the* Grandeur of the Seas *(Royal Caribbean).*

The aeroplane and the ship, which as recently as the 1970s were deadly enemies, have long since found their way to becoming a lucrative, mutually beneficial partnership. The airlines fly the cruise passengers to the port of embarkation and fetch them once they have disembarked. Maritime mass tourism would be inconceivable today without wide-body jets; oddly enough, these are religiously following the example of the liners with the three-class system which ships gave up long ago – champagne, caviar and lots of room at the front, whilst at the back, space is at a premium and the fare meagre.

As in the air, there is also first class, business class and economy class at sea – although not on the same cruise ship. The 'music steamers' cover these three market segments more or less fully. The *Europa*, the *Royal Viking Sun* and the *Crystal Symphony* are the equivalent of first class, the *Century*, the *Norwegian Dream*, the *Royal Princess* and the *Noordam* equate to business class and the *Costa Allegra*, the *Bolero* and the *Monterey* to tourist class.

The various cruise lines are also differentiated by the comfort, atmosphere, service and entertainment provided on their floating 'holiday hotels' or 'holiday islands'. Like hotel groups on land, they have their own specific style and their special target market: the Seabourn Cruise Line is the equivalent of a Ritz-Carlton, the Royal

Grandeur of the Seas – 73,600 GT, 1,950 passengers, built in 1996 – a typical Caribbean mega-cruiser: a compact design and lots of spacious windows.

Continued on 233

225

The high-tech four-master Wind Song cruises through the island world of the French Polynesians and anchors in Moorea's picturesque Cook's Bay.

Wind Song - South Sea dreams under sail

The Wind Song *and its two sister ships combine state-of-the-art computer technology with the romanticism of sail. Modern technology dominates on the bridge, and monitors indicate the positions of the sails. Passengers can swim, surf and snorkel from the platform at the stern of the ship.*

In 1789 the three-master *Bounty* is en route in the Pacific to the Caribbean islands, laden to the brim with breadfruit seedlings. The dissatisfied crew, led by the ship's mate Fletcher Christian, mutinies and takes over command. Whilst Captain William Bligh is expelled from the ship with a handful of loyal crew and put out in a small boat, the rebels enthusiastically call out, 'Onwards to Tahiti!' The 'Mutiny on the *Bounty*' made headlines, was filmed three times and helped Tahiti gain the fame of being the last paradise on earth.

Two hundred years later, on a Saturday afternoon in Tahiti's capital city Papeete, the snow-white *Wind Song* glides elegantly out of the harbour and heads on a north-westerly course.

Like the *Bounty*, she is a sailing ship, and like her predecessor she cruises around French Polynesia, sailing when the wind is up and using the engines when it is calm.

But this is where the parallels end. Captain Bligh's ship was a clumsy Royal Navy transporter armed with twelve cannons – extremely cramped, uncomfortable and only 27 metres in length.

The *Wind Song*, on the other hand, is a streamlined, 134 metre four-master with an elegant casino, a swimming pool and a piano bar. Captain Dag Dvergastein proudly shows off the bridge with its state-of-the-art equipment. At the touch of a button, the six giant, computer-controlled sails are unfurled as if by a ghostly hand. Numerous sensors control their position fully automatically, trimming them when the wind freshens and activating the engine when it is calm. The days when seafaring required hard, gruelling manual work which took all one's effort, when sailors climbed the rigging and pulled on sheets, are over.

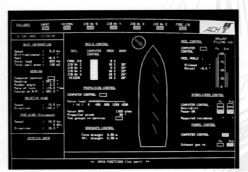

The *Wind Song* approaches Raiatea, continues to Huahine and anchors off Bora Bora. When Captain James Cook

The South Sea dreams of palms and lagoons come true in Polynesia: globe-trotters believe Moorea (top) and Bora Bora to be the most beautiful islands in the world – a paradise for cruise passengers and drop-outs alike.

Only 148 passengers travel on the Wind Song. *Evenings are spent in the piano bar, trying one's luck in the casino or watching a folklore show with Tamure dances.*

visited the island on his second journey round the world in 1774, the German scientist Georg Forster, who was accompanying him, noted in his diary: 'One of the most beautiful corners of the earth, one of the most beautiful areas I know.'

Today our idea of South Sea dreams is also connected with Bora Bora; drop-outs feel happy here and all the clichés are confirmed – gently waving coconut palms, lonely beaches and a turquoise-blue lagoon. Passengers snorkel and wind-surf from the lowered stern platform or cycle along the 32 km traffic-free coast road which is one long avenue of palms, and feel as if they are in a botanical garden.

On Thursday the *Wind Song* anchors in Moorea's Cook's Bay. An exquisite bay with crystal-clear water surrounded by green hills and grey mountains towering up to altitudes of 1,200 metres. In 1980, when Hollywood filmed the 'Mutiny on the *Bounty*' for the second time, the filming was done here on location. The bay was just as picturesque as it was at the time of the legendary mutiny.

On the eighth day of the cruise, the *Wind Song* docks once more in Papeete harbour. The trip was a Polynesian 'island hopping' following in the tracks of Captain Bligh and Captain Cook.

WIND SONG
SAILING AT 4.30 PM HRS
NEXT PORT OF CALL
OPUNOHU BAY

The Norwegian Cruise Line's Dreamward *(since 1998* Norwegian Dream*) lies off George Town, the capital of the Cayman Islands.*

For Americans, the motto of a Caribbean cruise is 'sun and shopping' – 'dolce far niente' on board, duty-free shopping in Charlotte Amalie in St. Thomas, one of the most popular Caribbean destinations.

Caribbean a Hyatt Regency, WinStar Cruises are Relais & Chateaux with stabilisers, Carnival Cruise Lines stands up to any comparison with glitzy hotels such as the Excaliber, the Luxor or the Treasure Island in Las Vegas.

These days there are cruise ships to suit every taste and every purse – from the nostalgic four-master *Sea Cloud* to the science-fiction catamaran *Radisson Diamond*, from a day trip from Miami for a fistful of dollars to a 99-day round-the-world trip on the *Queen Elizabeth II* where a luxury cabin costs DM 209,700. Whilst the Caribbean mega-cruise ships are built 'for sea, sun and fun', expedition ships like the *World Discoverer* boldly head for the Arctic and the Antarctic. There are also theme cruises which are aimed specifically at special interest groups – Oktoberfest Cruises and Alcoholics Anonymous cruises, cruises for amateur golfers, nudists, computer freaks, classical music lovers or amateur archaeologists.

Cruises are holidays with no tiresome packing and unpacking of suitcases – once you are ensconced in your cabin, you can travel without stress from town to town or from island to island for days or weeks on end, getting to know countries and their people on excursions ashore and retiring afterwards to your air-conditioned island of comfort on which you are spared the realities of everyday life. Just as Thomas Mann noted on the crossing to New York on the *Volendam* in the spring of 1934: 'Everything on a journey such as this is designed to make you forget, to create a carefree attitude."

The Americans are the undisputed cruise record holders. In 1996 they made up 70 per cent of all the world's passengers, and a massive 90 per cent in the Caribbean. Europe trailed a long way behind with just 20 per cent, and Asia and Australia brought up the rear with the remaining 10 per cent. Mega-cruise ships are, therefore, at least for the time being, primarily designed for the American market in the Caribbean, in which maritime marketing planners see absolutely unlimited potential.

Whilst Americans take cruises in a very relaxed way and 'just for fun', some Europeans continue to regard them with much more scepticism. The dream world of the soap opera *Das Traumschiff* can act as a deterrent; they stubbornly hold onto the belief that people who take part in cruises are ageing snobs.

Likewise, the Caribbean giant ships seldom venture to Europe; the cruising season is also very short in Europe so that small to medium size units tend to dominate. But things are different in the Far East: here, shipping magnate Eddy Lee is transforming the city state Singapore into a hub for Asian cruise tourism. His company Star Cruise, which started out modestly in 1993 with second-hand ships, is expanding and is now having 75,000 tonne ships

"**THE MOST BEAUTIFUL CARIBBEAN ISLAND HAS PROPELLERS AND IS A CRUISE SHIP**".

JOHN MAXTONE-GRAHAM IN "LINERS TO THE SUN"

Three ships, three styles: The Monarch of the Seas, *a floating skyscraper (left). – The* Radisson Diamond, *a catamaran with an innovative design – the* Ausonia, *an old-timer with a classical silhouette (bottom).*

There are lavish shows on offer every evening on Celebrity Cruises' Century. – The lobby, which stretches over several decks, is the social centre with its bars and boutiques.

built. In the meantime more and more of the old favourites are being withdrawn from service. They are getting old and expensive to maintain, they often do not meet the expectations of a younger market and they do not fulfil the ever more stringent safety and environmental regulations. There is no doubt that the age of classic cruising with traditional ships is coming to an end. Apart from the niche markets, the future belongs to the mega-ships.

An elongated hull with circular portholes. Above that, low superstructures towered over by at least two mighty funnels billowing clouds of smoke. This is how children have been drawing these ocean giants for decades. The image of the cruise ship of today has nothing in common with that of the liner; a new concept also necessitates a new design.

Once ships were floating representatives of their countries, elegantly and robustly built to carry passengers from A to B according to the timetable, whatever the seas. These days, they are 'floating holiday islands' carrying experience-hungry holidaymakers and sailing to sunny climes. The stern has been chopped off, the front of the ship shortened, the streamlined funnels moved right to the back. High super-structures do away with any remaining elegance in the silhouette, and the old guard of seafarers and cruise-goers speak disparagingly of 'shoeboxes with the charm of a container ship'. The loss of external beauty, however, is frequently made up for in other ways: managers are pleased because the rectangular designs enable them to maximise the number of cabins, which increases profits. Passengers are offered a level of comfort that not even first-class used to be able to provide. Panoramic windows have

Continued on page 241

THE EUROPA – GERMANY'S NUMBER ONE CRUISE LINER

'Temperature: 34º. Relative humidity: 89%. Water temperature: 28º.' Channel 1 of the ship's on-board television provides every cabin with this information. On channel 2, the TV camera positioned on the mast shows the bow of the ship, a perfect blue sky and lots of milky brown water. A few hours later the German satellite television reports snow storms in southern Germany. The *Europa*, Germany's number one cruise liner, which belongs to the world's top-class of liners and is known by its regular guests as 'our *Europa*', is en-route from Santarém to Manaus on the Amazon.

The Europa *is one of the top-class of cruise liners and combines tradition with modern design – a classic ship with many regular guests.*

When Hapag-Lloyd announced a new *Europa* for 1982, which was to be the fifth ship bearing this name, the shipping line advertised using the slogan 'A luxury hotel with a ship built round it'. Its predecessors were first and foremost ships and then hotels. But priorities have changed. The 316 cabins, for example, were pre-fabricated as completely furnished residential units, completely sound-proofed and installed individually. What is more, the inside of the ship is not laid out in the usual horizontal way but vertically: all the cabins are in the front, quieter part of the ship, whilst the engine room, the main public rooms, the refrigeration rooms and stores are all in the slightly noisier rear part of the ship. The area of the decks is the size of about five football pitches, giving each of the 600 passengers 64 square metres of space. Even the 300-man crew has the use of a swimming pool, a sauna and a fitness room, which is unusual on a cruise liner.

The *Europa* is a German ship for German passengers, efficiently organised, with good plain cuisine and draught beer as a matter of course. Everything runs like clockwork, although there are innumerable little surprising details: the cabin steward will shine your shoes without being asked to do so, and at night you will find a goodnight chocolate bar on your pillow. There is even an umbrella in the cupboard just in case. The daily programme politely suggests 'evening dress please' for the gala dinner. And in the boxes of *Europa* matches there is one single orange-headed match amongst all the matches with blue heads – a discreet display of the Hapag-Lloyd house colours, as the funnel is blue and orange, as are the decorative stripes on the hull.

The *Europa* wends its way along the lazily winding Amazon, lined on the left and the right by dense rain forests, to its destination, Manaus. Passengers play shuffleboard, stand chatting along the railings, take part in flower arranging courses, sit enjoying a drink in the 'Delfter Krug' bar or are hidden away behind a door with the sign: 'Nudist deck. No peeking.' Captain Uwe Bech plays table-tennis with the chief engineer on the sports deck. An old lady in a white *Europa* dressing-gown watches with concern and asks her friend: 'So who's steering the ship?'

In the 1930s, Europa III *was one of the 'speed queens' on the Atlantic (top right),* Europa IV *was the Swedish American Line's former* Kungsholm *(top left), and* Europa V *travels all over the world as a cruise liner and here celebrates crossing the Equator (bottom left).*

Modern cruise ships such as the Horizon *have wind-protected pool landscapes amidships with bars, whirlpools and a bandstand. One deck above the joggers do their rounds – on the* Sovereign of the Seas *in our picture.*

replaced cabin portholes, more and more cabins have balconies, and at the top amidships there are swimming pools, whirlpools, baths and jogging circuits. Multi-storey lobbies with bars and boutiques form the social heart of the ship, and the restaurant, which used to be accommodated deep down in the belly of the ship, now offers unprecedented views of the sea, as do the fitness and wellness centres. A casino and nightly shows in the theatre add a touch of Las Vegas.

Despite the radical break with the past, not all traditions have been thrown overboard. The captain still invites passengers to captain's cocktails and the captain's dinner, the midnight buffets are still held, and towards the end of the voyage stewards still parade in the darkened dining room bearing Baked Alaska, and, though hardly noticed by the passengers, the laundry is still operated by Chinese. The designers of the ships, who go for sheer functionality on the outside, like to replicate historical models on the inside. The *Splendour of the Seas*, built in 1995, has a Pompeii-style bath with pseudo-Roman columns and statues, as did the *Imperator* built in 1913. Grand staircases leading to the double-storey dining room, once the pride of transatlantic steamers like the *Ile de France*

On the Celebrity Cruises' Century a wide staircase leads to a dining room with lots of large windows in the aft of the ship. Crystal candelabras and art-deco columns lend it a touch of 'retro-chic'.

and the *Normandie*, are once more regarded as chic today. Even 'steamship baroque' is making a comeback. Joe Farcus, *Carnival's* in-house designer, is transforming their fun ships into neon-bathed pleasure parks.

The future of maritime tourism has been a reality for some time, at least on the drawing board. The Japanese Mitsubishi Group's Dream Ship project envisages a giant streamlined cruise ship behind whose glass-and-aluminium façade are concealed three hotel towers containing cabins for 5,000 passengers. The designers even want to run a monorail railway on the roof, 18 storeys above the sea.

The *Phoenix-Projekt*, a giant ship about 350 metres long and 77 metres wide, which bears no similarity to anything that has ever sailed the world's oceans before, has been afloat since 1983, although thus far purely as a model: on the deck, three giant residential blocks with cabins for 6,200 passengers tower up to 64 metres above the surface of the water. Between them are helicopter landing areas, shopping boulevards, tennis and squash courts, palms and swimming pools surrounded by sand. When the ship is anchored, the stern doors open and four high-speed tenders carrying 400 passengers each flit to land. The idea comes from Knut

SEA AIR MAKES YOU HUNGRY AND THIRSTY

This is what the 700 passengers on the Vistafjord *consume on average during a 14-day cruise:*

36,000 eggs; 10,540 bottles of beer

10,170 bottles of soft drinks

9,545 kgs fruit

9,060 kgs meat

7,730 kgs vegetables

4,200 litres milk

3,640 kgs potatoes

2,140 kgs fish and seafood; 1,900 litres cream

1,700 litres ice-cream

1,590 kgs flour

1,500 litres fruit juice

1,400 bottles of champagne and sparkling wine

1,500 bottles of table wine

815 kgs cheese; 730 kgs sugar

410 kgs coffee; 400 bottles whisky

270 kgs salt; 85 bottles of cognac

70 bottles of rum; 105 kgs cooking chocolate

24 kgs caviar

In the same period, the engine devours 4 tonnes of lubricating oil, 59 tonnes of diesel oil and 634 tonnes of heavy oil.

A roguishly blinking eye on the side of the ship indicates that the Aida *regards itself as a floating holiday club and not as a traditional 'music steamer' (top). The* Legend of the Seas *even has cabins at the stern to increase passenger capacity (centre). – The* World of ResidenSea *is Knut Kloster Junior's latest project. Apartments and penthouses between 102 and 213 square metres in area are available for sale for prices starting at $1.2 million (bottom).*

Utstein Kloster, the man who started the Caribbean cruising boom in the 1960s.

As clever as the concepts for maritime mass tourism in the 21st century may be, Jules Verne's vision at the end of the 19th century was much more adventurous. The imaginative Frenchman, who often went on cruises in his small steamer the *Saint-Michel III* and repeatedly chose ships as the scene of the action in his novels, had already created the giant ships of the future in 1895 in *The Propeller Island*. His *Standard Island* is seven kilometres long, five kilometres wide and has space for 10,000 passengers, 'exclusively Americans'; it is a floating island, 'an artificial paradise', which cruises the Pacific driven by a 1,000,000 hp engine and meets a tragic ending: first 'bloodthirsty Malayans' board the ship, then it goes down in a storm. But Jules Verne comforts himself: 'It will be crawling with these islands by the end of the 20th century'.

Jules Verne was wrong. The giant ships are by no means as gigantic as the visionary author had imagined. Not yet anyway.

Norwegian Knut Kloster's Phoenix Project offers space for 6,200 passengers.

"IT TOOK FOUR YEARS TO BUILD THE ISLAND.
STANDARD ISLAND WAS CONSTRUCTED WITH PLATES OF STEEL.
THE OVAL CONSTRUCTION MEASURED SEVEN KILOMETERS
IN LENGTH, FIVE IN WIDTH; IT'S CIRUMFERENCE WAS
THUS 18 KILOMETERS. (...)
ALMOST 10,000 PEOPLE INHABITED THE ISLAND,
ALL AMERICAN.
THE YANKEES FROM THE NORTH OCCUPIED THE PORT SIDE,
THE SOUTHERNERS THE STARBOARD SIDE".

JULES VERNES, IN
"THE PROPELLER ISLAND", 1895

The Carnival Destiny, *a superlative fun ship which has been sailing in the Caribbean since autumn 1996, is a $400 million ocean-going skyscraper. The giant 272-metre-long ship has four swimming pools, six restaurants, seventeen bars and cabins for 2,642 passengers. The lobby (right) is nine decks high, the theatre (left) holds 1,500 visitors and offers Las Vegas-style shows every evening. In the casino there are 23 gaming tables and 324 one-armed bandits.*

THE SOVEREIGN OF THE SEAS – A SHIP SETS NEW STANDARDS

The Sovereign of the Seas *was, in 1988, not only the biggest cruiser ever built, it was also a trendsetter in maritime tourism: after the converted liners and 'floating holiday hotels', there now came the 'floating holiday islands' for 2,000 and more passengers. The Viking Crown Lounge (right), a bar 12 storeys above the sea, is the symbol of all the units in the Royal Caribbean Fleet.*

26 June 1634. England's King Charles I visits the Woolwich shipyard and commissions ship's architect Phineaus Pett to build the biggest ship the world has ever seen. Pett sits down at the drawing board and designs a ship which was for those times a veritable maritime giant: 39 metres long, 14 metres wide, with 4 masts and 100 cannons. *Sovereign of the Seas* was launched in 1637, cost £65,586, joined the fleet of the Royal Navy and engaged the Dutch fleet in some bitter duels.

16 January 1988. Passengers in Miami enter a giant foyer five storeys high, and blink in amazement: glass-fronted lifts waft silently upwards, sweeping staircases wend their way upwards to the left and to the right, a cascade murmurs gently, a pianist quietly plays on the white grand piano. What seems to describe the lobby of a Hyatt Hotel is however the showpiece of Norway's *Sovereign of the Seas*: the biggest passenger ship in the world and, until 1988, the biggest cruise ship ever built, with some impressive vital statistics: 266 metres in length, 32 metres in width, 14 decks high, 2,276 passengers. Tens of thousands of people line the port's narrow exit, several helicopters carrying television crews circle overhead, a brass band belts out the 'River Kwai March'. Slowly the $185 million *Sovereign of the Seas* leaves the quay and embarks upon her maiden voyage to the Caribbean. 'Our passengers should be able to choose what they want to do on board. That is why we built the ship so big,' explains Captain Eigil Erikson. They have two swimming pools to splash around in, three restaurants to dine in and ten bars to order their drinks from. They sweat

The lobby with its glass-fronted lifts is 5 decks high (above). Here people meet to go to the captain's dinner in dinner jackets and evening dresses (left), then to see fast-moving shows in the theatre and to try their luck in the casino (far left).

Passengers sunbathe on the sundeck (left). One deck higher, basketball players practise shooting goals.

The section shows the interior of the Sovereign of the Seas:
1 fitness centre, 2 night-club and disco, 3 theatre, 4 dancing, 5 Center for Kids,
6 Viking Crown Lounge, 7 dancing, 8 casino, 9 two restaurants, 10 champagne bar, 11 lobby,
12 boutiques and shops, 13 Windjammer Café, 14 two cinemas, 15 cabins.

away in the fitness centre, jog along the jogging path, play the one-armed bandits in Casino 170 and amuse themselves in the evening with an abridged version of the musical 'On the Town' in the Follies Theatre.

The *Sovereign of the Seas* heralds the beginning of the era of the mega-cruise ship and the computer is not only a feature on the bridge but for the passengers as well. At the touch of a button on the monitor in their cabins, they can book excursions ashore, order the wine for their evening meal or find out the quickest way of getting to the Viking Crown Lounge, a cocktail bar located round the funnel 50 metres above sea level. A plan of the *Sovereign of the Seas* showing the fastest route there through the labyrinth of corridors, halls and decks also appears on-screen.

The efforts to keep the traditions of seafaring alive on a cruise ship at the end of the 20th century are almost touching: telescopes and sextants, maritime charts and nostalgic photographs of windjammers hang in the many public rooms. And a model of the first *Sovereign of the Seas* is on display in a glass cabinet in the Schooner Bar on the ShowTime deck.

Simply doing nothing or getting your exercise? The benefits of a cruise lie not least in the fact that everyone can do whatever he or she wants.

Liners that made History

BREMEN

Shipping Line	Norddeutscher Lloyd
Shipyard	Deschimag AG 'Weser', Bremen
Commissioned	1929
Tonnage	51,656
Length/width	286.1 metres/31.3 metres
Horse power	130,000
Service speed	27 knots
Passengers	2,228 (811 first-class, 500 second-class, 300 tourist-class, 617 third-class)
Crew	990
Sister ship	*Europa*
Decommissioned	Laid up in Bremerhaven in 1939, used as a barracks for the German navy in 1940, destroyed by arson in 1941

BRITANNIA

Shipping line	British and North American Royal Mail Steam Packet Company
Shipyard	Robert Duncan, Greenock
Commissioned	1840
Tonnage	1,154
Length/width	63.1 metres/10.4 metres
Horse power	420
Service speed	8.5 knots
Passengers	115
Crew	89
Decommissioned	Sold to the German *Bundesflotte* in 1849 and renamed the *Barbarossa*, taken over by the Prussian navy in 1852, used as a target ship and sunk in 1880

GREAT EASTERN

Shipping line	Great Ship Company
Shipyard	John Scott Russell, Millwall, Isle of Dogs
Commissioned	1860
Tonnage	18,915
Length/width	210.9 metres/25.2 metres
Horse power	2,600
Service speed	14 knots
Passengers	4,000 (800 first-class, 2,000 second-class, 1,200 third-class)
Crew	400
Decommissioned	Exhibition ship in 1886, scrapped in 1889

ILE DE FRANCE

Shipping line	Compagnie Générale Transatlantique
Shipyard	Chantiers de Penhoët, Saint-Nazaire
Commissioned	1927
Tonnage	43,153
Length/width	241.3 metres/28 metres
Horse power	60,000
Service speed	24 knots
Passengers	1,586 (670 first-class, 408 second-class, 508 third-class)
Crew	800
Decommissioned	Scrapped in 1959

IMPERATOR

Shipping line	Hapag
Shipyard	Vulkan, Hamburg
Commissioned	1913
Tonnage	52,117
Length/width	277.1 metres/29.9 metres
Horse power	74,000
Service speed	23 knots
Passengers	4,594 (908 first-class, 972 second-class, 942 third-class, 1,772 fourth-class)
Crew	1,180
Sister ship	*Vaterland*, *Bismarck*
Change of ownership	Given to the USA as reparation in 1919, bought by Cunard and renamed the *Berengaria* in 1921
Decommissioned	Laid up in 1938 after fire, scrapped in 1939

MAURETANIA

Shipping line	Cunard Line
Shipyard	Swan, Hunter & Wigham Richardson, Newcastle
Commissioned	1907
Tonnage	31,938
Length/width	240.8 metres/26.8 metres
Horse power	78,000
Service Speed	25 knots
Passengers	2,335 (560 first-class, 475 second-class, 1,300 third-class)
Crew	812
Sister ship	*Lusitania*
Decommissioned	Laid up in 1934, scrapped in 1935

NORMANDIE

Shipping line	Compagnie Générale Transatlantique
Shipyard	Chantiers de Penhoët, Saint-Nazaire
Commissioned	1935
Tonnage	83,423
Length/width	313.8 metres/35.9 metres
Horse power	160,000
Service speed	29 knots
Passengers	1972 (864 first-class, 654 tourist-class, 454 third-class)
Crew	1,345
Decommissioned	Laid up in 1939 in New York, taken over by the USA in 1941 and renamed the *Lafayette*, capsized after a fire in 1942, scrapped in 1946

QUEEN ELIZABETH

Shipping line	Cunard White Star
Shipyard	John Brown & Company, Clydebank
Commissioned	1940 (Troop transporter), 1946 (Liner)
Tonnage	83,673
Length/width	314.3 metres/35.5 metres
Horse power	200,000
Service speed	28.5 knots
Passengers	2,283 (823 first-class, 662 cabin-class, 798 tourist-class)
Crew	1,318
Decommissioned	Sold to Hong Kong as a floating university in 1967, capsized after a fire in 1972, scrapped in 1974

QUEEN ELIZABETH 2

Shipping line	Cunard Line
Shipyard	John Brown & Company, Clydebank
Commissioned	1969
Tonnage	65,836 (1969) 70,327 (since 1994)
Length/width	293.5 metres/32.1 metres
Horse power	110,000
Service speed	28.5 knots
Passengers	2,005 (564 first-class, 1,441 tourist-class (1969), 1,715 in various cabin categories (since 1998)
Crew	1,000

QUEEN MARY

Shipping line	Cunard White Star
Shipyard	John Brown & Company, Clydebank
Commissioned	1936
Tonnage	80,774
Length/width	310.5 metres/36 metres
Horse power	200,000
Service speed	28.5 knots
Passengers	2,139 (776 first-class, 784 cabin-class, 579 tourist-class)
Crew	1,100
Decommissioned	1967
Change of ownership	Bought by the City of Long Beach, California in 1967, museum and hotel ship since May 1971, taken over by the Disney Corporation in 1988

REX

Shipping line	Italia Flotte Riunite
Shipyard	Ansaldo, Genoa
Commissioned	1932
Tonnage	51,062
Length/width	268.2 metres/29.5 metres
Horse power	142,000
Service speed	28 knots
Passengers	2,258 (604 first-class, 378 second-class, 410 tourist-class, 866 third-class)
Crew	810
Decommissioned	Laid up in 1940, shelled, set on fire and sank in 1944, scrapped in 1947

TITANIC

Shipping line	White Star Line
Shipyard	Harland & Wolff, Belfast
Commissioned	1912
Tonnage	46,329
Length/width	269.1 metres/28.2 metres
Horse power	46,000
Service speed	22 knots
Passengers	2,603 (905 first-class, 564 second-class, 1,134 third-class)
Crew	900
Sister ship	*Olympic*, *Britannic*
Decommissioned	Sank on 15 April 1912

UNITED STATES

Shipping line	United States Lines
Shipyard	Newport News Shipbuilding & Drydock Company, Newport News, Virginia
Commissioned	1952
Tonnage	53,329
Length/width	301.8 metres/31 metres
Horse power	240,000
Service speed	31 knots
Passengers	2,008 (913 first-class, 558 cabin-class, 537 tourist-class)
Crew	1,093
Decommissioned	Laid up in 1969, sold to US Cruises in 1981 and Marmara Marine Inc. in 1992

Milestones in Cruising History

CARNIVAL DESTINY

Shipping line	Carnival Cruise Lines
Flag	Panama
Shipyard	Fincantieri Cantieri Navali, Trieste (Italy)
Commissioned	1996
Tonnage	101,353
Length/width	272.2 metres/35.3 metres
Passengers	2,642
Crew	1,050

NORWAY

Former name	*France*
Shipping line	Norwegian Cruise Line
Flag	Bahamas
Shipyard	Chantiers de l'Atlantique, Saint-Nazaire (France)
Commissioned	1962 (*France*), 1980 (*Norway*)
Tonnage	66,438 (*France*), 76,049 (*Norway*)
Length/width	315.5 metres/33.5 metres
Passengers	1,914 (*France*), 2,044 (*Norway*)
Crew	950 (*France*), 875 (*Norway*)

PACIFIC PRINCESS

Former name	*Sea Venture*
Shipping line	Princess Cruises
Flag	Great Britain
Shipyard	Rheinstahl Nordseewerke, Emden
Commissioned	1971 (*Sea Venture*), 1975 (*Pacific Princess*)
Tonnage	20,636
Length/width	168.7 metres/24.6 metres
Passengers	610
Crew	350
Sister ship	*Island Princess* (ex *Island Venture*)

PRINZESSIN VICTORIA LUISE

Shipping line	Hapag
Flag	Germany
Shipyard	Blohm & Voss, Hamburg
Commissioned	1901
Tonnage	4,419
Length/width	124 metres/14.3 metres
Passengers	180
Crew	161

QUAKER CITY

Shipping line	Leary Bros. Line
Flag	USA
Commissioned	1854
Tonnage	1,426
Length/width	81.4 metres/12.2 metres
Passengers	200

RADISSON DIAMOND

Shipping line	Radisson Seven Sea Cruises
Flag	Finland
Shipyard	Rauma Yards, Ruma (Finland)
Commissioned	1992
Tonnage	20,295
Length/width	129 metres/32 metres
Passengers	354
Crew	192

ROYAL VIKING STAR

Present name	*Black Watch*
Shipping line	Royal Viking Line (to 1991), now Fred Olsen Cruise Lines
Flag	Norway
Shipyard	Wärtsilä, Helsinki (Finland)
Commissioned	1972
Tonnage	28,221 (to 1981: 21,847)
Length	205.5 metres (to 1981: 177.7 metres)
Width	25.2 metres
Crew	375 (to 1981: 326)
Passengers	700 (to 1981: 375)
Sister ships	*Royal Viking Sky, Royal Viking Sea*

SEA GODDESS I

Shipping line	Sea Goddess Cruises, Cunard since 1986
Flag	Isle of Man
Shipyard	Wärtsilä, Helsinki (Finland)
Commissioned	1984
Tonnage	4,260
Length/width	104.8 metres/14.6 metres
Passengers	116
Crew	90
Sister ship	*Sea Goddess II*

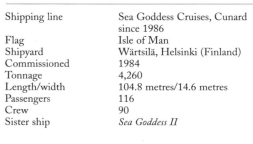

SONG OF NORWAY

Present name	*Sundream*
Shipping line	Royal Caribbean Cruises Line
Flag	Norway
Shipyard	Wärtsilä, Helsinki (Finland)
Commissioned	1970
Tonnage	32,005 (to 1978: 18,416)
Length	194.3 metres (to 1978: 168.3 metres)
Width	24 metres
Passengers	1,004 (to 1978: 724)
Crew	420 (to 1978: 320)
Sister ships	*Nordic Prince* (*Carousel* since 1995), *Sun Viking*

SOVEREIGN OF THE SEAS

Shipping line	Royal Caribbean Cruises Line
Flag	Norway
Shipyard	Chantiers de l'Atlantique, Saint-Nazaire (France)
Commissioned	1988
Tonnage	73,192
Length/width	266.3 metres/32.2 metres
Passengers	2,276
Crew	808
Sister ships	*Monarch of the Seas*, *Majesty of the Seas*

VISTAFJORD

Shipping line	Cunard, Norwegian American Cruises to 1983
Flag	Bahamas
Shipyard	Swan Hunter Shipbuilders, Wallsend-on-Tyne (Great Britain)
Commissioned	1973
Tonnage	24,492
Length/width	191 metres/25 metres
Passengers	677
Crew	380
'Almost sister ships'	*Sagafjord*, *Saga Rose* since 1997

WIND STAR

Shipping line	Windstar Cruises
Flag	Bahamas
Shipyard	Ateliers et Chantiers du Havre, Le Havre (France)
Commissioned	1986
Tonnage	5,703
Length/width	134.2 metres/15.8 metres
Sail area	1996 m^2
Passengers	148
Crew	90
Sister ships	*Wind Song*, *Wind Spirit*

Chronicle

1818

The Black Ball Line commences regular passenger voyages between New York and Liverpool with four sailing ships. The average crossing time is 24 days (west to east) and 40 days (east to west).

1819

The *Savannah*, a three-master with steam-driven propellers, crosses the Atlantic in 29 days and 11 hours.

A new law in England reduces daily working hours to twelve and prohibits child labour.

1825

The first railway line opens between Stockton and Darlington in England.

1837

The Peninsula Steam Navigation Company, later the Peninsula and Oriental Steam Navigation Company, P&O for short, established.

Samuel Morse invents the telegraph.

1840

The British and North American Royal Mail Steam Packet Company, later the Cunard Line, established. The *Britannia* commences scheduled voyages between Liverpool and Boston.

England issues the world's first postage stamp.

1844

P&O invite author William Makepeace Thackeray to take a 'cruise' in the Mediterranean.

1847

The Hamburg-Amerikanische Packetfahrt-Actien-Gesellschaft, or Hapag for short, established. First transatlantic voyages the following year.

The first horse-drawn double-decker buses take to the streets in London.

1857

Norddeutscher Lloyd established.

First Alpine Association established in London.

1860

Maiden voyage of the *Great Eastern*. Until 1901, she was the biggest ship in the world.

1861

Compagnie Générale Transatlantique (Transat) established.

1861–1865

American Civil War.

1862

The travel agency Thomas Cook organises a round-the-world trip using four different passenger ships.

1867

Mark Twain takes a pleasure trip to the Old World on the *Quaker City* and describes it in 'The Innocents Abroad'.

José Monier invents reinforced concrete, Alfred Noble invents dynamite, Karl Marx writes 'Das Kapital'.

1869

The Ocean Steam Navigation Company, later to become the White Star Line, established. Suez Canal opened.

The Central Pacific Railway links the east and west coasts of the USA. First cogwheel railway on Mount Washington, New Hampshire.

1890

Norddeutscher Lloyd runs a cruise to the Norwegian fjords on the *Kaiser Wilhelm II*.

1891

The *Augusta Victoria* (Hapag) sails on a 58-day 'pleasure trip' to the Mediterranean

Otto Lilienthal makes the first glider flight.

1897

The *Kaiser Wilhelm der Große* (Norddeutscher Lloyd) is the first four-funnel steamer and the first 'floating palace' on the Atlantic.

Rudolf Diesel presents the first diesel engine.

1901

The *Prinzessin Victoria Luise* (Hapag) is the first passenger ship built specifically for cruises. J. Pierpont Morgan establishes the Mercantile Marine Company, to which the White Star Line, amongst others, belonged. Hapag and Norddeutscher Lloyd are the biggest shipping lines in the world, with 117 and 113 ocean-going ships respectively.

Guglielmo Marconi sends a wireless telegraph across the North Atlantic between England and Newfoundland.

1903

The Wright Brothers make the world's first flight in a motor-driven aeroplane.

1905

The *Amerika* (Hapag) is the first 'Grand Hotel of the seas'. Climax of the emigration wave: 1,027,421 arrivals in New York, of which 90,772 arrive in September alone.

Albert Einstein develops the Theory of Relativity.

1907

Cunard's *Lusitania* and *Mauretania* undertake their maiden voyages.

First projects for a tunnel under the English Channel.

1909

The *Mauretania* (Cunard) crosses the Atlantic in 4 days, 10 hours and 51 minutes, wins the Blue Riband and remains the fastest passenger ship until 1929.
The *Cleveland* (Hapag) sets out on a three-month round-the-world voyage starting in New York and ending in San Francisco.
The *Mauretania* (Cunard) wins the Blue Riband.

Louis Blériot flies across the English Channel. The American Robert Peary is probably the first person to reach the North Pole.

1912

The *Titanic* (White Star Line) sinks on its maiden voyage after colliding with an iceberg; more than 1,500 fatalities.

The first *Titanic* film comes to the cinemas. Robert Scott, who reached the South Pole one month after Roald Amundsen, dies along with his team on their return journey.

1913

Maiden voyage of the *Imperator* (Hapag). It carries 4,594 passengers in four classes.
In London the International Conference for Safety of Life at Sea (the 'Titanic Conference') lays down binding safety regulations.

Ford introduces the assembly line for car production.

1914

The Panama Canal opens.

Alexander Behm invents the echo-sounder.

1914–1918

Passenger ships are used as troop transporters, auxiliary cruisers and floating barracks in World War I.

1915

A German U-boat sinks the *Lusitania*, 1,195 fatalities.

Towing research institute for model ships established in Hamburg.

1920

Booze cruises and Caribbean cruises become popular in the USA during Prohibition.

1922

The *Laconia* (Cunard) leaves New York in November, travels round the world and arrives back in New York at the end of March 1923.

Howard Carter discovers the tomb of the pharaoh Tutankhamun.

1927

The *Ile de France* (Transat) introduces the 'style paquebot'. First ever take-off of an aeroplane from a passenger ship, the *Leviathan* (United States Lines).

Charles Lindbergh crosses the Atlantic on a solo flight from New York to Paris. The age of the talkies begins with the film 'The Jazz Singer'.

1928

Norddeutscher Lloyd and Lufthansa offer a 'fly and cruise' programme: across the Atlantic on the *Columbus*, and across Europe by plane.

Mickey Mouse appears in a sound film for the first time as a helmsman in Walt Disney's cartoon 'Steamboat Willie'.

1929

The *Bremen* (Norddeutscher Lloyd) breaks the *Mauretania*'s 20-year-old speed record on its maiden voyage. The company owns the first ship with a streamlined silhouette, the *Europa* (1930).

The airship *Graf Zeppelin* flies round the world from Friedrichshafen in 3 weeks.
First regular television broadcasts by the BBC in England. World economic crisis after Black Friday on 24 October.

1931

The world economic crisis causes transatlantic passenger numbers to fall from 1.1 million in the previous year to 685,000.

The airship *Graf Zeppelin* commences an air service between Germany and Brazil.

1932

The *Rex* and the *Conte di Savoia*, which crossed the Atlantic by the southern route, are advertised with the slogan 'The Lido Crossing'.

Amelia Earhart is the first female pilot to fly across the Atlantic.

1934

Nazi Germany popularises holidays at sea with its cheap 'Power Through Pleasure' cruises.

Cole Porter's musical 'Anything Goes', which takes place on a luxury liner, has its premier on Broadway.

1935

The *Normandie* (Transat) wins the Blue Riband on its maiden voyage.

The first line in the Moscow underground is opened.

1936

The *Queen Mary* (Cunard) is the first passenger ship to cross the Atlantic in less than 4 days. West to east in 3 days, 23 hours and 57 minutes.

The airship *Hindenburg* starts regular passenger services across the North Atlantic.

1937

Hamburg-Süd 'invents' the holiday formula 'Cruise and Stay': to Rio on the *Cap Arcona*, a 10-day stay in Brazil and back to Europe by ship.

The Hindenburg explodes on landing at Lake Hurst. This marks the end of regular Zeppelin passenger services.

1939–1945

Passenger ships are used as troop transporters, auxiliary cruisers and floating barracks in World War II.

1945

A Soviet submarine torpedoes the *Wilhelm Gustloff*, British fighter planes sink the *Cap Arcona*. More than 10,000 fatalities.

Four-engine DC-4s fly across the Atlantic with three stop-overs.
The first atomic bomb is exploded at a testing ground near Los Alamos in New Mexico.

1952

Unbeaten passenger ship record: the *United States* (United States Lines) crosses the Atlantic in 3 days, 10 hours and 40 minutes.

Beginning of the jet age: the first passenger flight by a de Havilland Comet 1 from London to Johannesburg.

1956

The *Andrea Doria* sinks after colliding with the *Stockholm* east of New York.

1957

Record year on the Atlantic, with more than 1 million passengers.

First journey into space: the Soviet satellite *Sputnik* circles the earth.

1958

For the first time ever, aircraft carry more passengers across the Atlantic than do liners.

Boeing 707s cross Atlantic on scheduled flights in seven hours. First American satellite launched.

1962

Maiden voyage of the *France* (Transat), the last transatlantic liner.

The *Telstar* news satellite enables television signals to be transmitted between Europe and the USA.

1965

Maiden voyage of the *Michelangelo* and the *Raffaello*. Princess Cruises established.

First major deployment of American troops in Vietnam.

1966

First Caribbean cruise of the *Sunward* (Norwegian Caribbean Lines) from Miami.

1967

Queen Mary decommissioned.
Launch of the *Queen Elizabeth 2* (Cunard), which was designed as a liner and a cruise ship.

1968

Last transatlantic voyage of the *Queen Elizabeth*.

1969

Maiden voyage of the *Queen Elizabeth 2*.
The *United States* decommissioned.

Neil Armstrong and Edwin Aldrin are the first people to land on the moon.

1970

Song of Norway (Royal Caribbean) is the first passenger ship built exclusively for Caribbean Cruises. Hapag and Norddeutscher Lloyd merge to form Hapag-Lloyd.

First transatlantic flight by a Boeing 747 from New York to London.

1972

The *Mardi Gras* (Carnival Cruise Lines) travels on its first Caribbean cruise.

The USA withdraws from Vietnam.

1973

Royal Viking Line runs luxury world cruises with three identical ships.

Federico Fellini pays homage to the *Rex* in his film 'Amarcord'.

1974

The *France* is laid up in Le Havre. P&O group acquires Princess Cruises.

US President Nixon resigns after Watergate scandal.

1975

Raffaello and *Michelangelo* laid up.

A Soyuz and an Apollo capsule link up in space.

1976

First scheduled Concorde flights across the Atlantic in just 3 hours.

Bill Gates sets up Microsoft.

1980

The *Norway*, formerly the *France*, travels on its first Caribbean cruise for Norwegian Cruise Line.

Two Russian cosmonauts spend 185 days on board *Salyut 6*.

1982

Queen Elizabeth 2 and *Canberra* are used as troop transporters in the Falklands War.

1983

Knut Kloster presents his Phoenix Project for a cruise ship to carry 6,200 passengers.

1984

The *Sea Goddess I* and *Sea Goddess II* travel on exclusive cruises with just 116 passengers.

1985

Palestinian terrorists hijack the *Achille Lauro* in the Mediterranean and murder a passenger.

1986

Windstar Cruises run luxury sailing cruises on three high-tech four-masters.

1988

The era of the mega-cruiser begins with Royal Caribbean's *Sovereign of the Seas*.
34,000 passengers cross the Atlantic on ships, 30 million in aeroplanes.

1991

The atomic ice-breaker *Sovietsky Soyuz* takes tourists to the North Pole for the first time.

1992

5.5 million people go on cruises.
The Italian speedboat *Destriero* crosses the Atlantic in the record time of 2 days, 10 hours, 34 minutes and 4 seconds.

1994

The *Achille Lauro* sinks after a fire.

The Channel Tunnel between France and England opens.

1996

7.2 million cruise passengers worldwide. Miami is the 'cruise capital of the world' with 1.5 million passengers a year.

1997

Queen Elizabeth 2 crosses the Atlantic forty times on scheduled trips. The royal yacht *Britannia* is decommissioned.

Premier of the musical 'Titanic' on Broadway, and new *Titanic* film. Space probe Pathfinder lands on Mars.

1998

Ten new cruise ships commissioned, including the *Disney Magic* (Disney Cruise Line), the *Deutschland* (Peter Deilmann-Reederei) and the *Grand Princess* (Princess Cruises) of 109,000 GT.

The Silver Cloud *leaves Lisbon and passes the city's landmark, the Tower of Belém. The* Silver Cloud *has 140 cabins, of which 102 have balconies.*

The Norwegian Cruise Line's Windward (since 1998 Norwegian Wind), cruises off the coast of Alaska.

Index

A Brief Nautical Glossary

ACCOMMODATION LADDER – ladder let down side of ship to allow access e.g. from a small boat

AFT – at the back of the ship

AMIDSHIPS – the middle of the ship

BERTH – to attach a ship to a pier

BLUE PETER – flag raised on a ship leaving the port

BOLLARD – iron, concrete or wooden post to which ships' ropes are attached

BOW – front of the ship, opposite of stern

BOWSPRIT – a spar running out over the bow of a sailing ship

BRIDGE – navigation and command centre

BULKHEAD – fire and water-resistant partition inside the ship. There are transverse, longitudinal and collision bulkheads, amongst others.

BUNK – bed

BUNKER – to take fuel on board

CABLE – thick rope for fastening and pulling along a ship

CALM – period with no wind

CAPSIZE – (of a ship) to upset or overturn

CAPTAIN'S DINNER – a festive dinner

CATAMARAN – a boat with twin hulls in parallel

CHARTROOM – room behind the bridge in which maritime charts and nautical instruments are kept

CLIPPER – fast streamlined sailing ship from the 19th century with 3-4 masts

COMPANIONWAY – stairs leading down to cabins

COURSE – direction in which a ship travels

DAVIT – crane for suspending or lowering lifeboats and dinghies

DAY'S RUN – distance a ship has travelled between 12 noon one day and 12 noon the next day

DECK – a storey on a ship

DIE DOWN – (of wind) to become less strong

DRAUGHT – depth of a ship from the water line to the lower edge of the keel

ECHO DEPTH SOUNDER – electronic device for measuring water depth

FATHOM – 6 feet

FORWARD QUARTER – the front of a ship

GALLEY – ship's kitchen

GANGWAY – a bridge laid from ship to shore

HEAVE – to lift or haul with great effort

HELMSMAN – a member of the crew who operates the rudder in accordance with the commands of the officer on watch

HOIST – to lift or pull up

HULL – the body of the ship without superstructures and masts

JACOB'S LADDER – rope ladder with wooden steps

KEEL – lengthwise structure along the base of a ship

KNOT – a) rope knot
b) speed of ship measured in nautical miles per hour

LASH – to tie together

LAUNCH - the sliding of the named but unfinished ship into the water

LEE – the side of the ship away from the wind

LIST – (of a ship) to lean over to one side

LOG BOOK – ship's diary in which all information relating to the management of the ship is entered

MAIDEN VOYAGE – first voyage after completion of ship

MARINA – small harbour for sport and sailing boats

MARITIME – collective term for anything to do with marine travel

MASTHEAD – the top end of the mast

MESS – crew's dining-room

MOOR – to fasten

NAUTICAL MILE – 1,852 metres

NAVIGATION – the art of planning a ship's course

PIER – landing stage

PITCH – movement of a ship along its width

PORT – the left-hand side of the ship, looking in the direction of travel

PORTHOLE – a round window in the side of a ship

PULL – to row

PUT TO SEA – to leave a port

QUARTER-DECK – upper deck near the back of the ship

RAILING – a balustrade

RAM – to collide, crash

REEF – to shorten the sails

RIGGING – collective description for masts, yards, sails etc. on a sailing ship

RISE – (of wind) to increase in strength

ROAD – sheltered piece of water near the shore in which ships can ride at anchor

ROLL – to sway to and fro along the ship's length

RUDDER – device on the back of a ship for steering

SCREW – the ship's propeller

SHEET – rope for securing or controlling the sails

SHUFFLEBOARD – deck game on which wooden discs are pushed over a marked surface

SHROUD – set of wire ropes supporting the mast

SISTER SHIP – ship of an identical design

SPLICE – method of connecting two ends of rope together without knots

STABILISERS – floats which are extended amidships below the water line in choppy seas to reduce the rolling of the ship

STARBOARD – right-hand side of a ship, looking in the direction of travel

STERN – back end of the ship, opposite of bow

STEWARD – waiter

SWING – the turning of a ship around a buoy or anchor caused by the wind and current

TENDER – onboard motor boat

TONNAGE – ship's internal cubic capacity

WEIGH ANCHOR – to wind up the anchor with the anchor winch (see winch)

WINCH – winding gear

WINDJAMMER – large sailing ship

WINDWARD – the side of the ship facing the wind

WING – side part of the bridge

Bibliography & List of Illustrations

BIBLIOGRAPHY

Lothar-Günther Buchheim: Der Luxusliner.
© Verlag Albrecht Knaus, Hamburg 1980:
p. 197.
Paul Claudel: Mittagswende.
© Herle Verlag, Heidelberg 1959: p. 131.
Charles Dickens: American Notes. © J.M. Dent,
London 1997: p. 41.
Federico Fellini: Amarcord.
© Diogenes Verlag AG, Zurich 1974: p. 92
Federico Fellini: E la nave va.
© Diogenes Verlag AG, Zurich 1984: p. 201.
Richard Gordon: Käpt'n Ebbs – Seebär und
Salonlöwe. © Rowohlt Verlag GmbH,
Hamburg 1959: p. 210.
Erik Fosnes Hansen: Choral am Ende der Reise.
© Kiepenheuer & Witsch Verlag, Cologne 1995:
p. 67.
Heinz G. Konsalik: Promenadendeck
© Blanvalet Verlag GmbH, Munich 1985:
p. 192.
Alphonse de Lamartine: Voyage en Orient.
© Edition d'Aujourd'hui, Paris 1978: p. 26.
Anita Loos: Gentlemen prefer blondes.
© Diogenes Verlag AG, Zurich 1987: p. 83.
Thomas Mann: Meerfahrt mit Don Quijote.
© Bermann-Fischer, Stockholm 1945:
p. 120, 166.
Sandra Paretti: Das Zauberschiff.
© Droemersche
Verlagsanstalt, Munich 1977: p. 55.
Rainer Maria Rilke: Rainer Maria Rilke/André
Gide, Briefwechsel 1906-1926. © Insel Verlag,
Frankfurt am Main: p. 4.
Joachim Ringelnatz: Segelschiffe. © Henssel,
Berlin o.D.: p. 31.
Joachim Ringelnatz: Mein Leben bis zum
Kriege.
© Henssel, Berlin o.D.: p. 74.
Jeraldine Saunders: The Love Boats.
© Pinnacle Books, New York 1974: p. 205
Danielle Steel: Crossings.
© Goldmann Verlag GmbH, Munich 1984:
p. 96.
Mark Twain: Reise durch die Alte Welt.
© Verlag
Hoffmann und Campe, Hamburg 1964: p. 156.
Jules Verne: Une Ville Flottante.
Pawlak, Berlin Herrsching 1984: p. 50
Evelyn Waugh: Labels. A Mediterranean Journal.
© Penguin Books, London 1985: p. 168, 179.

PHOTOGRAPHS AND ILLUSTRATIONS

American Merchant Marine Academy Museum,
Kings Point: p. 106 t.
Berlin Art and History Archive: p. 12 b.r.,
13 t.l. and b.l., 14 (2). 15, 20/21 b., 24/25, 26 b.,
28 (background), 30 b.l. and b.r., 38 t., 54,
58 b.l., 59 t., 62/63, 65 (3), 66 b. and r., 67 (2),
74, 75, 77, 78, 87 b.l. and r., 90, 116, 120 b.l.,
130 (2) 131 (2), 172, 175 (5), 250 b.r.
Udo Bernhart, Langen: p. 198 b.l.. and t.r., 199 b.
Engelmeier Picture Archive, Munich: p. 82 (3), 83
Berlin Picture Archive of Prussian Cultural Pro-
perty: p. 121, l.
and t.r., 13 r., 32, 76, 84, 88, 89 l., 117 b., 199 b.,
56
Bucher Picture Archive, Munich: p. 52 t.l. and b.,
56 t., 57 t.l., t.r. and b., 84 b., 101 b., 110 t.l.,
166 (3), 176/177 (12)
Blohm & Voss, Hamburg: p. 87 t., 91
Henry Braunschweig, Frankfurt: p. 242 M.
Matthias Breiter, Walldorf: p. 258/259
Carnival Cruise Line, Miami: p. 242 b., 243 (3),
251 t.l.
Christa Elsler – Historical Colour Picture Archive,
Norderney: p. 21 b (2)
Collection of Business Americana/Smithsonian
Institution, Washington D.C.: p 50
Corbis-Bettmann, New York: p. 61, 86 b., 97 b.,
107 t.b., 110 b., 110/111 (background), 118,
119 t., 120 t. and b.r., 129 t., 248 t.l.
Cunard, Hamburg: p. 150 t.r., 152 t., 153 t.M. (2)
and b., 216/217, 250 t.l.
German Maritime Museum, Bremerhaven:
p. 3, 28 b., 49 t., 85 t., 106 l., 128, 153 t.l.,
248 b.l., 249 b.l. and t.r.
German National Library at the Foundation of
Prussian Cultural Property, Berlin: p. 166/167
Richard Faber Collection, New York and Bill Miller
Cruises Everywhere Inc., Secaucus: p. 59 b.l.
and r., 92 t.l., 95 b., 142 b., 154 t., 167, 168,
169 r., 195 t.r., 208 b., 218 t.l., 224 t.l., 236 t.l.,
237 t.l.
Filmbild Fundus Robert Fischer, Munich: p. 9 b.r.
Focke-Museum, Bremen: p. 34/35
Hapag-Lloyd AG, Hamburg: p. 237 b.
Hapag-Lloyd AG Historical Archive,
Hamburg: p. 42/43, 47 b., 53 b., 55, 69, 70 l. and r.,
71 b., 79 (2), 86/87 (background), 89 b., 126 b.,
159, 160, 173
Hulton-Getty, London: p. 111 t., 125 t.l. and r.,
126 t.
IFA-Bilderteam, Munich: p. 128/129 (background)
Interfoto, Munich: p. 29 b., 64 t., 64/65
(background), 68, 70/71 (background), 109,
111 b., 112 (2), 113, 161, 251 b.

Arnold Kludas, Bremerhaven: p. 163 b., 164 (2),
208 t.
Arnold Kludas, Bremerhaven / with the kind
permission of the Hapag-Lloyd Archive,
Hamburg: p. 1, 47 t., 165 (4)
Franz Lazi, Stuttgart: p. 198/199 (background)
Library of Congress, Washington D.C.: p. 22:
2nd row from bottom (3), 23: 2nd row from
bottom (3)
The Mark Twain House, Hartford Ct.: p. 252
Mary Evans Picture Library, London: p. 31 (3), 40
Mauritius, Mittenwald: p. 38/39 (background),
55 (background)
H.P. Merten, Saarburg: p. 37
Musée de Quebec: p. 30 t.
Museum of the City of New York: p. 36 M.
National Maritime Museum, Greenwich, p. 39,
48/49 b. (2)
The New York Historical Society: p. 26/27
New York Partnership and Chamber of Commerce:
p. 43 r.
The New York Public Library/Astor, Lenox and
Tilden Foundations: p. 23 r., 41, 248 t.r.
The Oakland Museum, Museum Donors'
Acquisition Fund: p. 33 t.
Peabody Essex Museum, Salem, Mass.: p. 17 b.,
24 b., 33 b., 51
Alain Roman, Copenhagen: p. 66 t., 107 (5), 143 b.
Royal Caribbean Cruise Line, Miami: p. 246/247 b.
Saxony State Library/National and University
Library/German Photographic Library, Dresden:
p. 72/73 (8)
Jürgen Saupe, Osterode am Harz: p. 174 t.
Seatours International GmbH, Frankfurt:
p. 252 b.r.
Slg. Bildpostkarten Axel Schenck, Bruckmühl:
53 t., 56 l., 56/57, 57 M.r., 71 r., 114 b.
Designed by H.A. Muth/„ Schuler Verlag
Stuttgart GmbH: p. 16 t., 17 t.
Schuler Verlag GmbH: p. 18/19
Hamburg State Picture Archive: p. 154 b.,
157, 158, 162, 163
Süddeutscher Bilderdienst, Munich: p. 64 b.,
106 b., 108, 110 M.l., 114 t., 115 b., 121, 122,
123, 124 (3), 125 b.l., 169 l., 250 M.l. and t.r.
Peter Tönnishoff, Augustdorf: p. 80, 81 (4), 90 b.,
94 l., 94/95, 98/99, 100 b., 102/103, 104/105,
111 M., 117 t., 129 b., 132 M. and b., 113 t.,
136/137, 138 l. (2), 139 (6), 140/141 (10),
186/187, 248 b.r.
The University of Liverpool Archives: p. 38 b., 44,
60 l. (2), 127, 249 t.l.

All photographs not listed above belong to
Kurt Ulrich, Zurich.

Picture legends:
Page 1: The Hapag high-speed steamer
Normannia, built in 1890
Pages 2/3: Promenade deck of the four-master
sailing ship Sea Cloud. Captain and officers of
the Bremen. Cruise ship Silver Cloud
(from left to right).

All the information in this book has been carefully
researched by the author and checked by the
publishing house for accuracy and topicality.
However, no liability can be accepted for the
accuracy of the information. We are always pleased
to receive any suggestions or information you may
have. Please write to: C.J. Bucher Verlag GmbH
& Co. KG, Lektorat, Goethestrasse 43,
80336 Munich, Germany

Published in the UK in 1998 by Tauris Parke Books
an imprint of I.B.Tauris & Co. Ltd.
Victoria House, Bloomsbury Square,
London WC1B 4DZ

© 1997 by Verlag C.J. Bucher GmbH & Co.
KG, Munich

Translation © I.B.Tauris & Co. Ltd., 1998

Printed and bound in Italy
ISBN 1-86064-373-6

ACKNOWLEDGEMENTS

The author would like to thank the crews of liners
and cruisers who always answered his many
questions with great patience. He would also like to
thank marine historians John Maxtone-Graham,
Arnold Kludas, Frank O. Braynard and William H.
Miller, without whose standard works this book
would not have been possible. His thanks also go to
Gudrun Schlüter, Gerhard Simonsen, Rolf Junker
and Urs Rychener for reading the manuscript.